D1498177

JUDGING WAR CRIMINALS

Judging War Criminals

The Politics of International Justice

Yves Beigbeder
Adjunct Professor
Webster University
Geneva
Switzerland

Foreword by Theo van Boven

First published in Great Britain 1999 by
MACMILLAN PRESS LTD
Houndmills, Basingstoke, Hampshire RG21 6XS and London
Companies and representatives throughout the world

A catalogue record for this book is available from the British Library.

ISBN 0–333–68153–3

First published in the United States of America 1999 by
ST. MARTIN'S PRESS, INC.,
Scholarly and Reference Division,
175 Fifth Avenue, New York, N.Y. 10010

ISBN 0–312–21649–1

Library of Congress Cataloging-in-Publication Data
Beigbeder, Yves.
Judging war criminals : the politics of international justice /
Yves Beigbeder ; foreword by Theo van Boven.
p. cm.
Includes bibliographical references and index.
ISBN 0–312–21649–1 (cloth)
1. International criminal courts.   2. War criminals.   I. Title.
K5000.B45   1998
341.7'7—dc21   98–25629
                                                                                CIP

This book is printed on paper suitable for recycling and made from fully managed and
sustained forest sources.

10   9   8   7   6   5   4   3   2   1
08   07   06   05   04   03   02   01   00   99

Printed and bound in Great Britain by
Antony Rowe Ltd, Chippenham, Wiltshire

*To the memory of Henri Donnedieu de Vabres
(1880–1952), French judge at the Nuremberg
War Crimes Trial, 1945–6*

Contents

List of Tables and Presentations

Foreword

This book conducts the reader through areas which are at the borders of hope and despair. The darker side of the spectrum is filled with accounts of man's inhumanity to man and with the apparent failure on the part of responsible actors to prevent, to counteract and to restore. Yet, at the other end of the spectrum, significant glimpses of hope are on the horizon. Women and men, individually and jointly, with roots in different cultures and societies, have over the ages lived and acted in the belief that the forces of evil and destruction should not be allowed to prevail and, instead, that respect for human dignity and for a just society should be the standard of conduct and achievement.

Yves Beigbeder recounts in this book many dark and desperate episodes of the world's recent history, but his main objective is to open up perspectives for remedy, response and renewal which are made visible by the proclamation and the enforcement of the basic premises of the rule of law. With this objective in mind, the author invests much confidence in the work of non-governmental organizations and groups that have gained great strength in the past few decades as moral and public actors on the national and international scene. Moreover, as a true internationalist, Beigbeder relies on the potentials of international co-operation as a means of creating conditions that foster the progressive development, the acceptance and the enforcement of standards of elementary justice. In this respect, he is a strong advocate of independent and impartial judicial institutions whose task it is to render justice and to defeat the cynical patterns of impunity and indifference.

Yves Beigbeder has written this book at the time when individuals accused of having committed war crimes and crimes against humanity in the former Yugoslavia, or of having participated in the genocide in Rwanda, are being brought to justice before international tribunals established by the United Nations Security Council. The creation and the functioning of these unique, special (*ad hoc*) institutions for the enforcement of international criminal law have spurred the wish to see a permanent International Criminal Court established, and the prospects that decisive steps will be taken shortly in that direction appear to be fairly positive. This book comes therefore in a timely manner, inasmuch as it sheds much light on a long process of diplomatic and legal efforts that have, directly or indirectly, hinted at a permanent International Criminal Court as the realization and the culmination of an idea that has been strongly in the minds of political leaders and international lawyers in the wake of World War II.

As was at the time quite aptly emphasized by the International Military Tribunal at Nuremberg, crimes are not committed by abstract entities but by human persons, who are held to be criminally responsible. It is quite significant that in recent years a clear shift is visible from merely factual reporting of violations of human rights and humanitarian law to bringing into focus the persons behind the facts: the perpetrators of international crimes and, on the other side, the victims of gross violations and grave breaches. Prosecution and punishment of the perpetrators is an important and essential means of rendering justice. Reparation in the form of compensation, rehabilitation and other ways and means of satisfaction for the victims is no less an important requirement of justice. Beigbeder reviews a wide gamut of experiences, at national and international levels, aimed at rendering justice and providing redress. He certainly envisages a preferential role for independent judicial organs, but he quite rightly also points at other institutions that may be instrumental in bringing about a process of retribution and healing, such as the various truth and reconciliation commissions established in recent years. It should be well understood, however, that these different institutions and mechanisms are not alternative devices but, rather, supplementary means of doing justice, and that all of them have to be guided by basic human rights and humanitarian standards.

The author comes across in this book as an informed observer and as a dedicated internationalist who shares with the readers his rich experience and his insights and who conveys, willingly or unwillingly, a vision. The book makes good and interesting reading because it avoids technicalities, it is informative and in its analysis it is realistic and balanced – and, last but not least, it is moderately visionary in its thread and its thrust. I wish to see this book in the hands of many and that it may effectively serve as a source of information, orientation and guidance.

Maastricht, December 1997 Theo van Boven
Professor of International Law, University of Maastricht;
former Director of the United Nations Centre for Human Rights

Preface and Acknowledgements

The rational way to stop war crimes is to stop wars – the utopian, pacifist attempt of the Kellogg-Briand Pact of 1928 to outlaw aggressive war – was an expected failure. In the 19th and early 20th centuries, the Geneva and Hague Conventions tried to 'humanize' war, an apparent oxymoron, in the vain hope that countries and their armies would abide by their obligations.

History has shown the fragility of international humanitarian law when confronted with aggressive ambitions of political or military leaders, and with the recurring natural barbarism of organized or uncontrolled armed combatants. At least, as in the general area of human rights, rules and standards have been defined. However, treaty obligations, discreet diplomatic persuasion, appeals to public opinion, mild monitoring and verbal condemnations are not enough. War criminals should be arraigned, tried and, if found guilty, punished, in 'a fair and public hearing by an independent and impartial tribunal', in the words of the Universal Declaration of Human Rights (Article 10). The Geneva and Hague Conventions left it to states, i.e. to national civil, criminal or military courts, to prosecute their war criminals, or those from other countries fallen in their hands. However, national justice has often been loath and slow to judge its country's nationals, out of political, military or class solidarity with those accused, or through an apparently more worthy, but also misplaced, will to forget all past offences and facilitate national reconciliation. International justice may then be brought in where and when national justice has failed.

The crimes against peace, war crimes and crimes against humanity committed by or allowed to be committed by high-level German and Japanese politicians and military commanders before and during World War II were reviewed and adjudged by the temporary military tribunals of Nuremberg and Tokyo. For the first time in history, prominent officials were held personally accountable for their decisions, and not the abstract, irresponsible state. However, the punishment of leaders of defeated enemies by the Allies' judges was rightly criticized as victors' justice, although legitimate judiciary procedures were duly applied. It took fifty years before genuine, international criminal tribunals were created in order to judge and sanction the perpetrators of war crimes and other grave violations of international humanitarian law in ex-Yugoslavia and those responsible for the Rwanda genocide. Their international composition and fair statute should give assurance of a substantial advance of international criminal justice, but the obstacles are considerable. The Tribunals are facing major difficulties in securing custody of indicted individuals, and they suffer from financial strictures and other administrative problems. Will these tribunals overcome the blatant lack of co-operation and support of those same governments which have created the tribunals? Will international politics continue to override the requirements of international justice, in a cynical disregard for the fundamental rights of victims: the right to know, the right to justice and the right to reparation? Even if the lonely appeals of the persistent international judges and prosecutors are finally heard, these tribunals are temporary, *ad hoc* courts with limited place and time jurisdiction. Why only for ex-Yugoslavia and Rwanda? Past genocides and mass slaughters have occurred in many other countries and have remained unpunished. Many of those crimes are cynically denied by their authors or their successors, conveniently ignored or deliberately hidden. The need for a permanent, international criminal court has finally emerged: a diplomatic conference has approved the statute of the court on 17 July 1998. The court will judge individuals, not states. The simple fact that a large majority of countries now support this creation, after decades of neglect or opposition, is in itself a major event.

Why now? Among the causes for this change of heart on the part of democratic and non-democratic governments, public opinion pressures probably have played the largest part, thanks to the recurrent media exposition of killings, atrocities and ill-treatment of combatants, prisoners of war, civilians and refugees. The crucial role of national and international non-governmental organizations and their networks and coalitions in exposing violations, in chastising guilty governments and groups, in promoting international human rights legislation and in lobbying governments in United Nations committees for the establishment of the International Criminal Court cannot be underestimated. The slow world evolution towards greater democracy in a larger number of countries has allowed more people to express their views and feelings freely and has encouraged national

judges to investigate the illegal transactions or conduct of powerful and well-protected high officials. Members of the branch of
government generally considered as its weakest part, the judiciary,
have developed, in such countries as Italy and France, the courage
and the skills to assume and apply all their legal powers, with the
indispensable support of the media, thus enhancing their own credibility. As a consequence, in an increasing number of unlikely countries, high-level politicians, state officials and business figures have
recently been indicted for corruption and other misdemeanours or
crimes. If these very important persons are losing their prior taken-
for-granted impunity, why should those who have committed, ordered or allowed the commission of war crimes and crimes against
humanity not be judged? If national courts cannot or will not judge
them, why should they not be subjected to international justice?
Could Truth and Reconciliation Commissions on the South African model usefully supplement national and international justice,
or are they only imperfect substitutes for justice? Has the independent International Peoples' Tribunal played a useful role? Is
there a place for such a Tribunal besides the proposed international
criminal court?

The creation and installation of the international criminal court
will take years, if not one or two decades. It would then be naive
to think that its existence will serve as an effective deterrent to
more atrocities, and that all high-level war criminals will be indicted, held in custody and judged. The present difficulties experienced by the ex-Yugoslavia Tribunal show the obstacles that the
future court will face: among these, rejection of international justice on the basis of national sovereignty and national pride, lack of
effective means to enforce extradition and obtain custody, the interference and prevalence of national and international politics over
justice, and the willing or forced trade-in of amnesty and impunity
in exchange for civil peace through national reconciliation.

The French philosopher and scientist Blaise Pascal wrote: 'Justice without force is powerless – force without justice is tyrannical.
One should bring justice and force together.' International criminal justice is in the process of being born on a permanent basis
but will lack force: like the International Court of Justice, the new
Court will have to rely on the co-operation of states, but, more
than the International Court of Justice, it may benefit from the
open support of a number of governments, international organizations, public opinion and friendly groups. In spite of its imperfect

nature, the creation of the Court will be taken as a sign that, at last, governments are intent on judging and condemning the individuals mainly responsible for the grave violations of international humanitarian law. More concretely, the public indictment of some of those individuals, and their condemnation, may be a signal to other perpetrators or potential offenders that they may face justice: in the words of Amnesty International, the 'vicious cycle of impunity that often transforms sporadic human rights violations into a systematic practice of abuse' may be interrupted.

The tone of the preceding remarks leaves no ambiguity as to the general purpose of this book: to make a small contribution to the on-going efforts to create an effective, permanent, international criminal court by recalling past and present attempts to try war criminals at the international level and also to recall a few of the recurring cases of unpunished, sometimes hidden or denied, massacres and other atrocities. This is not a legal treatise, although references are made to legal texts and interpretations. The author is not a specialist in this domain, but a concerned, perhaps partial, independent observer. The book is an attempt to provide a relatively short and referenced description of the historical background to and development of international criminal law and institutions, with their imperfections, failures and expectations, in relation to national and international politics. References are made only to some of the more recent publications on the subjects covered, publications which generally provide for an extensive bibliography. A number of like-minded governments, politicians, scholars, legal practitioners and international officials, supported by a coalition of non-governmental organizations and, more generally, by the new awareness, indignation and cry for justice of many peoples in many countries, are applying pressure for determined international action in this domain, an action which is constrained, if not openly opposed, by other governments under the well-worn cloth of national sovereignty, which often hides sins and crimes which present or past leaders would rather leave hidden.

The author's interest in this field stems generally from a long-term career in international organizations dedicated to international peace and co-operation, as well as research, writing and teaching on international relations and institutions. More to the point, this book was caused by the horror and frustration felt by many in this continent when fellow Europeans were seen practising with neither hesitation nor remorse a Nazi-type barbarism, in a continent where democracy and political compromise were thought to have consigned dictatorships and one-party regimes to history. It is also related to the author's brief assignment at the Nuremberg trial – from March to June 1946 – as a young (and inexperienced) legal assistant to the French judge, Henri Donnedieu de Vabres, to whom this book is dedicated. The views and assessments expressed in this book, which are sometimes unorthodox, are personal to the author: they do not necessarily reflect the views of organizations with which he has been associated. Finally, many thanks are expressed to those who have given me advice and reviewed this text, including Theo van Boven who has kindly written a foreword to this book, Chris de Cooker, and the most helpful UN library staff in Geneva and the Webster University library staff in Geneva and St Louis. The editing skills of Mandy Eggleston are, again, gratefully acknowledged.

Thonon-les Bains, France
July 1998 Y.B.

List of Abbreviations

ANC	African National Congress (South Africa)
COPAZ	National Commission for the Consolidation of Peace (El Salvador)
FMLN	Frente Farabundo Marti para la Liberacion Nacional (El Salvador)
ICC	International Criminal Court
ICJ	International Court of Justice
ICRC	International Committee of the Red Cross
IHT	International Herald Tribune
ILC	International Law Commission
ILO	International Labour Organisation
MINUGUA	United Nations Mission for the Verification of Human Rights and of Compliance with the Commitments of the Comprehensive Agreement on Human Rights in Guatemala
ONUSAL	United Nations Observer Mission in El Salvador
SPO	Special Prosecutor's Office (Ethiopia)
TOIP	Trial Observation and Information Project (Ethiopia)
TRC	Truth and Reconciliation Commission (South Africa)
UN	United Nations
UNGA	United Nations General Assembly
URNG	Unidad Revolucionaria Nacional Guatemalteca

1 Humanitarian Law: From Normative Thrust to Criminal Enforcement

Pictet has defined humanitarian law as 'a branch of public international law which owes its inspiration to a feeling for humanity and which is centered on the protection of the individual'. Its purpose is 'to alleviate the sufferings of all the victims of armed conflicts who are in the power of their enemy, whether wounded, sick or shipwrecked, prisoners of war or civilians' More formally, he has completed this definition as follows:

> By 'international humanitarian law applicable in armed conflicts', the International Committee of the Red Cross means international rules, established by treaties or custom, which are specifically intended to solve humanitarian problems directly arising from international or non international armed conflicts and which, for humanitarian reasons, limit the right of parties to a conflict to use the methods and means of warfare of their choice or protect persons and property that are, or may be, affected by conflict.

While these rules – the law of Geneva – provide legal protection to victims of armed conflicts, the law of the Hague regulates the conduct of states and combatants, and aims at prohibiting or restricting the use of cruel or indiscriminate weapons, as measures to prevent the excessive use of violence in warfare.[1]

Effective law and order at the national level requires the setting of norms, defining the rights and obligations of the state, other entities and citizens, i.e. what is allowed and what is forbidden, and what sanctions may be applied when the law is violated – enforcement of the law through police, including the taking of alleged offenders into provisional custody, trial by independent and impartial tribunals – the effective implementation of tribunals' judgments, acquittal or financial sanctions, imprisonment or other sentences, including the death penalty in a number of countries. International law, which was originally limited to relations between sovereign states, defines norms of conduct which states should respect through international conventions, negotiated by states and submitted to them for their ratification. However, there is no international police to force states to abide by their own commitments and to be judged, nor to ensure the implementation of judgments of international courts. States only submit to international justice with their own consent, and judgments of international courts are at times rejected or disregarded by indifferent or discontented states. States can only be sanctioned through economic sanctions, which they still have to accept, or by public reprimands, or, outside the realm of judiciary settlement, by bilateral or multilateral political, economic or military sanctions.

International humanitarian law, as part of international law, is also 'soft law', an imperfect law which sets norms and defines crimes but relies entirely on states to respect these norms. At the global level, the International Court of Justice is competent to judge legal disputes between states, but it cannot entertain individual complaints from nor judge individuals: it is only open to the states that are parties to its statute. No permanent international criminal court has yet been established. At the regional level, the American and European Courts of Human Rights also judge countries, not individuals, and also rely on their member states' willingness and good faith to implement their judgments. International criminal law is a law in the making, an imperfect and soft law, a law in slow evolution. It should ultimately list and define crimes committed in war or peace to be sanctioned under international humanitarian and human rights law, define the sanctions, or range of sanctions, applicable to specific crimes, assign criminal responsibility to states and/or individuals for such crimes, and determine the competence of national or international jurisdictions called upon to judge alleged criminals and applicable procedures.

While humanitarian concerns are as old as mankind itself, humanitarian law was only codified at the international level in the second half of the 19th century. Its evolution, since the First Geneva Convention was approved in 1864, has been considerable. Born on the battlefield to 'humanize' war, and initially concerned with the protection of wounded and sick soldiers and sailors, prisoners of war and medical personnel, international humanitarian law now also applies to civilians and 'civilian objects'. While this law was to ensure such protection only during international armed conflicts, it now applies to the more frequent non-international (internal) conflicts. Within the context of the international protection of human rights, it should also apply to crimes committed in peacetime, in circumstances not necessarily related to external or civil war. The protection of the non-combatants of the Geneva law was developed concurrently with the law of the war, now called the law of armed conflict, of the Hague Conventions, for instance through restraints on the use of force and the use of certain weapons. After World War II, the United Nations has either initiated or supported the negotiation and adoption of a number of international arms control agreements, which fall under the Law of War.

The Nuremberg Tribunal created a conceptual revolution in several ways: first, in spite of its imperfect composition, it was the first international tribunal to judge high-level individuals convicted of violations of international humanitarian law. Individuals were now accountable at the international level for their criminal decisions and could no longer hide behind the legal abstraction of the 'State'. The list of crimes was enlarged from war crimes to crimes against peace, and more importantly, to crimes against humanity, thus identifying a need to include the protection of human rights in war and in peace within the international humanitarian law. The creation of the Tribunal, its statute and its judgments have influenced the development of this law, creating a third 'branch', the 'Nuremberg law' – grafted on to the Geneva and Hague laws. This will be discussed further in Chapter 2.

The Genocide Convention, adopted in 1948 as a Resolution of the UN General Assembly, was a direct consequence of the Nuremberg trials. In the same year, the adoption of the Universal Declaration of Human Rights, and of later human rights instruments, gave the UN a central role in the development of human rights law, within which international humanitarian law should take its legitimate place.

The unexpected creation of the Tribunals for ex-Yugoslavia and Rwanda has caused another advance: for the first time, genocide was formally identified as another crime worthy of sanction. The planned creation of the International Criminal Court on a permanent basis will crown all these developments, which led from norm-setting with discreet monitoring of the conduct of states to individual repression through international tribunals.

THE ORIGINS OF INTERNATIONAL HUMANITARIAN LAW

Humanitarian concerns about the conduct of war go back many centuries, although international codification only started in the 19th and 20th centuries. Moral, philosophical or religious considerations led to setting unilateral limits to barbary and cruelty in battles, by instructions or advice given to commanders. Bilateral agreements based on reciprocity between enemies tried to avoid similar excesses. Sun Tzu, in *The Art of War*, a Chinese classic on military strategy, written in about 500 BC defined humanitarian guidelines: a commander must respect prisoners of war, he should avoid using needless violence, he should not seek the total annihilation of an enemy. The Indian Code of Manu, developed between 200 BC and AD 200, referred in part to the protection of war victims: a soldier must not kill an enemy by using a hidden weapon, he must not attack an enemy who has surrendered nor an enemy who is not ready for combat, who is severely wounded or is fleeing. In Japan, the spirit of Bushido, an unwritten law, dictated the duties of noblemen from the 12th century onwards. In battle, human conduct towards the weak and the defeated was highly praised by the Bushido moral code. Soko Yamaga (1622–85) the founder of modern strategy in Japan, advocated as the basic object of strategy the attainment of justice, humanity, peace and order, and avoiding unnecessary killing.[2]

In Europe, the oldest known condemnation of war crimes occurred in the 4th century: Ambrose, bishop of Milan, solemnly condemned Emperor Theodosius the First for the slaughter carried out by his armies of some 7000 inhabitants of the town of Thessalonia in 390.[3] The Christian doctrine of charity and brotherhood was instrumental in the creation of religious orders that gave care to the sick and the wounded. For instance, the Order of Malta, created in 1099, gave religious and hospital care to Christian pilgrims and crusaders in Jerusalem. Typical of the contradictions of humanitarian assistance, military and chivalrous duties were added to its original functions in 1126. In the 20th century, the Order continues its charitable duties at the international level, particularly for those stricken by natural disasters or war.[4]

In the 12th and 13th centuries, the Church tried to exclude non-combatants from conflicts: the Peace of God (*Pax Dei*) was to provide protection to monks, travellers, merchants and peasants as well as to churches, graveyards, monasteries and so on. During the 17th and 18th centuries, as noted by Partsch,[5] there were numerous agreements among Christian princes regarding the exchange of prisoners, the protection of the sick and wounded, respect for hospital sites and for medical personnel who were not to be made prisoners of war. Seven of the 150 *Articles of War* decreed in 1621 by King Gustavus II Adolphus of Sweden contain humanitarian rules: the rape of women was punished by death, and soldiers should not 'tyrannize over any Churchman, or aged people, men or women, maids or children, unless they first take arms against them'. Setting fire upon a town in the enemy land, or upon a church, hospital, school or mill, or pillaging a church or hospital would have to be commanded by higher authority. While these limited rules were an innovation and served as a model for the later development of the law of war in Europe, Ögren adds that the conduct and reputation of Swedish troops in that period was all but humanitarian.[6]

While instances of war crimes trials were rare, Sunga[7] recalls the Breisach Trial of 1474, which underlines one of the issues raised during the 20th-century international war crimes trials:

> Hagenbach, a knight, was charged with responsibility for the commission by those under his command of murder, rape, perjury and other serious crimes in his attempt to subjugate the citizens of Breisach in the Upper Rhine, following the instructions of his master, Duke Charles of Burgundy. Before the *ad hoc* international tribunal composed of twenty-eight judges, Hagenbach's counsel pleaded that Hagenbach had been following orders from his superior, Duke Charles, and that he therefore had no right to question or disobey those orders. This defence of superior orders was rejected. Hagenbach was found guilty, stripped of his knighthood and condemned to death.

The 18th century was that of the Enlightenment, which saw reason and the law of nature replace religion as a basis for the rights and freedoms of citizens within the state, and as a basis to place limits on the rules of war. In 1762, Jean-Jacques Rousseau wrote:

> Since the aim of war is to subdue a hostile State, a combatant has the right to kill the defenders of that State while they are armed; but as soon as they lay down their arms and surrender, they cease to be either enemies or instruments of the enemy;

they become simply men once more, and no one has any longer the right to take their lives. 'These principles' are derived from the nature of things; they are based on reason.[8]

Regulations on the lawful use of force during armed conflict are found in diverse military codes. In 1863, President Lincoln issued Army Order No. 100, entitled *Instructions for the Government of the United States Armies in the Field*, or the 'Lieber Code', which codified the customary law of land warfare, in the context of the American Civil War. This national code inspired later international efforts to codify and develop the rules of the law of war.

THE LAW OF GENEVA

The move from local *ad hoc* agreements, national military codes and bilateral agreements to international humanitarian codification during conflicts was due to the initiative of Henry Dunant and his Swiss friends to create, in 1863, the International Standing Committee for Aid to Wounded Soldiers, later called the International Committee of the Red Cross (ICRC), a Swiss non-governmental organization. Motivated by Christian beliefs and humane compassion, the Red Cross Movement was set up as a group of secular, neutral organizations which pursued dual objectives: the creation, promotion and development of international humanitarian law, and the provision of relief assistance in war and peace at both national and international levels.

In 1864, twelve states signed the first Geneva Convention for the Amelioration of the Condition of the Wounded in Armies in the Field, the first instrument of international humanitarian law. In 1899, at the Hague, another Convention was signed, adapting the principles of the Geneva Convention to warfare at sea. In 1906, the provisions of the 1864 Convention were improved and supplemented. In 1907, the Fourth Hague Convention defined the categories of combatants entitled to the status of prisoner of war when captured, and to a specific treatment during their captivity. In 1929, a revised Geneva Convention for the Relief of the Wounded and Sick in Armies in the Field was signed. In 1949, the four Geneva Conventions which are now in force were adopted, supplemented in 1977 by two Protocols.[9] The Geneva Conventions are founded on the principle of respect for the individual and his dignity.

Persons not directly taking part in hostilities and those put out of action through sickness, injury, captivity or any other cause must be respected and protected against the effects of war; those who suffer must be aided and cared for without discrimination. The Additional Protocols of 1977 extend this protection to any person affected by an armed conflict. They further stipulate that the parties to the conflict and the combatants shall not attack the civilian population and civilian objects and shall conduct their military operations in conformity with the recognized rules and laws of humanity. Prohibited at any time and in any places are: murder, torture, corporal punishment, mutilation, outrages upon personal dignity, the taking of hostages, collective punishments, execution without regular trial and all cruel and degrading treatment. Reprisals are prohibited against the wounded, the sick and the shipwrecked, medical personnel and medical services, civilian defence personnel and services, prisoners of war, civilian persons, civilian and cultural objects, the natural environment, and works and installations containing dangerous forces. Massive air bombardments, indiscriminate attacks, attacks on non-defended localities or demilitarized zones are also forbidden.

The first important innovation of the 1949 Conventions and the 1977 Protocols was the adoption of rules to protect civilian populations, who have become more vulnerable in the new types of conflicts. The second one was to provide more detailed protection in non-international armed conflicts, a more frequent occurrence since World War II. Protocol II supplements and develops article 3 common to the four Geneva Conventions of 1949 – the only provision until then applicable to armed conflicts of a non-international character.[10]

The Conventions and Protocols commit those states which have ratified them, or which have acceded to them, to specific humanitarian obligations. At the same time, their provisions confer on the ICRC certain rights: the right to visit prisoners of war and civilian persons protected by the Fourth Geneva Convention, a right of humanitarian initiative in situations not covered by the Conventions or Protocols. Such rights do not amount to a systematic and public monitoring of states' respect for their humanitarian obligations. The ICRC delegates' reports on their visits to prisoners or detainees are confidential: they are first submitted to the ICRC headquarters in Geneva, and then to the detaining authority. In the case of prisoners of war, the reports are also sent to the government of the prisoner of war's home country. As a rule, the confidential reports are not divulged to other governments or to third parties. As a well-established principle of its action, the ICRC maintains a strict neutrality and discretion, and abstains from making public pronouncements about specific acts committed in violation of law and humanity and attributed to belligerents. As stated by Pictet:[11] 'One cannot be at one and the same time the champion of justice and of charity. One must choose, and the ICRC has long since chosen to be a defender of charity.' States are financially accountable for violations of the provisions of the Conventions and of Protocol I and they are responsible for all acts committed by persons forming part of their armed forces (Article 91 of Protocol I). States are to enact any legislation necessary to provide effective penal sanctions for persons committing, or ordering to be committed, any of the 'grave breaches' of the Conventions. The concept of 'grave breaches' is another important innovation of the 1949 Conventions. States must search for such persons and bring them, regardless of their nationality, before their own courts. A State may also, if it prefers, hand such persons over for trial to another State concerned, provided that the latter has made a *prima facie* case. The accused persons must benefit by safeguards of proper trial and defence. Grave breaches of the Conventions and Protocols are regarded as war crimes.[12]

Article 90 of Protocol I provides for the establishment of an International Fact-Finding Commission consisting of fifteen members of high moral standing and acknowledged impartiality. This Commission is competent to enquire into any facts alleged to be a grave breach or other serious violation of the Conventions of Protocol I. It should facilitate, through its good offices, the restoration of an attitude of respect for the Conventions and Protocol. The Commission held its initial meeting in March 1992. By 1997, the Commission had not yet initiated any investigation.

The definition of grave breaches and war crimes in the Conventions and Protocols has been inspired by the numerous violations of international humanitarian law committed during World War II and by the Nuremberg law. However, the Geneva law leaves entirely to states the responsibility for searching for violators of the Conventions and Protocols, for judging them, and if warranted, to sanction them. A senior Red Cross official recently recognized that the international system of repression of war crimes under the Geneva Conventions, namely the obligation to judge or extradite war criminals (*aut dedere aut judicare*) has not, in practice, been implemented.[13] The Geneva law does not include any reference to a possible referral of war criminals to an international penal tribunal.

THE LAW OF THE HAGUE

While the law of Geneva is directed towards the protection of military personnel placed *hors de combat* and persons not taking part in hostilities, the law of the Hague, or the law of warfare, has determined the rights and duties of belligerents in the conduct of operations and limits the choice of warfare methods: one of its main objectives was to fix 'the technical limits at which the necessities of war ought to yield to the requirements of humanity ... in time of war between civilized nations', in the words of the 'Declaration of St. Petersburg of 1868 to the effect of prohibiting the use of certain projectiles in wartime'. The 'de Martens Preamble' inserted in the Hague Convention No. IV of 1907[14] has defined the general intent of all humanitarian law as an attempt to accommodate military 'necessities' to the principle of humanity in war and an appeal to the 'dictates of public conscience' 'among civilized peoples', i.e. to universal moral imperatives:

> ... these provisions, the wording of which has been inspired by the desire to diminish the evils of war, as far as military requirements permit, are intended to serve as a a general rule of conduct for the belligerents in their mutual relations and in their relations with the inhabitants,

> ... Until a more complete code of the laws of war has been issued, the High Contracting Parties deem it expedient to declare that, in cases not included in the Regulations adopted by them, the inhabitants and the belligerents remain under the protection and the rule of the principles of the law of nations, as they result from the usages established among civilized peoples, from the law of humanity, and the dictates of the public conscience ...

In spite of their different approach, both laws apply to armed conflict, which cannot be effectively banned or prevented but whose evil consequences may be alleviated – both attempt to protect military

personnel, prisoners of war and civilians against the effects of war
– and both laws rely on states to ensure the respect of ratified
Conventions. One important difference is that the law of Geneva
has a permanent institution, the ICRC, as its custodian, promoter
and monitor, while the law of the Hague, made up of *ad hoc* Conventions, relies only on the text of each individual Convention for
its implementation. This explains in part that some of the Hague
law has been taken over by the Geneva law, in 1929 and 1949,
on the status of prisoners of war, of the wounded and shipwrecked
in hostilities at sea, and of civilians in occupied territories. Later
on, the United Nations has taken over another part of the Hague
law, in attempts to ban or limit the use of cruel or indiscriminate
weapons.

The First Hague Peace Conference of 1899 was convened by Tsar
Nicolas II, during which four Conventions were adopted. At the
Second Hague Peace Conference held in 1907, for which the USA
shared the initiative with the Tsar, 13 Conventions were approved.
Of these, the most important for the development of international
humanitarian law was Convention No. IV of 18 October 1907 'concerning the laws and customs of war'. It dealt with, in part, the
protection of prisoners of war and established that 'The right of
belligerents to adopt means of injuring the enemy is not unlimited'
(Article 22). Under Article 23(e) it was forbidden, 'To employ arms,
projectiles, or material calculated to cause unnecessary suffering'.
Article 25 prohibited 'The attack or bombardment, by whatever
means, of towns, villages, dwellings, or buildings which are undefended'; Article 28 prohibited 'The pillage of a town or place, even
when taken by assault'. Convention VIII of 1907 regulated 'the
laying of automatic submarine contact mines', Convention IX referred to the 'bombardment by naval forces in time of war'. The
Hague Convention of 14 May 1954 ruled on 'the protection of cultural
property in the event of armed conflict'.

The Hague Conventions of 1899 and 1907 required the contracting Powers to 'issue instructions to their armed land forces which
shall be in conformity with the Regulations respecting the Laws
and Customs of War on Land, annexed to the present Convention'. In case of a violation of the provisions of the Regulations in
the Hague Convention of 1907, a belligerent Party 'shall, if the
case demands, be liable to pay compensation. It shall be responsible for all acts committed by persons forming part of its armed
forces' (Article 3). Under Article 41 of both Conventions, a violation

of the terms of the armistice by private persons acting on their own initiative only entitles the injured party to demand the punishment of the offenders or, if necessary, compensation for the losses sustained'. Under Article 56 of both Conventions, 'all seizure of, destruction or wilful damage done to institutions of this character, historic monuments, works of art and science, is forbidden, and should be made the subject of legal proceedings'. Under the title of 'Sanctions', Article 28 of the 1954 Hague Convention is more specific: it requires the High Contracting Parties to 'take, within the framework of their ordinary criminal jurisdiction, all necessary steps to prosecute and impose penal or disciplinary sanctions upon those persons, of whatever nationality, who commit or order to be committed a breach of the present Convention'.

As for the Geneva Conventions, under the Hague law, the state remains responsible under classical international law for the violations of the provisions of ratified Conventions, but it must submit the violator to national penal justice. The Hague Conventions do not refer to the possible referral of war criminals to an international penal tribunal.

OTHER LAW OF WAR CONVENTIONS

The main but unattainable purpose of both the League of Nations and the United Nations was, and is for the UN, to achieve international peace and security, by making member states accept 'obligations not to resort to war' (Preamble of the Covenant), or 'to ensure, by the acceptance of principles and the institution of methods that armed force shall not be used, save in the common interest' (Preamble of the UN Charter). The Kellogg–Briand Pact, or General Treaty for the Renunciation of War, was adopted in 1928 and was ratified by 64 states by 1939. Its principles were simple: war was renounced as an instrument of national policy, and the parties agreed to settle all disputes by peaceful means. Widely acclaimed as a landmark in the search of peace, it was soon shown to be an unrealistic and ineffective moral declaration, scorned by the dictators and military regimes. Short of banning war, disarmament was among the methods by which both the League and the UN could hope to prevent wars, or to limit their consequences on combatants and non-combatants. Between the two World Wars, besides the two Geneva Conventions of 1929, only two humanitarian instruments were adopted: the Geneva Gas Protocol of 1925 and the Protocol to the London Naval Agreement of 1936.

After World War II, a number of international arms control agreements were adopted, dealing primarily with the threat of nuclear weapons. The Treaty on the Non-Proliferation of Nuclear Weapons was adopted in 1968. The Convention on the Prohibition of the Development, Production, and Stockpiling of Bacteriological (Biological) and Toxin Weapons and on their Destruction has been in force since 1975. The General Assembly adopted in 1995 the text of a comprehensive nuclear test-ban treaty, opened for signature at UN Headquarters. The Chemical Weapons Convention came into force in 1997, following its ratification by 163 countries. As inter-state treaties or conventions, ratifications commit states to the respect of their obligations, without engaging the individual penal responsibility of their leaders or other officials to national or international tribunals.

THE CRIME OF GENOCIDE

On 9 December 1948, the UN General Assembly approved the Convention on the Prevention and Punishment of the Crime of Genocide. It entered into force on 12 January 1951. Due to the initiative, conviction and perseverance of Raphael Lemkin, a Professor of International Law at Yale University, the Convention is one of the 'products' of the Nuremberg judgments, which condemned, among other crimes, the crimes against humanity committed by the Nazis. On 11 December 1946, the General Assembly affirmed the 'principles of international law recognized by the Charter of the Nuremburg Tribunal and the Judgment of the Tribunal '(Res. 95/I). These principles, as formulated by the International Law Commission are as follows (UN Doc. A/CN.4/22/1950):

I. Any person who commits or is an accomplice in the commission of an act which constitutes a crime under international law is responsible therefor and liable to punishment.

II. The fact that domestic law does not punish an act which is an international crime does not free the perpetrator of such crime from responsibility under international law.

III. The fact that a person who committed an international crime acted as Head of State or public official does not free him from responsibility under international law or mitigate punishment.

IV. The fact that a person acted pursuant to order of his government or of a superior does not free him from responsibility under international law. It may, however, be considered in mitigation of punishment, if justice so requires.

V. Any person charged with a crime under international law has the right to a fair trial on the facts and law.

Also on 11 December 1946, the General Assembly declared that genocide was a crime under international law, contrary to the spirit and aims of the UN and condemned by the civilized world (Res. 96 (I)).

As a first innovation, the Genocide Convention (see Presentation 1.1) establishes that genocide, whether committed in time of peace or in time of war, is a crime under international law: the scope of international humanitarian law was thus extended from violations committed only in war to violations in war and in peace. Article 6(c) of the Nuremberg Charter referred to 'crimes against humanity . . . committed against any civilian population, before or during the war . . . in execution of or in connection with any crime within the jurisdiction of the Tribunal'. The Tribunal, in its judgment, stated that it 'cannot make a general declaration that the acts before 1939 were Crimes against Humanity within the meaning of the Charter': the Tribunal had to interpret the Charter as not having jurisdiction over these crimes unless they were connected with a war of aggression or war crimes, a pre-requirement which had not been met. In this respect, the Genocide Convention is therefore an advance over the Nuremberg Charter.

PRESENTATION 1.1
THE CONVENTION ON THE PREVENTION AND PUNISHMENT
OF THE CRIME OF GENOCIDE (Excerpts)

ARTICLE I

The Contracting Parties confirm that genocide, whether committed in time of peace or in time of war, is a crime under international law which they undertake to prevent and to punish.

ARTICLE II

In the present Convention, genocide means any of the following acts committed with intent to destroy, in whole or in part, a national, ethnical, racial or religious group, as such:
   (a) Killing members of the group;
   (b) Causing serious bodily or mental harm to members of the group;
   (c) Deliberately inflicting on the group conditions of life calculated to bring about its physical destruction in whole or in part;
   (d) Imposing measures intended to prevent births within the group;
   (e) Forcibly transferring children of the group to another group.

ARTICLE III

The following acts shall be punishable:
   (a) Genocide;
   (b) Conspiracy to commit genocide;
   (c) Direct and public incitement to commit genocide;
   (d) Attempt to commit genocide;
   (e) Complicity in genocide.

ARTICLE IV

Persons committing genocide or any of the other acts enumerated in article III shall be punished, whether they are constitutionally responsible rulers, public officials or private individuals.

ARTICLE V

The Contracting Parties undertake to enact, in accordance with their respective Constitutions, the necessary legislation to give effect to the provisions of the present Convention and, in particular, to provide effective penalties for persons guilty of genocide or any of the other acts enumerated in article III.

ARTICLE VI

Persons charged with genocide or any of the other acts enumerated in article III shall be tried by a competent tribunal of the State in the territory of which the act was committed, or by such international penal tribunal as may have jurisdiction with respect to those Contracting Parties which shall have accepted its jurisdiction.

ARTICLE VII

Genocide and the other acts enumerated in Article III shall not be considered as political crimes for the purpose of extradition.
   The Contracting Parties pledge themselves in such cases to grant extradition in accordance with their laws and treaties in force.

ARTICLE VIII

Any Contracting Party may call upon the competent organs of the United Nations to take such action under the Charter of the United Nations as they consider appropriate for the prevention and suppression of acts of genocide or any of the other acts enumerated in article III.

Source: Resolution No. 260 (III) approved by the UN General Assembly on 9 December 1948.

Article II of the Convention limits its scope to the destruction, in whole or in part, of 'a national, ethnical, racial or religious group'. The Nuremberg Charter had included 'political' persecutions in its Article 6(c), and Resolution 96 (I) of the UN General Assembly referred to 'political groups', and not to 'national groups'. After long discussions in the Sixth Committee of the Assembly, the Committee yielded to Soviet pressures and agreed not to include political groups among groups to be protected by the Convention. This unfortunate decision seemed to give impunity to governments intent on physically destroying their political opposition. The Convention confirms the key Nuremberg principle which establishes the individual penal responsibility of responsible rulers, public officials or private individuals.

The second major innovation is a reference to an international penal tribunal, a logical sequence to the Nuremberg and Tokyo *ad hoc* Tribunals. In the same resolution (260 (III) B), the General Assembly invited 'the International Law Commission to study the desirability and possibility of establishing an international judicial organ for the trial of persons charged with genocide or other crimes over which jurisdiction will be conferred upon that organ by international conventions'. Some 48 years later, the Commission finally submitted to the General Assembly a draft statute for an International Criminal Court.

As another follow-up to Nuremberg, the Convention on the Non-Applicability of Statutory Limitations to War Crimes and Crimes against Humanity was adopted by the General Assembly on 26 November 1968. In 1971, the Assembly expressed its conviction that the effective punishment of war crimes and crimes against humanity was important for ending such crimes and for promoting peace and international security. In 1973, it proclaimed certain principles of international cooperation in the detection, arrest, extradition and punishment of persons guilty of war crimes and crimes against humanity.

For the first time, charges of genocide were brought against individuals by the *ad hoc* Tribunals for ex-Yugoslavia and Rwanda. The Tribunal for ex-Yugoslavia, established in 1993, was given the power to prosecute persons committing or ordering to be committed grave breaches of the Geneva Conventions of 1949, violations of the laws or customs of war (the law of the Hague), genocide and crimes against humanity (the Nuremberg law). The Rwanda Tribunal was given similar power, except for the violations of war or customs of war.

THE LINK TO HUMAN RIGHTS

Both the humanitarian and the human rights movements have similar historical, religious and philosophical origins. However, the latter attempts generally to protect citizens from their own government's abuses at all times, while the former provides protection to military personnel placed *hors de combat* and non-combatants only in time of war. As noted by Pictet,[15] 'the principles of human rights are of a more general nature and application, whereas humanitarian law has a special and exceptional character, since it applies, in fact, when war prevents human rights from being exercised or limits their application'. The two systems are complementary: any advance in the protection and promotion of international human rights, applicable at all times and not only in times of conflict, should support and enhance the more specialized international humanitarian law. It would then appear logical to place humanitarian law within the general human rights regime, as a subsystem of the general system.

The freedoms granted by King John in 1215 to his subjects in the *Magna Carta* were a first sign that the power of the Prince had its limits in legality and fair justice. In 1354, King Edward III reaffirmed the Charter and undertook that no man, of whatever estate or condition, should be harmed except by due process of law. Charles the First completed this legal guarantee by *habeas corpus* in the Petition of Rights of 1628. In 1581, a group of the Dutch subjects of King Philip II of Spain, assembled in their States-General, asserted unequivocally[16] 'that God did not create the subjects for the benefits of the Prince, to do his bidding in all things whether godly or ungodly, right or wrong, and to serve him as slaves, but the Prince for the benefit of the subjects, without which he is no Prince'. In the 18th century, Jean-Jacques Rousseau developed the pre-revolutionary theory, derived from John Locke and Hugo Grotius, that a ruler could only derive his powers from a 'social contract' with his subjects, which imposed obligations on him as well as granting him rights. The American and French Revolutions produced another innovation, that of listing and defining for the first time the rights and freedoms of individuals within a state, incorporated in the constitutional texts of the state. The Declaration of Rights of the State of Virginia of June 1776, the French Declaration of the Rights of Man and the Citizen of 1789, and the first Ten Amendments to the US Constitution of 1791 generally included equality before the law, due process of law, freedom from arbitrary arrest and imprisonment, the presumption of innocence, fair trial, freedom of assembly, speech, conscience and religion. The effective implementation of these declaratory advances was, and remains, dependent on the varying degree of democratic progress in different countries.

Furthermore, human rights were originally viewed as an entirely internal political matter, protected from international intervention by the international law principle of national sovereignty: any human rights abuses could then be carried out with impunity behind national borders. The principal exception was the 19th century anti-slavery campaign. At the Congress of Vienna in 1815, major powers recognized an obligation to abolish the slave trade. In 1840, the Anti-Slavery Society, the world's oldest international human rights non-governmental organization, organized the First Anti-Slavery Convention in London. In 1885, the Berlin Conference on Central Africa affirmed that 'trading in slaves is forbidden in conformity with the principles of international law'.[17] Finally, in 1926, the League of Nations adopted the Convention on the Abolition of Slavery and the Slave Trade. The Supplementary Convention on the Abolition of Slavery, the Slave Trade and Institutions and Practices similar to Slavery was adopted on 25 September 1956 by a diplomatic conference convened by the UN. The Convention did not create any mechanism for its implementation. It should be noted that the Second Additional Protocol of 1977 to the Geneva Conventions prohibits slavery and the slave trade in all their forms in non-international armed conflicts (Article 4.2.f.).

The Covenant of the League of Nations did not mention human rights in general, but made sparse references to 'the prohibition of abuses such as the slave trade', the 'just treatment' of native inhabitants of dependent territories. It entrusted the League with general supervision over the execution of agreements with regard to the traffic in women and children. Its Members were to endeavour to secure and maintain fair and humane conditions of labour for men, women and children, a task which was assumed by the International Labour Organisation, also created in 1919. Among the conventions adopted by the ILO in this field before and after World War II: No. 29, concerning Forced Labour (1930) and No. 105 concerning the Abolition of Forced Labour (1957), No. 111, concerning Discrimination in Respect of Employment and Occupation (1958).

The United Nations and Human Rights

By contrast, the Preamble of the UN Charter reaffirmed 'faith in fundamental human rights, in the dignity and worth of the human person, in the equal rights of men and women'. One of the purposes of the UN is to encourage respect for human rights and for fundamental freedoms for all without distinction as to race, sex, language or religion (Article 1.3). The catalyst for making human rights a prominent issue in world politics was the horror and repulsion felt in most countries when the Holocaust and other crimes committed by the Nazi regime during World War II became fully known. On 10 December 1948, the Universal Declaration of Human Rights was adopted and proclaimed by the UN General Assembly 'as a common standard of achievement for all peoples and all nations'. Among the civil and political rights are included: the right to life, liberty and security of person; freedom from slavery, from torture or cruel, inhuman or degrading treatment or punishment, the right to effective judicial remedy, freedom from arbitrary arrest, detention or exile, the right to a fair trial and public hearing by an independent and impartial tribunal, and the right to be presumed innocent until proved guilty, freedom from arbitrary interference with privacy, family, home or correspondence, freedom of thought, conscience and religion, freedom of opinion and expression, the right to association and of assembly. Among the economic and social rights, the right to social security, to work, to an adequate standard of living, to education. Rights and freedoms should be enjoyed by all, without distinction of any kind, such as race, colour, sex, language, religion, political or other opinion, national or social origin, property, birth or other status.

The non-binding Declaration was followed in 1966 by two international Covenants, one on economic, social and cultural rights, and the other on civil and political rights. Both Covenants entered into force in 1976. Article 40 of the International Covenant on Civil and Political Rights provides for 'consideration' by the Human Rights Committee of reports submitted by States parties on measures taken to implement its provisions. Under the Optional Protocol to the same Covenant, the Committee also 'considers' communications (complaints) from individuals who claim to be victims of violations of any rights set forth in the Covenant. In 1970, resolution 1503 of the Economic and Social Council authorized the Commission on Human Rights to conduct confidential investigations of communications (i.e. complaints) that suggested 'a consistent pattern of gross and reliably attested violations of human rights and fundamental freedoms'. The UN has thus set minimum norms and has been authorized to monitor the respect of the Covenant by states. However, states' violations of the norms are not sanctioned except by the limited adverse publicity given in UN reports and by UN meetings, and by the more public and critical exposure given by non-governmental organizations and the media. The Convention relative to the Status of Refugees was adopted in 1951. One of the functions of the UN High Commissioner for Refugees, an Office established in 1951, is to provide international protection to refugees.

The International Convention on the Suppression and Punishment of the Crime of Apartheid adopted by the General Assembly on 30 November 1973 rejoins and adds to the Nuremberg precedent and emulates the Genocide Convention in several important ways. First, it includes apartheid among crimes against humanity, a crime that violates the principles of international law and constitutes a serious threat to international peace and security. While the Nuremberg Charter linked crimes against humanity to crimes against peace or war crimes, the Apartheid Convention sets no such limit. Secondly, it emulates the Genocide Convention and innovates in relation to all other UN human rights conventions in imposing international criminal responsibility on individuals for committing, participating in, directly inciting or conspiring in the commission of acts mentioned in Article II of the Convention, or directly abetting, encouraging or co-operating in the commission of the crime of *apartheid*: 'International criminal responsibility shall apply, irrespective of the motive involved, to individuals, members of organizations and institutions and representatives of the State'. The third legal progress over other conventions was to emulate the Genocide Convention in declaring that persons charged with *apartheid* acts may be tried either by a national tribunal or by an international penal tribunal. The decision by the General Assembly to include these provisions in the Convention may be explained by the extent of the hostility to *apartheid* felt and expressed by most UN members. While these provisions have not been implemented before *apartheid* ended, this Convention was another step towards the renewed recognition that individual perpetrators of crimes against humanity should be judged by an international penal tribunal.

The Convention against Torture and other Cruel, Inhuman or Degrading Treatment or Punishment, adopted by the General Assembly in 1984, entered into force in 1987. The Universal Declaration of Human Rights (Article 5), the International Covenant on Civil and Political Rights (Article 7), the European Convention for the Protection of Human Rights and Fundamental Freedoms (Article 3), the American Convention on Human Rights (Article 5.2) and the African Charter on Human and Peoples' Rights (Article 5) also prohibit torture and other cruel, inhuman or degrading treatment. Similar prohibitions apply in warfare: in international armed conflicts, the 'grave breaches' of the Geneva Conventions subject to penal sanctions include torture or inhuman treatment, including biological experiments, wilfully causing great suffering or serious injury to body and health (I, 50; II, 51; III, 129; IV, 147). Common Article 3 to the Geneva Conventions of 1949 prohibits violence to life and person, cruel treatment and torture, humiliating and degrading treatment, in the case of armed conflict not of an international character, for persons taking no active part in the hostilities, including members of armed forces who have laid down their arms and those placed *hors de combat*. The First Additional Protocol of 1977 protects the physical or mental health and integrity of persons who are in the power of the adverse Party or who are interned, detained or otherwise deprived of liberty (P.I, 11, 85). Protocol II prohibits, *inter alia*, violence to the life, health and physical or mental well-being of persons, in particular murder as well as cruel treatment such as torture, mutilation or any form of corporal punishment, outrages upon personal dignity, in particular humiliating and degrading treatment (P.II, 2). The

UN Convention against Torture requires states parties to take effective legislative, administrative, judicial and other measures to prevent acts of torture in any territory under their jurisdiction. This includes the obligation to ensure that all acts of torture are offences under their criminal law. The Convention requires that wherever the alleged torture occurred, and whatever the nationality of the torturer and the victim, parties must either prosecute the alleged torturers or extradite them to a country that will, thus giving universal jurisdiction to national courts. The Convention's Committee against Torture receives periodical reports from states on the measures they have taken to give effect to the Convention, reports on which the Committee may make general comments. The Committee may initiate, on a confidential basis, an investigation if it receives reliable information containing well founded indications that torture is being systematically practised in the territory of a state party. Under optional Article 21, the Committee may receive communications from or on behalf of individuals who claim to be victims of a violation by a state party of the provisions of the Convention. This Convention therefore includes reporting and monitoring mechanisms which may prove that a state party has violated the provisions of the Convention. However, there is no international mechanism to identify individual violators nor to submit them to international justice.

The implementation of other human rights Conventions, including the International Convention on the Elimination of All Forms of Racial Discrimination (1965), the Convention on the Elimination of All Forms of Discrimination Against Women (1979), the Convention on the Rights of the Child (1989), is monitored by committees with limited powers.

Human Rights in Regional Organizations

Three regional organizations have adopted human rights conventions: the European Convention for the Protection of Human Rights and Fundamental Freedoms (Council of Europe, 1950), the American Convention on Human Rights (1969) and the African Charter on Human and People's Rights (1981).

The first two Conventions have created a court of human rights, progress over the UN regime. Under the European Convention of the Council of Europe, as amended by its ninth Protocol of 6 November 1990, states parties, the Human Rights Commission – an expert group – and persons, non-governmental organizations or groups of individuals may submit a petition to the Secretary-General of the Council of Europe, and, following review by the Commission, have the right to bring a case before the Court of Human Rights. A new protocol (No. 11) signed on 11 May 1994, sets up a single permanent Court in place of the two-tier system of Commission and Court. If the Court decides that there has been a breach of the Convention, it can award compensation to the complainant. States are obliged to comply with the judgment against them. The implementation of judgments is supervised by the Committee of Ministers and the ultimate sanction for non-compliance could be expulsion from the Council of Europe.

The American Convention limits the right to submit a case to the Inter-American Court of Human Rights to states parties and the Commission: individual applicants have no such right. Neither the European Court, nor the Inter-American Court judge individuals, but countries: they do not assign individual penal responsibility to individual violators of the Conventions. The African Charter has not created a court of human rights.

The Draft Code of Crimes against the Peace and Security of Mankind

References to crimes against peace, war crimes, crimes against humanity and genocide are scattered in many legal instruments of various dates, Red Cross Conventions and Protocols, UN and ILO Conventions, and in the Statutes of War Crimes Tribunals. It is therefore desirable to update and codify all these diverse elements from diverse sources into one international text to be approved and ratified by a large majority of states. This text should, ideally, list and define the crimes to be sanctioned under international law, determine the competent national and/or international jurisdiction and decide which sanctions, or range of sanctions, would be applicable for each crime. Such a Code would be the necessary complement to the establishment of a permanent International Criminal Court.

In 1947, the UN General Assembly requested the International Law Commission to formulate the Nuremberg Principles and to prepare a Draft Code of Offences against the Peace and Security of Mankind.[18] A first draft was submitted in 1951 followed by a revised version in 1954. In 1957, the Assembly decided that the Commission should defer further work on the Draft Code until a definition of aggression was developed, deemed necessary for further progress to be made, particularly in respect of the various crimes against peace.[19] The Assembly completed a definition of aggression in 1974 and in 1981, the Assembly again referred the question to the Commission.[20] The last version of the Draft Code against the Peace and Security of Mankind was submitted to the General Assembly in July 1996.[21] The 1996 Draft Code establishes that crimes against the peace and security of mankind are crimes under international law and punishable as such, whether or not they are punishable under national law (Article 1.2). The Draft Code integrates the successive contributions to international humanitarian law.

The list of war crimes (Article 20) is based on both the law of the Hague and the law of Geneva. It includes acts committed in violation of the laws or customs of war, in violation of international humanitarian law applicable in armed conflict of an international character, or of a non-international character. From the Nuremberg law, the Draft Code re-affirms that the listed crimes entail individual responsibility, whatever the position of the individual, head of state or of government (Articles 2 and 7). However, individual responsibility is without prejudice to any question of the responsibility of states under international law (Article 4). The notion of conspiracy is included in Article 2.3.(e) but, contrary to the Nuremberg precedent, there is no reference to criminal organizations. An individual, who, as a leader or organizer, actively participates in or orders the planning, preparation, initiation or waging of aggression committed by a state, may be responsible for the Nuremberg crime against peace, now called crime of aggression (Article 16). A list of crimes against humanity, also inspired by Nuremberg, is in Article 18, without necessary link to the crime of aggression or war crimes. The Nuremberg position concerning superior orders is confirmed (Articles 5 and 6).

The crime of genocide in Article 17 is based on the Genocide Convention. References to an international criminal court are inspired by the Genocide Convention and the Convention against Apartheid. These references presuppose its establishment, without prejudging it (Articles 8 and 12). The same Articles 8 and 12 set out the conditions under which an individual may be tried by a national and/or by an international criminal court, by reference to the *non bis in idem* principle. National jurisdiction should apply to crimes set out in Articles 17, 18, 19 and 20, while a crime set out in Article 16 (crime of aggression) rests with an international criminal court. Article 12 prescribes that no one shall be tried for a crime of which he has already been finally convicted or acquitted by an international criminal court and specifies under what conditions an individual who has been finally convicted or acquitted by a national court may be tried again by an international criminal court or by a national court of another state.

Other legal principles are confirmed in the Draft Code: Obligation to extradite or prosecute (Article 9), judicial guarantees (Article 11) and non-retroactivity (Article 13). The Draft Code does not attempt to set sanctions, or ranges of sanctions as punishment for specific crimes against the peace and security of mankind, except to state that 'The punishment shall be commensurate with the character and gravity of the crime'. Such sanctions will therefore have to be part of the statute of the future International Criminal Court. An innovation is to include crimes against UN and associated personnel among crimes against the peace and security of mankind, when committed intentionally and in a systematic manner, with a view to preventing or impeding a UN operation from fulfilling its mandate (Article 19). Resolutions of the General Assembly have noted with grave concern the increasing number of fatalities and of cases of illegal arrest and detention of UN officials in violation of the privileges and immunities granted by Article 105 of the UN Charter.[22]

The Draft Code of 1996 has eliminated the following crimes included in the Draft Code of 1991: intervention (subversive or terrorist activities), colonial domination and other forms of alien domination, *apartheid*, recruitment, use, financing and training of mercenaries, international terrorism, illicit traffic in narcotic drugs and wilful and severe damage to the environment (Articles 17, 18, 20, 23, 24 and 25). In December 1996, the General Assembly drew the attention of states participating in the Preparatory Committee for the Establishment of an International Criminal Court to the relevance of the Draft Code to their work (Res. 51/160). The International Law Commission, in its 1996 report, had considered various forms which the Draft Code could take: an international convention, incorporation of the Code in the statute of an international criminal court, or adoption of the Code as a declaration by the General Assembly (paras 47–8). The second form would appear to be the most appropriate, as a Conference of Plenipotentiaries will be convened in 1998 to consider the text of a convention to establish an International Criminal Court. This would avoid holding two sets of parallel diplomatic negotiations, one for the Code and one for the court's statute.

CONCLUSION

This narrative shows that the nature of international humanitarian law, like that of international law in general, has changed and is changing in several respects. The first change, due to the increase of internal conflicts since the end of World War II, is that international humanitarian law, originally limited to conditions of international warfare, has extended its scope, since 1949, to non-international conflicts.

Originally limited to the relations of states, but concerned with victims, international humanitarian law has recognized the individual as a subject in his own right. This second change is due to a large extent to the development of the human rights regime since the Universal Declaration of Human Rights was approved in 1948. Human rights protect individuals against the power of the state, and this protection requires an interference with states' sovereignty. Even though the international monitoring of states' (governments) conduct versus their citizens is generally limited, this first breach of national frontiers has led to others. While international humanitarian law was developed essentially by the International Committee of the Red Cross as an independent and self-contained branch of international law, a law that protects non-combatants and war victims and a law of warfare, it may now be considered as a specialized part of the international human rights regime, which protects and promotes human rights at all times, in war and in peace. It is noteworthy that the United Nations has progressively taken over some of the legislative functions of the Red Cross and has continued, updated or developed the work of the Hague Conventions in old and new fields.

Thirdly, the grave violations of humanitarian law during World War II and during later international or local conflicts showed that humanitarian conventions are necessary but lack sanctions against those individuals who violate their rules. The traditional realm of international law, which had reluctantly admitted victims as subjects, then had to accept that individual perpetrators of war crimes or crimes against humanity should be held accountable for their decisions and replace the anonymous, irresponsible 'state' at the dock. Even at the present stage of a weak, diverse, conflicting, unorganized 'world community', the peoples' need for international criminal justice, even if imperfect, temporary and selective, has been strong enough to support the creation of the Tribunals for ex-Yugoslavia and Rwanda. A number of governments, other public and private constituencies and pressure groups are now supporting the current negotiations for the creation of an International Criminal Court.

These developments, which show that international humanitarian and human rights law is slowly evolving into international criminal law, would not have been possible if they had not built on the Nuremberg precedent: this will be discussed in Chapter 2.

2 The Nuremberg Precedent

For the first time in history, after World War II, an international tribunal judged and sentenced high-level politicians and senior military officers for their responsibilities, or their consenting part, in the commitment of crimes against peace, war crimes and crimes against humanity. The creation of this tribunal, its Charter and its judgments, have extended the traditional scope of international humanitarian law, in adding international criminal law and justice to the laws of Geneva and the Hague.

This significant innovation was made possible by the revelations of systematic mass atrocities committed by the Nazis before and during the war, which created both horror and an urge for revenge and punishment, and by the leadership of the USA in having its war allies agree to a judiciary process, rather than summary executions of those major war criminals detained by them. The failure of an effective judiciary process for alleged war criminals after World War I was another factor in the creation of the Nuremberg tribunal.

THE TREATY OF VERSAILLES AND THE LEIPZIG TRIALS

The violation of the neutrality of Belgium and Luxemburg by the German army in August 1914, the misery of refugees fleeing from occupied countries, pillage and destruction of cities, the sinking of the *Lusitania* and the use of poison gas during the battle of Ypres had aroused outrage and calls for revenge and punishment mainly from British and French public opinion, even though some of the accusations of indiscriminate murder, rape and infanticide were later shown to be the product of war propaganda. Charges were levelled against the Kaiser and other alleged war criminals.

The Paris Peace Conference, which started on 18 January 1919, established a Commission on the Responsibility of the Authors of the War and the Enforcement of Penalties.[1] The Commission's report submitted in March 1919 charged Germany and her allies with extensive violations of the laws of the war. The Commission recommended that '. . . all persons belonging to enemy countries, however high their position may have been, without distinction of rank, including Chiefs of State, who have been guilty of offences against the laws and customs of war or the laws of humanity, are liable to criminal prosecution'. However, the Commission's recommendation to submit Chiefs of State to criminal prosecution met with determined opposition from the US representatives. The US argued that subjection of Chiefs of State to this degree of responsibility was unprecedented in national or international law and would be contrary to the principle of national sovereignty: heads of state are agents of the people and only responsible politically to the people. A compromise led to Articles 227–230 in the Treaty of Versailles, signed on 28 June 1919. Under Article 227, the former German Emperor was to be tried by an international tribunal of five judges, one each from the USA, Great Britain, France, Italy and Japan. He was to be charged with a 'supreme offence against international morality and the sanctity of treaties'. The charge did not refer to violations of the laws of war nor to a penal responsibility: it was therefore to be a political trial, and not a judiciary process based on humanitarian conventions. The Kaiser had taken refuge in the Netherlands and the *pro forma* request of the Allies to make him available for trial was refused by the Dutch authorities, on the legal ground that the offence charged against him was unknown to Dutch law, was not mentioned in the treaties to which Holland was a party, and appeared to be of a political rather than of a criminal character. This outcome gave satisfaction to the USA, Italy and Japan who were opposed to the trial. By Article 228, the German Government had expressly recognized the right of the Allied Powers 'to bring before military tribunals persons accused of having committed acts in violation of the laws and customs of war'. The German Government was obliged to hand over German suspects to the Allied Powers for prosecution. By Article 229:

> Persons guilty of criminal acts against the nationals of one of the Allied and Associated Powers will be brought before the military tribunals of that Power.
>
> Persons guilty of criminal acts against the nationals of more than one of the Allied and Associated Powers will be brought before military tribunals composed of members of the military tribunals of the Powers concerned.

On 7 February 1920, the Allies submitted to Germany a list of 896 persons to be extradited, including many famous political and military figures: among others, Chancelor Bethmann, Hindenburg, Ludendorff and the Kronprinz. This list caused a violent reaction in Germany, and the Allies accepted a German proposal that those accused of war crimes would be tried before the German Supreme Court in Leipzig. The Allies then presented a list of 45 individuals for prosecution. Eventually, only 12 persons were tried. Of that number, only six were convicted and sentenced to terms of imprisonment of from two months to four years. In protest at this outcome, the Allied mission which had attended the Leipzig trials withdrew and the German Supreme Court thereafter proceeded to acquit persons charged and even to dismiss cases altogether – some 800 – either due to a failure to state crimes covered by German law or for lack of sufficient evidence.

Notwithstanding the expected, or even hoped-for, lack of co-operation of the Dutch government, the failure of this first attempt to set up an international tribunal to judge a Chief of State was due to a large extent to the lack of agreement among the main powers on the legality and the political wisdom of pursuing this line of action, at the risk of making a martyr of the Kaiser and creating more resentment among the German people. The USA kept to the traditional notion of national sovereignty and, in any case, did not sign the Versailles Treaty. The French were more interested in obtaining financial reparations from the Germans than in international justice. The reversion to national justice, in this case, essentially German justice to judge German alleged war criminals, proved to be totally ineffective, as the Germans perceived charges and trials as being imposed by the victors. While violations of the laws of the war were also committed by the Allies, there was no attempt on their part to investigate and sanction their own violations of international humanitarian law.

WORLD WAR II

The killings, devastations, losses and suffering caused by World War II, in the European theatre, were not only larger than in World War I – ten million deaths in World War I, over 50 million in World War II – but they took another dimension as a result of the racist ideology of the Nazis, which caused the persecution of the

Jews followed by their systematic extermination. The harassment
and mass murder of Soviet prisoners of war, another class of 'sub-
humans', was in part due to the racist theories of Aryan superiority over the Slavs, and in part to the political and military struggle
between Nazism and Communism. The Nazis had already tested
extermination methods on their own citizens, mentally ill, handicapped persons, the infirm and other 'worthless' lives, on the biological altar of 'racial hygiene': the so-called T4 programme killed
70 000 German victims from 1939 to 1941. Another 30 000 of those
'semi-humans' were eliminated in concentration camps in Mauthau-
sen, in Dachau from 1941 to 1945.[2]

Robert Daniell, who died in January 1997, was the British tank
commander who in 1945 smashed open the gates of the Nazi concentration camp at Bergen-Belsen, where inmates, most of them
Jews, had died for years of starvation, disease and torture. On
Daniell's arrival, the camp still held more than 60 000 prisoners.
In the first days of their liberation, 14 000 died and as many died
in the following weeks.[3]

It is probable that Hitler took the decision to exterminate the
Jews in August–September 1941, the implementation of which was
the objective of the Wannsee meeting of high Nazi officials on 20
January 1942. Rudolf Hoess was Commandant of the Auschwitz
concentration camp from May 1940 until December 1943. In his
testimony at the Nuremberg Tribunal on 15 April 1946 (Doc. 3868
PS), he estimated that 'at least 2,500,000 victims were executed
and exterminated by gassing and burning, and at least another half
million succumbed to starvation and disease, making about 3,000,000.'
Among them were 'approximately 20,000 Russian prisoners of war'.
'We executed approximately 400,000 Hungarian Jews in the single
Auschwitz camp in the Summer of 1944'. It is now estimated that
5 100 000 persons were murdered between 1941 and 1945 at the
instigation of the Nazi power for the only reason that they were
Jews. The victims represented about two-thirds of the Jewish population of Europe. As from the end of 1942, the Gypsies joined the
Jews as victims of the Nazi racist theories and cruelty: the numbers of deaths caused by this other genocide range from 200 000
to 500 000, a genocide which was ignored by the Nuremberg Tribunal.[4] According to a letter from Rosenberg to Keitel of February
1942, of 3 600 000 Soviet prisoners of war, 'only several hundred
thousand are still able to work fully'. The others have 'starved or
died because of the hazards of the weather'.[5] To these atrocities,

one should add the mass killings of Polish and Russian civilian populations, the deportation of political opponents from occupied countries and forced labour of civilians and prisoners of war to German factories, as only samples of a global picture of organized terror.

At least some of these crimes were known, at various times during the war, by the Allied leaders, the Vatican and the International Committee of the Red Cross.

THE NUREMBERG INTERNATIONAL MILITARY TRIBUNAL

The main promoter of the decision to create an international tribunal to judge the major German war criminals is properly credited to the USA, after a change of its initial position. Without US leadership, the Nuremberg trial might have never taken place. Even if it had, without the strong legal, material and financial support provided by the USA, the trial itself would probably not have been carried out with the same high professional standards.

Winston Churchill was originally opposed to trying the Nazis. In September 1942, when President Roosevelt and Prime Minister Churchill met in Quebec, they adopted in principle the 'Morgenthau plan'. Under this approach, as part of the denazification of Germany, major Nazi war criminals were to be shot on sight, and lesser Nazis sent to repair Allied lands damaged by the war. In a brief submitted to the British Foreign Office in February 1944, the viewpoint was expressed that an international trial would be too slow, its legality would be contested and it would give Nazi leaders an opportunity to engage in propaganda. Major Nazi leaders should be summarily executed, since their guilt was taken for granted. Roosevelt finally accepted somewhat reluctantly the contrary counsel of other advisers, including Cordell Hull, Secretary of State, Henry Stimson, Secretary of War, and Justice Felix Frankfurter of the US Supreme Court. His successor, Harry Truman, was strongly in favour of a trial, with the support of the USSR and of General de Gaulle, and the British government had to accept his position.[6] This was a complete reversal of British and US policies after World War I, when Prime Minister Lloyd George had pressed vigorously for the establishment of international tribunals to try the Kaiser and other German leaders, efforts which were blocked by American opposition. A series of declarations led progressively to the creation of an international tribunal. On 27 October 1941, Prime Minister Winston Churchill officially announced his commitment to the proposition that 'the punishment of these crimes must now be included among the major aims of the war'.[7] How the perpetrators of these crimes would be punished was, however, not specified.

The St James's Palace Declaration, issued by the representatives of nine governments-in-exile on 13 January 1942, explicitly repudiated retribution 'by acts of vengeance on the part of the general public' and declared that the 'sense of justice of the civilized world' required that the signatory powers

> place among their principal war aims the punishment, through the channel of organized justice, of those guilty of or responsible for these crimes, whether they have ordered them, perpetrated them or participated in them.

The terms of the Declaration were endorsed by Churchill, Roosevelt and Stalin in July 1942. However, another declaration issued on 1 November 1943 in the name of the same leaders, at the Moscow Conference of the Foreign Ministers of the UK, the USA and the USSR, referred only to the 'punishment' of the major criminals whose offences have no particular location, by a joint decision of the Allied governments, without reference to 'organized justice'. The communiqué published on 2 August 1945 by the three Allied powers – with two new actors, the British Prime Minister Attlee, and the US President Truman – specified that the method of punishment would be through 'swift and sure justice'. On 8 August, the UK, France, the USA and the Soviet Union signed the London Agreement, which provides that '. . . there shall be established after consultation with the Control Council for Germany an international military tribunal for the trial of war criminals whose offences have no particular geographical location'. The Nuremberg Charter was annexed to the London Agreement.

The Tribunal's Charter

The Charter is an international agreement signed in London by the US, French, British and Soviet representatives on behalf of their governments on 8 August 1945. Nineteen other countries later adhered to the Agreement, thus reinforcing its international credentials.[8] The Agreement established an 'International Military

Tribunal for the just and prompt trial and punishment of the major war criminals of the European Axis'. In effect, only high-level German officials were tried in Nuremberg. The permanent seat of the Tribunal was in Berlin, at the insistence of the Soviets, but the first and only international trial was held in Nuremberg. The trial lasted from 14 November 1945 to 1 October 1946.

One judge and one alternate were appointed by each of the four powers. Neither the Tribunal, its judges or alternates could be challenged by the prosecution, or by the defendants or their counsels. Convictions and sentences could be imposed only by affirmative votes of at least three judges. Lord Justice Geoffrey Lawrence of the Court of Appeal was the British Judge and Sir Norman Birkett, a barrister and Judge of the High Court, was his alternate. The US judge was Francis Biddle, a former Attorney General and a Democrat. His alternate was John Parker, a Republican, who had valuable experience as a jurist and judge. The Soviet judge was General I. T. Nikitchenko, Vice-Chairman of the USSR Supreme Court, and his alternate Colonel Volchkov, a professor of criminal law in Moscow. The French judge was Henri Donnedieu de Vabres, a renowned specialist in international criminal law, a professor at the Sorbonne Law School. His lack of judiciary practice was compensated by the long experience of his alternate, Robert Falco, a judge at the Cour de Cassation.

Each of the four signatories appointed a Chief Prosecutor for the investigation of the charges against and the prosecution of the defendants. The US Prosecutor, Robert H. Jackson, Associate Justice of the Supreme Court, played a major role in the preliminary negotiations which led to the approval of the Charter and in the trial itself. The trial took place in the US zone of defeated Germany and benefitted from substantial US legal expertise, documentation and financial resources and, not least, the determined US political will to overcome the many obstacles which threatened the course of the trial.

The jurisdiction of the Tribunal was based on a definition of the following crimes, 'for which there shall be individual responsibility':

(a) CRIMES AGAINST PEACE: namely, planning, preparation, initiation or waging of a war of aggression, or a war in violation of international treaties, agreements or assurances, or participation in a common plan or conspiracy for the accomplishment of any of the foregoing;

(b) WAR CRIMES: namely, violations of the laws or customs of war. Such violations shall include, but not be limited to, murder, ill-treatment or deportation to slave labor or for any other purpose of civilian population of or in occupied territory, murder or ill-treatment of prisoners of war or persons on the seas, killing of hostages, plunder of public or private property, wanton destruction of cities, towns or villages, or devastation not justified by military necessity;

(c) CRIMES AGAINST HUMANITY: namely, murder, extermination, enslavement, deportation, and other inhumane acts committed against any civilian population, before or during the war, or persecutions on political, racial or religious grounds in execution of or in connection with any crime within the jurisdiction of the Tribunal, whether or not in violation of the domestic law of the country where perpetrated.

Leaders, organizers, instigators and accomplices participating in the formulation or execution of a common plan or conspiracy to commit any of the foregoing crimes are responsible for all acts performed by any persons in execution of such plan.

The official position of defendants, whether as heads of state or responsible officials in government departments, would not free them from responsibility nor mitigate punishment. The fact that a defendant acted pursuant to order of his government or of a superior would not free him from responsibility, but may be considered by the Tribunal in mitigation of punishment. The Tribunal had the right to take proceedings and conduct a hearing against a defendant in his absence. Defendants were to receive a copy of the Indictment and other documents in their language. They had the right to conduct their own defence or to have the assistance of counsel, to present evidence in support of their defence, and to cross-examine any witness called by the prosecution. Anglo-American criminal procedures (the 'adversarial' system) were applied, whereby the evidence is presented in open court by the lawyers, who examine and cross-examine the witnesses. This placed at a disadvantage the French and Soviet judges and prosecutors, as well as the defendants' counsels, whose training and experience had been gained in the Continental 'inquisitorial' system.

The Tribunal had the right to impose upon a defendant, on conviction, death or such other punishment determined by it to be just. Judgments as to the guilt or innocence of any defendant were final. However, in case of guilt, the Allied Control Council for Germany could reduce or otherwise alter the sentences but could not increase their severity. In the event, the Control Council accepted without change the Tribunal's sentences.

The Defendants and their Sentences

Twenty-four individual defendants were indicted, as well as seven organizations.[9] The individual defendants represented different levels of responsibility in the Nazi regime and different civilian and military functions. The political need to start the trial without delay, and differences of opinion among the four powers did not allow them to define and apply clear criteria to the selection of the 'major war criminals'. Hitler's suicide in his Berlin bunker on 30 April 1945 enticed most defendants to blame him for most major decisions. Other senior officials were either dead – Goebbels and Himmler in May 1945 – or had escaped from Germany through friendly political and/or religious networks. Those in the docks had been arrested by the Allies or had surrendered to them. Robert Ley, Leader of the German Labour Front, committed suicide in his cell on 25 October 1945. Gustav Krupp von Bohlen und Halback, the industrialist, was not tried on account of his senility. The major figure was Hermann Goering, proud and unrepentant, loyal to his Führer and to the Nazi regime, rejecting the legality of the trial. A former World War I airpilot hero and Reich Marshall, he was to succeed Hitler. He was condemned to death by hanging, but committed suicide in his cell before the execution. Also condemned to the same sentence and executed (except for Bormann) were:

- Field Marshall Wilhelm Keitel, Chief of OKW, who recognized before the Tribunal that he had been 'carrying out criminal orders in violation of one of the basic principles of our professional soldiers' code'.[10]
- General Alfred Jodl, Chief of the OKW Operations General Staff.
- Hans Frank, Governor-General in Poland, who declared during the trial that 'after I have gained a full insight into all the horrible atrocities which have been committed, I am possessed by a deep sense of guilt ... A thousand years will pass and still the guilt of Germany will not have been erased'.[11]

- Wilhelm Frick, Minister of the Interior from 1933 to 1943, then Reich Protector of Bohemia and Moravia and Reich Minister without Porfolio.
- Ernst Kaltenbrunner, who replaced Reinhard Heydrich after the latter's assassination as Chief of the Reich Security Main Office (RSHA), where he was immediately responsible to Heinrich Himmler, the Head of the SS. As Chief of the RSHA, Kaltenbrunner had authority over both the SD (the Security Service) and the Gestapo (Secret State Police).
- Alfred Rosenberg, a theoretician and promoter of Nazi ideology. He was appointed in 1941 as Reich Minister for the Occupied Eastern Territories.
- Fritz Sauckel, appointed in 1942 as Plenipotentiary General for the Allocation of Labour. He declared that 'Out of the 5 million foreign workers who arrived in Germany, not even 200,000 came voluntarily'.[12]
- Julius Streicher, condemned for his violent incitement to the persecution and extermination of the Jews in his periodical, *Der Stuermer*.
- Arthur Seyss-Inquart, Governor of Austria after its annexation by Germany (Deputy to Hans Frank, the Governor-General of Poland) Reich Commissioner of the occupied Netherlands in 1940.
- Joachim von Ribbentrop, Hitler's Foreign Minister from 1938 to the end of the war.
- Martin Bormann, who succeeded Hess as Chief of the Party Chancellery. He was named Secretary to the Führer in 1943, the most powerful man in the Reich after Hitler. Having escaped, he was judged and sentenced to death *in absentia*.

Three defendants were condemned to life imprisonment:

- Rudolf Hess had been Hitler's deputy and the administrative head of the Nazi Party. He flew to Britain on 10 May 1941 with the intention of ending the state of war between Germany and the UK. His mental state was in question, and he attended the trial without any sign of interest or attention.
- Erich Raeder had been Commander in Chief of the Navy since 1935 and Grand Admiral since 1939.
- Walter Emmanuel Funk replaced Dr Schacht as Minister of Economics and President of the Reichsbank.

Time-limited sentences were given to the following:

- Twenty years to Albert Speer, Hitler's favourite architect, appointed Reich Minister for Armaments and Munitions in 1942 with the responsibility for the use of millions of foreign workers – and to Baldur von Schirach, Head of the Hitler Jugend, appointed as Gauleiter and Reich Governor in Vienna in 1940.
- Constantin von Neurath was sentenced to 15 years: he had been Hitler's Minister of Foreign Affairs as from 1933 and resigned in 1938. Hitler appointed him as Reich Protector of Bohemia and Moravia in 1939 but replaced him with Heydrich in 1941.
- Karl Doenitz was sentenced to ten years: he was Vice Admiral in 1940, then Admiral in 1942. In 1943, he replaced Raeder as Commander in Chief of the Navy.
  The Tribunal declared that three defendants were not guilty:
- Hjalmar Schacht was President of the Reichsbank from 1923 to 1930, and again from 1933 until 1939, Minister of the Economy (1934–37) and Plenipotentiary for War Economy (1935–37) and remained as a Minister without Portfolio from 1937 to 1943. In July 1944, after the attempt on Hitler's life, he was sent to concentration camps.
- Hans Fritzsche was a member of the Ministry for Peoples' Enlightenment and Propaganda. During the last two years of the war, he was Chief of the Radio Section of the Ministry. However, he was subordinated to Reich Press Chief Otto Dietrich, who in turn reported to Goebbels.
- Franz von Papen was briefly Vice Chancellor under Hitler, and German Ambassador to Turkey from 1939 to 1944.

Among the indicted organizations, the Leadership Corps of the Nazi Party, the Gestapo and the SD, and the SS were declared criminal. The Tribunal considered that the SA, the Reich Cabinet and the General Staff and High Command of the German Armed Forces were not criminal organizations under the Charter. The Soviet judge filed a separate Opinion concerning the acquittal of Schacht, von Papen and Fritzsche, the leniency of the punishment imposed on Hess and the refusal to recognize as criminal organizations the Reich Cabinet, the General Staff and High Command of the German Armed Forces.

38 *Judging War Criminals*

The sentences decided by the Tribunal on individual Defendants
are listed in Table 2.1. Count 1 is the common plan or conspiracy;
count 2, crimes against peace; count 3, war crimes; and count 4,
crimes against humanity.

Table 2.1
The Sentences of the Nuremberg Tribunal

Names	Charges under counts	Sentence
M. Bormann (*in absentia*)	3, 4	Death by hanging
H. Frank	3, 4	Death by hanging
W. Frick	2, 3, 4	Death by hanging
H. W. Goering	1, 2, 3, 4	Death by hanging
A. Jodl	1, 2, 3, 4	Death by hanging
E. Kaltenbrunner	3, 4	Death by hanging
W. Keitel	1, 2, 3, 4	Death by hanging
A. Rosenberg	1, 2, 3, 4	Death by hanging
F. Sauckel	3, 4	Death by hanging
A. Seyss-Inquart	2, 3, 4	Death by hanging
J. Streicher	4	Death by hanging
J. von Ribbentrop	1, 2, 3, 4	Death by hanging
W. Funk	2, 3, 4	Life imprisonment
R. Hess	1, 2	Life imprisonment
E. Raeder	1, 2, 3	Life imprisonment
A. Speer	3, 4	Twenty years
B. von Schirach	4	Twenty years
C. von Neurath	1, 2, 3, 4	Fifteen years
K. Doenitz	2, 3	Ten years
H. Fritzsche	Not guilty	Released
H. Schacht	Not guilty	Released
F. von Papen	Not guilty	Released

30 September 1946	1 October 1946
Sentences signed by the four Judges	Sentences pronounced by the President

Source: M. R. Marrus, *The Nuremberg War Crimes Trial, 1945–46, A Documentary History* (Boston/New York: Bedford Books, 1997), p. 261.

NUREMBERG CRITICIZED

Article 3 of the Charter prohibited the defendants or their counsels to challenge the Tribunal. A petition submitted by all defense counsels the day before the opening of the trial, on 20 November 1945, challenging the criminality of 'starting an unjust war' and complaining that the Tribunal was composed exclusively of judges from the victorious powers, was expectedly denied by the Tribunal. Following the trial, these and other criticisms have been addressed to the Tribunal and its Charter.

Victors' Justice

The historical origin of the Tribunal, its purpose, the nationality of its judges and prosecutors leave no doubt that the victorious nations had decided that the leaders of the vanquished nation should be judged and 'punished' for their responsibilities in the commitment of crimes. Only German war criminals were judged in Nuremberg and any charges that the Allies had also committed crimes against peace, war crimes or crimes against humanity were rejected by the Tribunal as outside the terms of the Charter and therefore outside their mandate.

A response to this charge is found first in the Charter's Preamble that, in creating the Tribunal to judge the major war criminals, the four powers were 'acting in the interests of all the United Nations', and therefore on behalf of the entire 'civilized world'. The adhesion of 19 nations to the London Agreement was a concrete sign of a general international support to the Allies' initiative. In its Judgment,[13] the Tribunal stated:

> The making of the Charter was the exercise of the sovereign legislative power by the countries to which the German Reich unconditionally surrendered; and the undoubted right of these countries to legislate for the occupied territories had been recognized by the civilized world. The Charter is not an arbitrary exercise of power on the part of the victorious nations, but in the view of the Tribunal, as will be shown, it is the expression of international law at the time of its creation; and to that extent is itself a contribution to international law.
>
> The Signatory Powers created this Tribunal, defined the law it was to administer, and made regulations for the proper conduct of the Trial. In doing so, they have done together what any one of them might have done singly; for it is not to be doubted that any nation has the right thus to set up special courts to administer law. With regard to the constitution of the court, all that the defendants are entitled to ask is to receive a fair trial on the facts and law.

Whether valid or not, this legal construction is based on the Allies' victory and assumption of all powers over Germany. It does not provide a satisfactory answer to the charge that four judges and four prosecutors of the four Allied Powers, prosecuting, judging and punishing only German defendants, cannot constitute an internationally representative Tribunal. A really 'international' tribunal would have to follow the model of the Permanent Court of International Justice, and of its successor, the International Court of Justice, i.e. 'a body of independent judges elected regardless of their nationality from among persons of high moral character, who possess the qualifications required in their respective countries for appointment to the highest judicial offices, or are jurisconsults of recognized competence in international law' (Article 2 of the Court's Statute). International representation would have required the appointment of a German judge, and judges from neutral and other countries from all parts of the world. However, which German judge would have accepted, in 1945, to sit in judgment of his former leaders? Neutral countries would undoubtedly have refused their participation on the simple ground of their neutrality and most other nations would probably not have been eager to join the victors in this uncertain and unprecedented venture.

The establishment of the Tribunal was undoubtedly a political process, which followed debates and controversies within each victor's nation, and was the result of difficult negotiations between their political and legal representatives. Its creation by a quadripartite agreement, even if later confirmed by 19 other countries, did not conform with the norms of customary international law, i.e. the negotiation and approval of an international treaty in an international conference and ratification by states' signatories, a process that would have taken ten to twenty years, without assurance that a sufficient proportion of states would support the creation of an international Court to judge the Nazi violators of international humanitarian law. This was the 'original sin' of the Nuremberg Trial, in the opinion of a number of international law specialists. The circumstances of the war, the need for urgent action and the claims for revenge and punishment did not allow for such guarantees and alternatives to be investigated: expediency prevailed.

In his opening statement to the trial, US Chief Prosecutor Robert E. Jackson recognized frankly that: 'Unfortunately, the nature of these crimes is such that both prosecution and judgment must be by victor nations over vanquished foes'. He added: 'If these men are the first war leaders of a defeated nation to be prosecuted in the name of the law, they are also the first to be given a chance to plead for their lives in the name of the law'.[14]

Count 1: Conspiracy

The concept of conspiracy was introduced in the Charter at the initiative of the Americans, against the objections of the French and the Soviets. As related by Taylor,[15] its author, Murray Bernays, a New York lawyer, promoted the conspiracy and 'organizational guilt idea with the purpose of obtaining a judgment of criminality in a single trial, following which convictions of members who had joined voluntarily would follow automatically and punishments could be imposed in summary proceedings against hundreds of thousands of members'. The French viewed this concept as 'a barbarous legal mechanism unworthy of modern law'.[16] The final draft of the Charter limited the impact of this concept to 'crimes against peace' (Article 6(a), and no explicit reference to conspiracy is found in Articles 6(b) and (c). It could then be deduced that only conspiracy to commit crimes against peace was a prosecutable offence. Conspiracy to commit war crimes or crimes against humanity were not. The Prosecution's Indictment still attempted to extend the application of the charge of conspiracy to any of the three basic crimes in the Charter.

At the first closed meeting of the Judges to consider their judgment, on 27 June 1946, the French judge, Henri Donnedieu de Vabres, moved that count 1, conspiracy, be rejected. This crime did not exist in international law and evidence had shown that there had been no common plan. No practical purpose would be served by a finding of conspiracy, since all the defendants had been involved under the other counts. This proposal was rejected by his colleagues and the judges decided to limit the application of conspiracy to the charge of waging aggressive war. In a final consensus, the Court declared that membership in one of the convicted organizations was criminal, *per se*, and could be punished by any sentence, including death. However, the Tribunal excluded from condemnation 'persons who had no knowledge of the criminal purposes or acts of the organization, and those who were drafted by the state for membership, unless they were personally implicated in the commission of acts declared criminal by Article 6 of the

Charter as members of the organization. Membership alone is not enough to come within the scope of these declarations.'[17] In a later writing, the French judge reiterated his doubts. He felt that 'the imputation of a conspiracy adorns the Hitlerian enterprise of a romantic prestige' but could hardly be deemed indispensable to ensure a just repression.[18]

A few years after Nuremberg, Justice Jackson, who had been a strong supporter of the conspiracy theory, criticized this same doctrine in a separate opinion in *Krulewitch v. United States*: 'The modern crime of conspiracy is so vague that it almost defies definition.'[19]

Count 2: Crimes against Peace

As did count 1, to which it is closely linked, count 2 also proved controversial. It was challenged by both the French and the Soviets when the text of the Charter was being discussed.

The French position was based on legal grounds. Professor André Gros affirmed that the launching of a war of aggression was not a crime under international law and could not assign criminal responsibility to individuals who launch aggressive wars. Deciding otherwise would constitute *ex post facto* legislation. Nazi leaders were criminals not because they launched aggressive wars, but because, in so doing, they committed war crimes. The American jurist Alwyn Vernon Freeman had supported this view: under international law, a violator of an agreement did not suffer criminal penalties and, unless the agreement concerned specified criminal penalties for its violation, no such penalties could legally be imposed.[20]

The Soviet view was not so clearly exposed, but its representative was probably and rightly fearing that past Soviet aggressions would be brought up during the trial: the joint German/Soviet aggression against Poland of August 1939 with the disclosure of the secret protocol attached to the non-aggression pact of 23 August 1939, and the Soviet aggression against Finland and the Baltic States, between November 1939 and June 1940.

In spite of these objections, the Allies decided to include the crimes against peace charge in the Charter. Under its Article 6(a), the defendants were charged by the prosecution with initiating war against Poland, the UK and France in September 1939, Denmark and Norway in April 1940, Belgium, the Netherlands and Luxemburg in May 1940, Yugoslavia and Greece in April 1941, the USSR in

June 1941 and the USA in December 1941. They were charged with violations of the Hague Conventions of 1899 and 1907, of the Treaty of Versailles of 28 June 1919, of the Kellogg–Briand Pact of 1928, of the Munich Agreement of 29 September 1939, of the non-aggression Treaty between Germany and the USSR of 23 August 1939 and others. In a 'Motion adopted by all Defense Counsels', the counsels argued that 'The present Trial can, therefore, as far as Crimes against Peace shall be avenged, not invoke existing international law; it is rather a proceeding pursuant to a new penal law . . . enacted only after the crime'.

In its judgment, the Tribunal affirmed

> that the maxim *nullum crimen sine lege* is not a limitation of sovereignty, but is in general a principle of justice. To assert that it is unjust to punish those who in defiance of treaties and assurances have attacked neighboring states without warning is obviously untrue, for in such circumstances the attacker must know that he is doing wrong, and so far from it being unjust to punish him, it would be unjust if his wrong were allowed to go unpunished.

The Tribunal pointed out that the Kellogg–Briand Pact had been ratified by 63 states, including Germany, Italy and Japan, at the outbreak of the war in 1939. In its opinion, the renunciation of war 'as an instrument of national policy necessarily involves the proposition that such a war is illegal in international law and that those who plan and wage such a war, with its inevitable and terrible consequences, are committing a crime in so doing'. In order to overcome the objection that the Pact (or other international treaties) did not expressly state that waging a war of aggression was a crime, or set up courts to try the individuals who engaged in such wars, the Tribunal invoked an 'adaptive', or 'evolutive' concept of international law:

> The law of war is to be found not only in treaties, but in the customs and practices of states which gradually obtained universal recognition, and from the general principles of justice applied by jurists and practised by military courts. The law is not static, but by continual adaptation follows the needs of a changing world. Indeed, in many cases treaties do no more than express and define for more accurate reference the principles of law already existing'.[21]

Jackson had publicly declared that the prime purpose of the trial was to establish the criminality of aggressive war under general international law.[22] One of the unstated US objectives in having the Nuremberg Tribunal declare that an aggressive war was an international crime was that the USA declared war on Germany without the traditional justification of self-defence. If the German leaders were condemned for having designed and carried out an illegal plan of aggression under the first two counts, this would have constituted *post facto* international approval for the US entry into the war.

It is doubtful, albeit unfortunate, that the criminality of aggressive war has now been firmly established under international law. It is also more than doubtful that the Nuremberg Tribunal's prosecution of individuals for the crime against peace was supported by pre-Nuremberg international law.

Count 3: War Crimes

If the American priority was to establish the criminality of aggressive wars under international law, for the French and the Soviets, war crimes were the major and crucial charge against the defendants. This count was based on well-established, traditional law of the war and was therefore less subject to legal controversies with regard to its substance, with a few exceptions. However, the relevant instrument, the Hague Convention of 18 October 1907 and Annexed Regulations concerning the Laws and Customs of War on Land, do not establish individual criminal responsibility at the international level for those who violate their provisions: states were to issue instructions to their armed land forces in conformity with these provisions and states could be liable to pay compensation for acts committed by persons forming part of their armed forces. It was the responsibility of contracting powers to introduce in their penal and/or military codes the definition of war crimes, relevant sanctions to be applied to violators and which national jurisdiction would be competent to judge them. The legal argument that the four powers that created the Tribunal assumed all powers in occupied Germany and did 'together what any one of them might have done singly' supports the validity of the Tribunal's competence on this count, by converting the competence of four national criminal jurisdictions into the competence of one international (quadripartite) military Tribunal. As stated earlier, this argument does not, however, alleviate the general charge that the Nuremberg Trial was 'Victors' Justice'.

In the indictment, the defendants were charged with the following war crimes:

1. Killing and cruel treatment of the civilian population on occupied territory and in the open sea;
2. Abduction of the civilian population of occupied territories into slavery and for other purposes;
3. Killing and cruel treatment of prisoners of war and other servicemen, with whom Germany found itself in a state of war, as well as persons in the open sea;
4. Killing of hostages;
5. Imposition of extortionate fines;
6. Senseless destruction of towns, settlements, and villages and devastation unjustified by military necessity;
7. Forced recruitment of civilian manpower;
8. Germanization of occupied territories.[23]

These war crimes were committed on a vast scale and amply documented during the trial. The Hague Convention of 1907 prescribes, *inter alia*, that 'Prisoners of war . . . must be humanely treated' (Article 4). Especially forbidden by Article 23 are:

b) To kill or wound treacherously individuals belonging to the hostile nation or army;
c) To kill or wound an enemy who, having laid down his arms, or having no longer means of defence, has surrendered at discretion;
d) To declare that no quarter will be given.

Under Article 25, 'The attack or bombardment, by whatever means, of towns, villages, dwellings, or buildings which are undefended is prohibited'. Under Article 28, 'The pillage of a town or place, even when taken by assault, is prohibited'.

Prisoners of war were also protected by the Second Geneva Convention of 1929, ratified by Germany in 1934. However, Germany withdrew this protection from countries that had lost their sovereignty, such as Poland, Yugoslavia or Greece. Having repudiated all the international commitments of tsarism, the USSR was unable to obtain the protection of its prisoners of war from Germany under the Hague and Geneva Conventions. Left without care and without sufficient food, millions of Soviet prisoners of war were subjected to extreme violence, deprivation and murders, amounting to a plan of political and racist extermination: about two-thirds of the 5.2 million Soviet prisoners taken by the Wehrmacht died.[24] Civilian populations who were victims of barbaric treatment and extermination were, however, not adequately protected under the international humanitarian law in effect in 1939.

The *Tu Quoque* Arguments

The debates on this count allowed the defence to use the *tu quoque* argument, even if charges against the victors were rejected by the Tribunal as being outside its competence. The mass execution by firing squads of more than 25 000 Poles, including thousands of Polish Army officers, policemen, land and factory owners, and clergymen held in prisoner-of-war camps or in jails, was ordered by the Soviet Politburo, meeting on 5 March 1940. Their bodies were dumped in a mass grave at Katyn. On 14 December 1992, Boris Yeltsin handed over to the Polish President, Lech Walesa, a copy of the document signed by Stalin ordering the massacre, after Gorbachev first admitted Soviet guilt in the Katyn massacre in April 1990. The false charge that the Katyn killings had been committed by the Germans had been included in the indictment at misdirected Soviet insistence, against the unanimous reticence of the other three prosecutors. The Tribunal allowed both German and Soviet witnesses to testify during two days, but made no mention of Katyn in its judgment.[25] This omission in effect cleared the Germans of this war crime, a war crime committed by the Soviets and never judged by a national or an international court.

On air bombing, the Luftwaffe attacks against Warsaw, London, Rotterdam, Coventry or Belgrade and their consequences were debated at length during the trial while the British and American strategic air bombing against Hamburg, Dresden and other German cities were only alluded to by some of the defendants. According to various estimates, from 1940 to 1945, between 305 000 and 650 000 German civilians were killed under the bombs, at least 758 000 were wounded and more than 7.5 million were without shelter. Luftwaffe attacks caused more than 51 500 British deaths, plus 8900 deaths due to the V-1 and V-2 rockets in 1944–5.[26] While the IVth Hague Convention of 1907 had forbidden the ' . . . bombardment, by whatever means, of towns, villages, dwellings, or buildings which are undefended' (Article 25), all attempts to legislate internationally in the domain of air war – the Washington Conference of 1922, a German proposal of 1929 to ban the use of aviation for military purposes and to ban air bombing, and a British draft convention for disarmament of 1933, aiming at a total prohibition of air bombing – failed. Under international law, air bombing could therefore not be labelled as 'war crime', even if terrorizing, maiming and killing the civilian population indiscriminately should be condemned on humane and moral grounds, besides having been shown to be an ineffective means of political and military pressure on the governments concerned.

Admirals Doenitz and Raeder were accused of violating the London Submarine Protocol of 1936, to which 36 nations, including Germany, had adhered by 1939. German submarines had sunk many British and other merchant ships without warning. The Protocol provided that a 'merchant vessel' could not be sunk by either surface vessels or submarines without the attacking vessel first placing 'passengers, crew, and ship's papers in a place of safety'. However, this specific charge could not be maintained by the Tribunal on another *'tu quoque'* basis. All belligerents violated the Protocol, and in particular, the British and the Americans. US Admiral Nimitz testified in writing to the Tribunal on 2 July 1946 that: 'The Chief of Naval Operations on 7 December 1941 ordered unrestricted submarine warfare against Japan', and 'On general principles, the US submarines did not rescue enemy survivors if undue additional hazard to the submarine resulted or the submarine would thereby be prevented from accomplishing its further mission.' American submarines had sunk 1944 Japanese merchant vessels.[27]

Count 4: Crimes against Humanity

Some of the atrocities committed by the Nazis in the name of racial purity, such as the planned and systematic persecution and extermination of the European Jews, of the Gypsies, and other inhuman acts committed against civilian populations on political, racial or religious grounds, were not directly related to nor caused by the war, and could therefore not be qualified as war crimes under the existing international law. Some were committed before the 1939 war. One could have expected that these crimes, which were in themselves a major justification for the creation of the Tribunal, would have taken precedence over the first three counts and acquired their autonomy in the new concept of 'crimes against humanity'. This was not the case. What could have been a major advance in international criminal law was narrowed down in the Charter and in the Judgment. In the words of Professor Donnedieu de Vabres (written in 1947), 'the category of crimes against humanity, which the Charter had introduced through a very small door, has, because of the judgment, gone into thin air'.[28] Article 6(c) of the Charter enumerated those crimes as 'murder, extermination, enslavement, deportation, and other inhumane acts committed against civilian population, before or during the war, or persecutions on political, racial or religious grounds' but linked them to 'any crime within the jurisdiction of the Tribunal', i.e. conspiracy, crimes against peace and war crimes. In its Judgment, the Tribunal excluded such crimes as the murder of political opponents, the persecution of the Jews, and the persecution, repression and murder of civilians in Germany before the war of 1939 from its purview within the meaning of the Charter. As from the beginning of the war in 1939, the Tribunal then linked crimes against humanity with war crimes: ' . . . War Crimes were committed on a vast scale, which were also Crimes against Humanity; and insofar as the inhumane acts charged in the Indictment, and committed after the beginning of the war, did not constitute War Crimes, they were committed in execution of , or in connection with, the aggressive war, and therefore constituted Crimes against Humanity'.[29]

NUREMBERG'S CONTRIBUTION TO INTERNATIONAL CRIMINAL LAW

Nuremberg had its warts, which have been recalled above: victor's justice, the application of *ex post facto* legislation and the *tu quoque* arguments. Former judge Donnedieu de Vabres candidly acknowledged, after the trial, the 'infirmity of human justice, in particular that of political justice, of which the Nuremberg is a manifestation'. He wrote that the Tribunal was an *ad hoc* jurisdiction, whose institution was subsequent to the offences it was mandated to judge. The charges were vague, the sanctions almost entirely left to the discretionary appreciation of the judges. On the other hand, he felt that the trial had brought morality into international law – no small feat.[30]

The trial played an important political role in reducing the tension between victors and the vanquished, by substituting a legal process for the victims' urge for revenge. By focusing the blame on important Nazi dignitaries, it decreased the risk that the whole German nation and population would be assigned the lasting burden of collective guilt, even if new claims that all the German people were 'willing executioners' of the genocide have recently been revived. A considerable amount of documentation on the Nazi era was researched and assembled for the trial, which has proved invaluable for historians, even if anti-semitic pseudo-historians have chosen to ignore the evidence and deny the Holocaust.

Even if it were an imperfect, political justice, Nuremberg made a significant contribution to international criminal law and justice. It established the principle and practice that individuals at the highest levels of government and armed forces could be prosecuted and punished by an international tribunal for serious violations of international humanitarian law. It thus established international individual responsibility for crimes against peace, war crimes and crimes against humanity. 'Obedience to superior orders' was no longer acceptable as an absolute defence in international law for these crimes. Even the limited application of the new concept of 'crimes against humanity' by the Tribunal served as a basis and an inspiration for the Genocide and the Apartheid Conventions, as well as for the institutionalization of the system of 'grave breaches' and the extension of protection to civilian populations in the four Geneva Conventions of 1949.[31]

Finally, the Nuremberg precedent, with its faults and achievements, has provided an essential historical, legal and judiciary basis for the later creation of the Tribunals for ex-Yugoslavia and Rwanda. It has also contributed to the elaboration by the International Law Commission of the Draft Code of Crimes against the Peace and Security of Mankind and to the drafting of the Statute of the future International Criminal Court.

3 The Tokyo Trial

On 14 August 1945, the Emperor of Japan informed his good and loyal subjects that he had decided the surrender of his country to the Allied forces, the USA, the UK, China, Australia, Canada, New Zealand and the USSR. He stated that Japan had declared war on America and Britain out of 'Our sincere desire to assure Japan's self-preservation and the stabilization of East Asia, it being far from Our thought either to infringe upon the sovereignty of other nations or to embark upon territorial aggrandizement' (the full text of the statement is in Presentation 3.1).

The Emperor's words hardly reflected historical facts.

THE MILITARY RISE AND FALL OF JAPAN

The Sino–Japanese War of 1894–5 had made Japan dominant in a still nominally independent Korea. The Chinese also ceded to them Taiwan (Formosa). The Russian–Japanese War of 1904–5 reinforced Japan's hold on Korea and gave it substantial influence in Southern Manchuria. In 1910, Japan annexed Korea. Japan joined the Allies in World War I: it had a permanent seat in the Council of the League of Nations. In 1928, Zhang Zuolin, the most powerful warlord in northern China, was murdered by the Japanese: he had threatened to side with the Chinese Nationalists rather than with the Japanese. While Japan never declared war on China, its involvement on the Chinese mainland increased. In 1931, the Manchurian Incident led to the occupation of all of Manchuria as 'Manchukuo', declared part of the Japanese Empire. In 1933, Japan left the League of Nations in protest against the Lytton Commission Report, accused to be biased against Japan. In 1937, came the Incident at Marco Polo Bridge and the outbreak of full hostilities between the Japanese army and those of both Jiang Jieshi (Chiang Kai-shek) and Mao Tse-tung. China had the support of the USA and the UK. Isolated from the international community, Japan joined the Axis Powers, signing the Tripartite Alliance in 1940. When Hitler invaded the Soviet Union in June 1941, Japan responded by concluding a neutrality pact with the USSR and invaded French-held

PRESENTATION 3.1
THE IMPERIAL RESCRIPT (JAPAN)

To Our good and loyal subjects:
   After pondering deeply the general conditions of the world and the actual conditions obtaining in our Empire today, We have decided to effect a settlement of the present situation by resorting to an extraordinary measure.
   ... We declared war on America and Britain out of Our sincere desire to assure Japan's self-preservation and the stabilization of East Asia, it being far from Our thought either to infringe upon the sovereignty of other nations or to embark upon territorial aggrandizement. But now, the war has lasted for nearly four years. Despite the best that has been done by everyone – the gallant fighting of military and naval forces, the diligence and assiduity of Our servants of the State and the devoted service of Our one hundred million people, the war situation has developed not necessarily to Japan's advantage, while the general trends of the world have all turned against her interest. Moreover the enemy has begun to employ a new and most cruel bomb, the power of which to do damage is indeed incalculable, taking the toll of many innocent lives. Should We continue to fight it would not only result in the ultimate collapse and obliteration of the Japanese nation, but also it would lead to the total extinction of human civilization. Such being the case how are We to save the millions of Our subjects or to atone Ourselves before the hallowed spirits of Our Imperial Ancestors? This is the reason Why we have ordered the acceptance of the Joint Declaration of the Powers ... We are keenly aware of the inmost feelings of all ye, Our subjects. However, it is according to the dictate of time and fate that We have resolved to pave the way for a grand peace for all the generations to come by enduring the endurable and suffering what is insufferable ...

The 14th day of the 8th month of the 20th year of Shōwa (August 14, 1945)

Source: Haruka Taya Cook and Theodore F. Cook, *Japan at War, An Oral History* (New York: The New Press, 1992) p. 401 by permission.

Southern Indochina. The USA then declared an embargo on oil, joined by the UK, China and the Netherlands: Japan was dependent on imported oil for 80% of its needs.
   When the Japanese–American negotiations of 1941 failed to satisfy its claims, Japan attacked Pearl Harbor in Hawaii on 7 December, without a declaration of war, as in 1895, 1904 and 1937. The USA declared war on the Axis (Germany, Italy and Japan) as well as on

the UK (against Japan). The Japanese conquests of Malaya, Burma, Indonesia and the Philippines followed. With the approval of the French Vichy authorities, Japan used the bases in French Indochina. Japanese forces captured Kuala Lumpur in January 1942, Singapore in February, Rangoon in March and Mandalay in May. The Dutch forces in Indonesia had surrendered in March. Heavy fighting in the Philippines led to surrender also in January 1942.

The tide turned against Japan with the naval battle of Midway in June 1942. The strongly defended islands of the western Pacific were retaken one by one by the Americans and Australians in fierce battles, with heavy losses on both sides. The Philippines were retaken by early 1945, and in June, Okinawa, part of Japanese home territory, fell to the Allies. Japan sent feelers for a possible surrender to the still neutral Russians in early 1945. Ignoring these, the USSR joined the victors' camp by declaring war on Japan on 8 August and invading Manchuria and North Korea. The atomic bombs were dropped on Hiroshima and Nagasaki respectively on 6 and 9 August.

Much of Asia had been devastated by World War II: there were more war casualties in Asia than in the European war. A total of 2.5 million Japanese military had died in the war and nearly one million civilians had perished in air raids. It is estimated that 10 million Chinese died as a result of the Japanese invasion, most of them civilians. Between 300 000 and one million Indonesians were mobilized as forced labour by the Japanese: of these, estimates of deaths range from tens of thousands to half a million. According to the UN Working Group for Asia and the Far East, 'the total number who were killed by the Japanese, or who died from hunger, disease and lack of medical attention is estimated at 3,000,000 for Java alone, and 1,000,000 for the Outer Islands'.[1]

Politically, Japan was different from Nazi Germany, for historical and cultural reasons, despite a few similarities. There was no one-man dictatorship, no Führer. The Emperor was revered as a sacred figure, but was not a political leader. Japan was ruled by a coalition of strongly nationalist military officials and politicians, whose objective was an expansionist Japan and the creation of a Greater East Asia Co-Prosperity sphere under exclusive Japanese domination. The Japanese people enthusiastically supported their leaders and their objectives, within the corset of intensive propaganda, strict censorship and repression of political and intellectual dissidence. There was no scapegoat group such as the Jews, although the Japanese believed in the superiority of their race over other Asian peoples, and over most of the European peoples, who were considered to be decadent. There was no genocide against a particular race or people, but terror and indiscriminate abuses were applied to both Asian and Anglo-Saxon military and civilian personnel.

WAR AND OTHER CRIMES

Japanese atrocities included massacres of non-combatants, the maltreatment and killing of prisoners of war, torture, forced labour and institutional murder in the form of lethal medical experiments. In their occupation of foreign countries and territories, the Japanese armed forces were ruthless: they exterminated whole villages as part of a policy of terror and slaughtered non-combatants indiscriminately. They often used prisoners of war as live targets for bayonet practice. They were the only belligerents to use biological warfare, dropping germs of bubonic plague and other epidemic diseases by air on Chinese cities. The bacteriological warfare research and experimentation carried out by the Japanese Unit 731 in Manchuria are referred to later in this chapter. Japanese brutality was assigned to their conviction of their own racial and cultural superiority and their contempt for those whom they had vanquished and had surrendered. They boasted of their flouting of the Geneva Convention on the treatment of prisoners of war, which they saw as a contemptible Western notion.[2]

Among the many recorded atrocities committed by the Japanese armed forces, the 'Rape of Nanking' stands out, although it has long been denied by the Japanese authorities and is still occulted in Japan. In October 1937, Japanese troops, with the full knowledge of their commanders, engaged in the widespread execution, rape and random murder of Chinese men, women and children. From 42 000 to 100 000 Chinese were killed during this 'incident', as a result of the shelling and subsequent atrocities.[3] Survivors described sights of raped women impaled on stakes and children burned to death or sliced in two. Stores and homes were systematically plundered and burned.

In order to consolidate their power over northern China, the Japanese turned to 'rural pacification' campaigns, which amounted to indiscriminate terror against the peasantry. By 1941–2, the anti-Communist pacification had evolved into the devastating 'three-all' policy: 'kill all, burn all, destroy all'. After the American defeat in the Philippines in 1942, from 5000 to 10 000 Filipino troops and 600 Americans died in the infamous Bataan Death March. As many as 300 000 Javanese, Tamil, Malayan, Burmese and Chinese labourers were mobilized to build the Burma-Siam railroad between October 1942 and November 1943, as well as 60 000–70 000 Allied prisoners of war, mostly Australian, British, Indian and Dutch: of the former group, an estimated 60 000 died and of the latter group, approximately 15 000 – 27% of Japan's Anglo-American prisoners of war died in detention.

Either as a response to well-publicized Japanese atrocities, or as a compelling part of warfare itself, the Allies also engaged in violations of humanitarian law on the battlefield, and they carried out extensive and intensive air bombing. However, they had not initiated a war of aggression against Japan.

THE CREATION OF THE TOKYO TRIBUNAL

On 8 August 1945, the quadripartite London Conference produced the Agreement that included the Statute of the Nuremberg International Military Tribunal and the guiding principles of the Trial. Two weeks before, on 26 July, China, the UK, and the USA – subsequently joined by the USSR – had issued the Potsdam Declaration, announcing their intention to prosecute high-level Japanese officials for the same crimes committed by the Germans in the European war. Articles 6 and 10 of the Declaration, entitled 'Proclamation Defining Terms for Japanese Surrender', stated, *inter alia*:

(6) There must be eliminated for all time the authority and influence of those who have deceived and misled the people of Japan into embarking on world conquest, for we insist that a new order of peace, security and justice will be impossible until irresponsible militarism is driven from the world.

(10) We do not intend that the Japanese shall be enslaved as a race or destroyed as a nation but stern justice shall be meted out to all war criminals, including those who have visited cruelties upon our prisoners . . .

On 2 September 1945, the signatories for Japan 'by command of and on behalf of the Emperor and the Japanese government' accepted the terms of the Potsdam Declaration by the Instrument of Surrender of Japan executed at Tokyo Bay. The authority of the Emperor and the Japanese government was then made subject to General MacArthur, the Supreme Commander for the Allied Powers. On 6 September 1945, the USA issued a 'Statement of the Initial Surrender Policy for Japan', followed on 21 September by a directive issued by the US Joint Chiefs of Staff, and approved by all nations taking part in the occupation of Japan. The directive ordered the investigation, apprehension and detention of all persons suspected of war crimes. The Supreme Commander was to appoint special international courts and to prescribe their rules of procedure. The directive, although known and approved by the other allied nations, represented unilateral action on the part of the USA. On 19 January 1946, MacArthur issued a Proclamation establishing an 'International Military Tribunal for the Far East for the trial of those persons charged individually, or as members of organizations, or in both capacities, with offences which include crimes against peace'.

As for Nuremberg, the intention was to assign criminality to individuals, and to reject the charge of collective responsibility of a whole nation and people. However, unlike Nuremberg, the drafting of the Charter of the Tokyo Tribunal was not submitted to an international conference: it was essentially an American project. The Tokyo Charter was drafted by the Americans only and was approved unilaterally on 19 January 1946 by the Supreme Commander for the Allied Powers in Japan, in the form of an executive order. The Allies were only consulted after its issuance, a subordinate position justified politically by the primary military role played by the USA in fighting the Japanese and in achieving victory.[4] The Charter, dated 26 April 1946, established the International Military Tribunal 'for the just and prompt trial and punishment of the major war criminals in the Far East'. Its permanent seat was set in Tokyo.

The supremacy of the USA was again asserted by the authority granted to the Supreme Commander of the Allied Powers to appoint the eleven members (judges) of the Tribunal from the names submitted by the Signatories to the Instrument of Surrender, i.e. the UK, Australia, China, the USSR, France, Canada, the Netherlands, New Zealand and the USA. India and the Philippines had been added to the initial list, although they were not yet sovereign states. There were no alternates. The Chief Supreme Commander also had the authority to appoint the President of the Tribunal among its members: he appointed to that position Sir William Webb, a former Justice High Court of the Australian Commonwealth and Australian war crimes commissioner during the war. The four Nuremberg judges and alternates had been appointed by the four Signatories, and their President appointed by the judges themselves.

Unlike Nuremberg, where there were four prosecutors, equal in rank if not in actual performance and influence, in Tokyo there was one Chief of Counsel (Prosecutor), an American, and ten associate counsels, each having the nationality of the ten countries other than the USA. Responsibility for investigation and prosecution rested solely on the Chief of Counsel: as an unusual departure of international judiciary practice, 11 nations had agreed to subordinate their sovereignty and to permit a national of one of them to have final direction and control. The crimes coming within the jurisdiction of the Tribunal were the same as those of the Nuremberg Charter: crimes against peace, conventional war crimes and crimes against humanity, including the participation in a common plan or conspiracy to commit those crimes. One difference compared with Nuremberg was that only persons charged with 'offences which included crimes against peace' were brought to trial. Another difference was that crimes against humanity were not limited to 'any civilian population', thus allowing the punishment for crimes against civilian and military personnel. Finally, no provision was made at Tokyo for the trial of allegedly criminal groups or organizations.

Fair trial procedures were essentially similar to those of Nuremberg. The proceedings were to be conducted in English and in Japanese. Each defendant had the right to be represented by counsel of his own selection, 'subject to the disapproval of such counsel at any time by the Tribunal'. In effect, Japanese and American lawyers represented the defendants. As for Nuremberg, sentences included the death penalty.

The Proceedings

The Tokyo Trial lasted more than twice the duration of Nuremberg: it opened on 3 May 1946 and the Tribunal delivered its majority judgment in November 1948. The defendants included Tojo Hideki, who was Prime Minister during the attack on Pearl Harbor; three others who had also been Prime Ministers, including one who had been Minister of Foreign Affairs from 1933 to 1936; the Commander-in-chief of the Japanese forces in Central China in 1937–8 and his successor in 1940–4; 11 other Army officers; three admirals; four diplomats; three bureaucrats; and the theoretician of Greater Asia.

Emperor Hirohito was not among the defendants, nor was he called as a witness. The decision to give him immunity was shared by most of the Allies, led by the Americans, and by the Japanese authorities: the Shidehara government, which assumed its functions on 5 October 1945, submitted that his quality as constitutional monarch made him unable to oppose the government's decisions during the war, in spite of his own feelings in favour of peace. The defendants held to that formal and respectful position throughout the Trial, with the exception noted hereunder.[5] As reported by Minear,[6] the US Chiefs of Staff had issued a secret order in January 1946 not to indict the Emperor, a position that had been strongly supported by MacArthur. This decision was endorsed by the Far Eastern Commission. The UK approved this decision and advised Commonwealth nations that prosecuting the Emperor would constitute a grave political error.[7] On the other hand, the USSR had insisted that the Emperor be tried: for Truman and MacArthur, this was a means of causing internal unrest in Japan.[8] This political decision had been taken in order to ensure an element of continuity in Japan's political life and to facilitate the task of the US occupation forces in the progressive democratization of the country's institutions, including the transformation of the status of the sacred Emperor into a real constitutional monarch. By leaving the Emperor in his position, MacArthur wanted to prevent a possible violent reaction from the Japanese people seeing their God-monarch in the dock of a Western-run trial.

Granting the Emperor immunity was not based on the merits of the case. The major defendant at the trial, Tojo, testified once that 'there is no Japanese subject who would go against the will of His Majesty; more particularly, among high officials of the Japanese government or of Japan . . .'. Tojo later corrected this statement, in order to protect the Emperor, by insisting on the Emperor's 'love for and desire for peace'. Both the President of the Tribunal, William Webb (Australia), and Justice Henri Bernard of France had serious reservations about the Emperor's immunity. For Webb, if the Emperor had not been indicted, none of his ministers should suffer the death penalty. Bernard held that the failure to indict the Emperor was one of three serious defects that nullified the trial. No member of the industrialist groups was indicted, as no evidence

was produced that any of them occupied the position of a principal formulator of policy.

   In the two years following the opening of the trial, the judges
heard testimony from more than 400 persons and received more
than 4000 items of documentary evidence. Altogether, the trial
generated a transcript of over 45 000 pages. The judges spent seven
months writing their opinions. Their judgment was rendered on
1 November 1948.

THE JUDGMENT

In Nuremberg, one of the four judges filed a separate Opinion. In
Tokyo, the Tribunal's majority judgment was followed by four separate or dissenting Opinions and one concurring Opinion.[9] At the
commencement of the proceedings, the nine judges then present
had unanimously decided to abandon separate or dissenting opinions. Only one judgment was to be delivered, reflecting the opinion of the majority, and the secrecy of the deliberations *in camera*
was to be respected. The Indian judge, when he arrived later, declared himself not bound by the agreement, since he would thus
forfeit his right to a dissenting opinion. The agreement was thereby
cancelled.

   The judges found all the defendants guilty by a vote of eight to
three – the three dissenters were Justice Bernard of France, Justice Pal of India and Justice Röling of the Netherlands. All defendants but two (Matsui, Commander-in-Chief of the Japanese
Forces in Central China in 1937–8 and Shigemitsu, Foreign Minister in 1943–5) were found guilty of 'conspiracy to wage aggressive
war'. These two defendants were found guilty, the first of war crimes
only – for which he was hanged – and the second of six other counts
of aggressive war and war crimes, for which he was sentenced to
seven years' imprisonment. Five defendants were found guilty of
'atrocities', namely crimes against humanity, in addition to other
crimes, chiefly the 'over-all conspiracy' – they were all hanged. In
summary, seven defendants were condemned to death by hanging
– two of them politicians, Hirota and Tojo, both former Prime
Ministers – and five generals. The others were given jail sentences
ranging from life to seven years. None was acquitted. In contrast,
at Nuremberg, there were three acquittals, but 12 of the 22 defendants were condemned to death.[10] In a separate opinion, the

Australian President did not record any formal dissent with the sentences pronounced by the majority, but offered some reasons why imprisonment for life could have been preferred to the death sentence, including a parallel with Nuremberg sentences. Affirming the undoubted authority of the Emperor, he felt that his immunity should be taken into consideration when determining the punishment of the accused found guilty.[11]

In his 'Judgment', Justice Pal held that all the accused must be found not guilty of all charges in the indictment and should be acquitted of all those charges; for him, the 'name of Justice should not be allowed to be invoked only for the prolongation of the pursuit of vindictive retaliation.' Röling noted that Justice Pal emerged as the judge who represented the real Asian attitude: he resented colonial relations and the Japanese slogan 'Asia for the Asians' struck a chord with him.[12] In his Dissenting Judgment, Justice Bernard concluded that 'a verdict reached by a Tribunal after a defective procedure cannot be a valid one'. He believed that guarantees for their defence were not granted to the accused. The eleven judges were never called to meet to discuss orally a part of or, in its entirety, the part of the judgment relative to the findings of fact. He reached the conclusion that the culpability of the accused regarding the accusation of crimes against peace could not be regarded as certain. The declaration of the Pacific war had a 'principal author who escaped all prosecution and of whom in any case the present defendants could only be considered as accomplices'. He had no doubt that certain defendants bore a large part of the responsibility for the 'most abominable crimes' committed on the largest scale by the members of the Japanese police and army, and that others were guilty of serious failings in the duties towards the prisoners of war and towards humanity. However, he 'could not venture further in the formulation of verdicts, the exactitude of which would be subject to caution or of sentences, the equity of which would be far too contestable'.[13]

In his Opinion, Justice Röling asserted that, from the law as it now stands, no one should be sentenced to death for having committed a crime against peace: internment for life would be the appropriate punishment for this crime. Those found guilty of conventional war crimes should be punished with the supreme penalty. In consequence, he agreed with six of the seven death penalties. As for the seventh defendant, Hirota, Röling felt that he had not been proved guilty of any charge. Three military defendants

(Oka, Sao and Shimada) should have been sentenced to death instead of to life imprisonment, as they were guilty of conventional war crimes. Finally, he stated that four other defendants (one military man, Hata, and three politicians, Kido, Shigemitsu and Togo), condemned by the Tribunal to either life imprisonment or shorter sentences, should have been acquitted.[14] In his Concurring Opinion, Justice Jaranilla endorsed the majority judgment, although he differed on some of the penalties imposed by the Tribunal, which were, in his view, too lenient, not exemplary and deterrent and not commensurate with the gravity of of the offence or offences committed.[15]

On 24 November 1948, General MacArthur, after having consulted with the diplomatic representatives in Japan from each of the nations represented on the Far Eastern Commission, confirmed the convictions, and directed the sentences to be executed.

THE CRITICISMS

From the above, and in comparison with Nuremberg, the Tokyo Trial suffered from a number of flaws, in addition to those already mentioned for the former. At the same time, one should recall that the demand from many nations for retribution for the Japanese wars, war crimes and crimes against humanity was as great and as urgent as that for Nuremberg. In common with Nuremberg, and for similar reasons, the Tokyo Tribunal was not created by an international treaty, which would have taken too long to negotiate, without assurance of a successful outcome. This was their common 'original sin', in the view of international law specialists. This 'sin' was however aggravated in the case of Tokyo by the cavalier fashion in which the American authorities drafted the Tribunal's Charter without prior consultation with their Allies, and had it promulgated as an American executive order by the American Supreme Commander for the Allied Powers in Japan. The order did not have the substance nor the form of a multilateral, freely negotiated, agreement among these Allied Powers: at least the London Agreement had been negotiated by the four Allied Powers, and later endorsed by 19 other governments.

Victors' and American Justice

As for Nuremberg, Tokyo was justice decided upon by Allied Powers and rendered only by judges of Allied countries. There was no attempt nor intent to broaden the composition of the Allied Tribunal into a genuine international tribunal. Only Japanese officials were judged in Tokyo. As for Nuremberg, the prosecution was entirely in the hands of Allied Powers' representatives, with the difference that, for Tokyo, the Americans chose to create a post of Chief Prosecutor, filled by an American, in a position of authority over the ten associate prosecutors. As noted above, the American Supreme Commander had the authority to appoint the judges and to nominate the Tribunal's President, in another difference from Nuremberg. The immunity granted to the Emperor was essentially an American decision.

The formal and real American domination and control of the trial was finally asserted by the authority given to the Supreme Commander by the Tokyo Charter to 'reduce or otherwise alter the sentence [of the Tribunal], except to increase its severity' (Article 17). As already noted, this American control of the Tokyo trial is easily explained by the US political and military supremacy in the Asian War over its Allies, and its determining role in achieving victory. While the overt objective of the trial was to punish those who had started an aggressive war, an international crime under the Tribunal's Charter, one of the judges later affirmed that MacArthur's real aim was to avenge the treacherous attack on Pearl Harbor, which had brought humiliation on the US nation and its military forces, an attack which should be branded as an 'enormous crime, a grave violation of the laws of war'. In doing so, and in exposing the Japanese atrocities, it would take the blame off the American government and the American military commanders for the use of atomic weapons at Hiroshima and Nagasaki.[16]

The Uncertain International Law

The Tokyo Tribunal suffered from the same weaknesses as Nuremberg, in so far as neither the law of Geneva nor the law of the Hague had established that high-level leaders would be made responsible before an international tribunal for alleged war crimes, nor that such an international tribunal would apply sanctions to these individuals for crimes which were previously considered as 'acts of states', for which only states could be blamed and possibly condemned to only financial sanctions. The Geneva and Hague Conventions relied on states to sanction individual perpetrators of violations of humanitarian law, i.e. on national, not international, justice. As noted in the previous chapter, the legal concept of 'conspiracy', contained in both Tribunals' Charters is peculiar to Anglo-Saxon legal systems, and was resisted in Nuremberg by the French and Soviet representatives at the London Conference. In Tokyo, both President Webb and Judge Pal rightly asserted that conspiracy had never been a part of international law, although the Chief prosecutor and the majority judgment held the opposite view.[17] There was no agreement among all the judges that conspiracy had been proved beyond doubt, and that conspiracy was a crime under international law. The majority judgment held that aggressive war was an international crime, basing itself on part of the Nuremberg judgment, with the latter's interpretation of the legal effect of the Pact of Paris of 1928: its text has been quoted in Chapter 2.[18]

That crimes were committed as a consequence of aggressive wars is beyond doubt: in fact, any war, an aggressive or a self-defence war, is the cause of crimes; that the Pact of Paris made aggressive wars illegal under international law was more than doubtful; and, finally, that those individuals who initiated such wars committed crimes under the then applicable international law, and were to be sanctioned by an international tribunal was highly questionable and was rejected by Judge Pal. Judge Bernard appealed to natural law to conclude that aggressive war was illegal. Judge Röling held that aggressive war was not a crime under international law at the beginning of the Second World War: it was an innovation of the Nuremberg and Tokyo trials. He conceded to the victorious Allies the right to create such a crime even after the fact.[19]

War crimes came under the jurisdiction of the Geneva and Hague laws, with the reservations expressed above. The legal notion of crimes against humanity was another innovation created by the Nuremberg Charter and reproduced in the Tokyo Charter. The issue of negative criminality was another ground for discord. The defendants at Tokyo (not at Nuremberg) were accused of having 'deliberately and recklessly disregarded their legal duty to take adequate steps to secure the observance and prevent breaches' of the law and customs of war (Count 55 of the indictment). Justice Pal argued that this did not constitute a crime under the Charter, while Justices Bernard and Röling sought to narrow its scope.

On the general question of the alleged retroactive application of the Tokyo law, the majority judgment also relied on Nuremberg: the Allies had acted within the limits of existing international law in establishing the Charter: its definition of crimes was decisive and binding. Quoting again the Nuremberg judgment (see Chapter 2), the majority held that 'The maxim "nullum crimen sine lege" is not a limitation of sovereignty but is in general a principle of justice.' The problem with this affirmation is that the maxim is more than a 'principle of justice': non-retroactivity of criminal laws is an essential legal principle that applies without exception to national criminal law and justice, as a fundamental guarantee for defendants.

JUDICIARY PROCEDURE

Besides the 'disability' of the judges of being citizens of the victor or aggrieved nations, Minear has identified their vulnerability to specific challenges: the Chinese justice was not a judge in his own country; the Soviet judge did not understand English or Japanese, the two official languages of the trial; and the Philippino, the second American and the Australian justices had prior involvement in the issues to come before the Tribunal. Many observers have contended that President Webb conducted the trial in a manner prejudicial to justice, a charge which was never levelled against the respected and equanimous President at Nuremberg, Sir Geoffrey Lawrence. The French judge at Nuremberg had no judiciary experience, but his alternate had a considerable amount of such experience. On language qualifications, the problem at Tokyo seemed to be a lack of appropriate interpretation facilities in languages other than English and Japanese, justified at the time by the difficult translation problems of the Japanese language. Again, adequate interpretation facilities in English, French, Russian and German had been available in Nuremberg. Finally, the 'prior involvement' charge would not necessarily be an impediment in legal proceedings in Europe.

Three of the judges, Justices Bernard, Röling and Pal, found that the defendants were not granted sufficient guarantees for their defence, or that the Tribunal unfairly construed the evidence, or ignored it, or that the Tribunal's method of procedure and rulings crippled the defence. In his defence appeal to General MacArthur of 21 November 1948, defence counsel for all defendants claimed that 'The trial was Unfair' and 'The Verdict is Not Based on Evidence'. As an example, he said that

> The Tribunal accepted from the prosecution 'evidence' in the form of newspapers reports, second-hand findings and verdict on the basis of such 'evidence'; it ignored all defence evidence in its verdict, saying that the evidence of Japanese witnesses (although not those who testified for the prosecution) was unsatisfactory and unreliable'.[20]

While there were a few procedural flaws at Nuremberg, they never amounted to the levels reached in Tokyo.

TU QUOQUE

While the sequence of Japanese aggressions against Asian nations and the USA cannot be refuted, the USSR Declaration of War against Japan, on 8 August 1945, was also an act of aggression, breaching the non-aggression pact with Japan of 1941. As legitimate self-defence could not be argued, it was also a breach of the 1928 Pact of Paris, a key element in the prosecution of the German and Japanese leaders for crimes against peace at Nuremberg and in Tokyo. Furthermore, the responsibility for the Soviet Declaration of War rested in part on the USA: at Yalta and at Potsdam, the US civilian and military leaders had sought an early Soviet involvement in Manchuria as a way of reducing their own casualties. The Soviets then asked for a formal request to that end from the Allies, a request that was satisfied by President Truman.[21] Joining the Allies in the war against Japan at this late stage – the Emperor announced Japan's surrender on 14 August – allowed the USSR to be among the victors and to have a judge at the Tokyo Tribunal. As the Tokyo Tribunal only judged Japanese crimes, the allegation that the USSR also committed a crime against peace was not raised at the trial.

AIR BOMBARDMENT OF JAPAN

Leaving aside Japan's crimes, the USA has been accused of having carried out intensive and extensive bombing of undefended Japanese cities with large civilian populations, unrelated to military necessity. This was alleged to be in violation of the Hague Convention of 1899, although the 1907 revision was deemed to be only an 'empty shell', and the Geneva Conference failed in 1933 to obtain an agreement on a prohibition of air bombing on civilian populations.[22] Even if such bombing was not formally prohibited under the existing laws of the war, and thus could not be labelled as a war crime, the resulting extensive suffering and large number of deaths of non-combatants can only be the object of severe criticisms on a humane basis.

When the Japanese began bombing Chinese cities in 1937, Japan was condemned by an advisory committee to the League of Nations and by the US Department of State. President Franklin D. Roosevelt condemned this barbarity in October 1937 and again in 1939:

> The ruthless bombing from the air of civilians in unfortified centers of population during the course of the hostilities which have raged in various quarters of the earth during the past few years, which has resulted in the maiming and in the death of thousands of defenseless men, women and children, has sickened the hearts of every civilized man and woman, and has profoundly shocked the conscience of humanity.

The German bombing of Warsaw in 1939, and Rotterdam, London and Coventry in 1940 was denounced as wanton terror. In 1940, Winston Churchill denounced it as a 'new and odious form of attack'.

By 1942, the situation had been reversed: the Royal Air Force and the US Air Forces promoted strategic bombing and perfected the technique of massive urban destruction with incendiary bombs, war practices then firmly denounced by the Axis Powers. Following the Quebec Conference of August 1943, the British Minister of Information reported that the Allies intended to 'bomb, burn and ruthlessly destroy' both Germany and Japan.[23] In Japan, the USA first adopted a strategy of high-altitude daytime 'precision' bombing of military and industrial targets, as from late 1944. It was replaced by massive, indiscriminate bombing when, on 9–10 March 1945, 334 aircraft attacked Tokyo at low altitude with incendiary bombs, destroying nearly forty square kilometres of the city and killing close to 100 000 civilians. The Army Air Force Chief of Staff, General Henry A. (Hap) Arnold, sent congratulations to General Curtis Le May, who ordered the raid. Over the next nine days, additional B-29 raids burned an additional 80 square kilometres in Japan's four largest cities, causing 150 000 more deaths.[24]

The Atomic Bombing

On 6 August 1945, at 8:15 a.m., one of a group of three B-29s, the Enola Gay, released an atomic bomb over Hiroshima. It was the first use of this new weapon in warfare: its immediate effect was to cause death and destruction, in a way similar to incendiary bombs, but it also caused long-term suffering due to the irradiation of the survivors. Its expressed political motivation, a terror raid to force Japan to surrender and thus save Allied soldiers' lives, was similar to that of massive air bombing in Germany and Japan, but the horror created by the new weapon, its extraordinary power and its unknown consequences initiated a yet unfinished controversy over President Truman's decision and more generally on the legality of the use of nuclear weapons. As described by Cook:[25]

[The first bomb] was detonated at an altitude of 590 meters. The fission of the 0.85 kilograms of uranium contained in the bomb released energy equivalent to the explosive force of 13,000 tons of TNT. At the instant of the explosion, a fireball of several hundred thousand degrees centigrade formed . . . [which] attained a temperature on the surface of 7,000 degrees centigrade . . . Those exposed to the heat rays within one kilometer [from the hypocenter] were killed by intense burns and the rupture of internal organs. Burns were caused to the bodies of those within 3.5 kilometers of the hypocenter, and clothes and wooden houses were ignited . . . An intense blast was also created at the time of the explosion . . . The explosive wind reached a distance of eleven kilometers about thirty seconds after the explosion. The blast stripped people of clothing, tore up burned skin, ruptured the internal organs of some victims, and it drove glass and other debris into their bodies. Wooden buildings within a radius of 2.3 kilometers were leveled and over half of such buildings within 3.2 kilometers were destroyed. Even concrete buildings near the hypocenter were smashed by the blast.

The third major effect of the detonation after heat and blast was radiation. Gamma rays and neutrons emitted within one minute of the bombing inflicted a wide variety of physical damage to people as far as 2.3 kilometers from the hypocenter. Those within one kilometer received intense radiation doses. Residual radiation caused many who entered the area within 100 hours of the explosion to suffer exposure to gamma rays. Moisture condensing on rising ash and dust fell as the 'black rain' that began falling within thirty minutes of the explosion and continued to come down for some ninety minutes. It contained huge amounts of radiation that damaged not only humans, but plants and animals as well, over a large area. Long-term effects of radiation, including diseases like leukemia and the development of cancers, are still [in 1992] claiming victims . . .

It is estimated that by the end of December 1945, approximately 140,000 persons had died from effects caused by the single atomic bomb dropped on Hiroshima August 6. The blast in Nagasaki three days later had claimed 60,000 to 70,000 by year's end.

On 10 August 1945, the Imperial Government filed a protest to the US government and instructed its Minister to Switzerland to advise accordingly the International Committee of the Red Cross. The protest referred to the fundamental principle of international law in time of war according to which a belligerent does not have an unlimited right in choosing the means of injuring the enemy, and should not use such weapons, projectiles and other material as cause unnecessary pain, as expressly stipulated in the Hague Conventions. Since the beginning of the present war, the US government had repeatedly declared that the use of poison or other inhumane methods of warfare had been regarded as illegal by public opinion in civilized countries, and that the USA would not use these methods of warfare unless the other countries used them first. The new bomb far exceeded the indiscriminate and cruel character of efficiency of poison and other such methods. The US use of the new bomb

has indiscriminate and cruel character beyond comparison with all weapons and projectiles of the past. This is a new offence against the civilization of mankind. The Imperial Government impeaches the Government of the US in its own name and the name of all mankind and of civilization, and demands strongly that the Government of the USA give up the use of such an inhumane weapon instantly.[26]

Secretary of War Henry L. Stimson had encouraged the new incumbent of the US Presidency, Harry S. Truman, to consider the use of 'special weapons' as a way to end the war. During a meeting held on 31 May and 1 June 1945, the Interim Committee – an eight-man panel of top officials and scientists charged with drawing plans for the bomb to recommend to Truman – agreed that the atomic bomb would be used against Japan 'as soon as possible against a dual target, i.e. military or war plant surrounded by adjacent houses most susceptible to damage and used without prior warning'. On the Committee, only the Undersecretary of the navy, Ralph A. Bard, disagreed with this recommendation and resigned: he wanted a specific warning given to Japan about the bomb before it was used. In a speech to the nation after Nagasaki, Truman justified the use of the bomb 'in order to shorten the agony of war, in order to save the lives of thousands and thousands of young Americans'. In the words of Dr Karl Compton – quoted by Stimson – 'it was not one atomic bomb, or two, which brought surrender; it was the experience of what an atomic bomb will actually do to a community, plus the dread of many more, that was effective'. Stimson added, *post facto*, 'The bomb thus served exactly the purpose we intended. The peace part was able to take the path of surrender, and the whole weight of the Emperor's prestige was exerted in favor of peace.'[27]

The British Nobel prize winner H. M. S. Blackett questioned why the USA had to use the bomb so hastily. If the primary purpose was to save American lives, Washington could have deferred both the bomb and the invasion of Japan until the Soviet offensive had run its course. He felt that the bombs were in fact a display of power more directed at the Soviets than at the Japanese.[28]

The Tribunal held that evidence concerning the use of the atomic bombs was inadmissible, and the majority judgment did not mention the issue. Two justices did, holding opposing views. Judge Jaranilla, in his Concurring Opinion, wrote: 'If a means is justified by an end, the use of the atomic bomb was justified, for it brought Japan to her knees and ended the horrible war.' Justice Pal condemned the use of the atomic bombs: 'As a matter of fact, I do not perceive much difference between what the German Emperor is alleged to have announced during the First World War in justification of the atrocious methods directed by him in the conduct of that war and what is being proclaimed after the Second World War in justification of these inhuman blasts.' Referring to the charge of execution of Allied airmen by the Japanese, Justice Pal asserted that

the real horror of the air warfare is not the possibility of a few airmen being captured and ruthlessly killed, but the havoc which can be wrought by the indiscriminate launching of bombs and projectiles. The conscience of mankind revolts not so much against the punishment meted out to the ruthless bomber as against his ruthless form of bombing'.[29]

In his reflections published in 1993, Justice Röling stated: 'I am strongly convinced that these bombings [including both traditional air bombing and atom bombing] were war crimes . . . It was terror warfare, "coercive warfare" . . . forbidden by the laws of the war'.[30]

The Legality of Atomic Bombing

On 7 December 1963, the Tokyo District Court rejected the claims of R. Shimoda and four others for financial compensation for damages suffered by them as a result of the atomic bombing of Hiroshima and Nagasaki, alleged to be an illegal act of hostility contrary to the positive international law of that period. In the same judgment, the Court referred, *inter alia*, to Article 25 of the Hague Regulations which provides that 'the attack or bombardment, by any means whatever, of towns, villages, habitations, or buildings, which are not defended, is prohibited'; and to the Draft Rules of Air Warfare which prohibit useless aerial bombardment and provide for the principle of military objectives, which constitute international customary law. The Court then 'safely' said that 'it is a long-standing, generally recognized principle of international law respecting air raids, that indiscriminate aerial bombardment is not permitted on an undefended city and that only aerial bombardment on military objective is permitted'. The Court concluded that 'an aerial bombardment with an atomic bomb on both cities of Hiroshima and Nagasaki was an illegal act of hostility as the indiscriminate aerial bombardment on undefended cities'. Furthermore, 'the pain brought by the atomic bombs is severer than that from poison and poison-gas [prohibited by the Hague Regulations and the 1925 Protocol] . . . the act of dropping such a cruel bomb is contrary to the fundamental principle of the laws of war that unnecessary pain must not be given'.[31] While this national judgment has no effect on international law, it represents widely held popular convictions in a number of countries, as well as the position of a number of governments, mainly in non-nuclear countries.

On 15 December 1994, the UN General Assembly requested the International Court of Justice for an urgent advisory opinion on the question: 'Is the threat or use of nuclear weapons in any circumstance permitted under international law?' (Res. 49/75K). The controversial resolution, which followed intense lobbying by pacifist and human rights non-governmental organizations, was adopted by less than a two-thirds majority and opposed in particular by

France, Russia, the UK and the USA. The Court's divided and inconclusive advisory opinion of 8 July 1996 reflected the division of the international community on this issue. The main opposition was between those states who condemn the use or threat of nuclear weapons as illegal in any circumstances whatsoever and those, led by the USA, who consider that events have demonstrated the legality of the threat or use of nuclear weapons in extraordinary circumstances, and that nuclear deterrence is 'not only eminently lawful but intensely desirable'. In its advisory opinion, the Court held:

(A) unanimously, that neither customary nor conventional international law specifically authorizes the threat or use of nuclear weapons;

(B) by eleven votes to three, that neither customary nor conventional international law comprehensively and universally prohibits the threat or use of nuclear weapons;

(C) unanimously, that a threat or use of force by means of nuclear weapons that is contrary to Article 2, paragraph 4 of the UN Charter and that fails to meet all the requirements of Article 51 is unlawful;

(D) unanimously, that a threat or use of nuclear weapons should be compatible with the requirements of the international law applicable in armed conflict (including international humanitarian law) and specific obligations under treaties and other undertakings expressly dealing with nuclear weapons;

(E) by seven votes to seven, by the President's casting vote, that the threat or use of nuclear weapons would generally be contrary to the rules of international law applicable in armed conflict, and in particular the principles and rules of humanitarian law, but that in view of the current state of international law and the facts before the Court, it could not conclude definitively whether the threat or use of nuclear weapons would be lawful or unlawful in an extreme circumstance of self-defense, in which the very survival of a state would be at stake; and

(F) unanimously, that there exists an obligation to pursue in good faith and bring to a conclusion negotiations leading to nuclear disarmament in all its aspects under international control.[32]

While refraining from a determination that the threat or use of nuclear weapons was illegal, the Court provided all the basic elements for such a determination.

In applying the relevant law, the Court 'considered it imperative to take into account certain unique characteristics of nuclear weapons, in particular their destructive capacity, which can cause untold human suffering for generations to come' (paras 34–36). The Court noted that certain specific treaties dealing with the acquisition, manufacture, possession, deployment and testing of nuclear weapons, 'point to an increasing concern in the international community' with nuclear weapons and concluded they 'could therefore be seen as foreshadowing a future general prohibition of the use of such weapons, but they do not constitute such a prohibition by themselves' (para. 62). By reference to its 1986 Judgment in *Nicaragua v. USA*, the Court made clear that, notwithstanding the absence of specific mention of proportionality in Article 51 of the UN Charter, 'there is a specific rule whereby self-defense would warrant only measures which are proportional to the armed attack and necessity to respond to it, a rule well established in customary international law' (para. 41). The Court stated that the cardinal principles of international humanitarian law prescribing the conduct of military operations are (1) the protection of the civilian population and civilian objects and the prohibition of the use of weapons incapable of distinguishing between combatants and non-combatants, and (2) the prohibition on causing unnecessary suffering to combatants by using certain weapons (para. 78). While the Court affirmed that these constitute intransgressible principles of international customary law, to be observed by all states whether or not they have ratified the conventions that contain them (para. 79), it refrained from drawing the obvious conclusions from its previous findings on the ground that they were controversial.

Even though the Court made the unusual, non-legal recommendation that states had an obligation to pursue in good faith and bring to a conclusion negotiations leading to nuclear disarmament, a number of participants at the opening session of a UN Conference on Disarmament Issues held in Hiroshima expressed dismay at the Court decision. Yuzan Fujita, governor of the Hiroshima Prefecture, said that the Court's decision 'was a bitter disappointment for the people of Hiroshima, who have consistently insisted that the use and the threat of use of nuclear weapons violate international law'.[33]

UNIT 731: THE HIDDEN ATROCITIES

A particularly atrocious Japanese war crime, similar to the medical experiments carried out in Nazi concentration camps under the direction of Josef Mengele, was deliberately withheld from the Tribunal by the American authorities, for political–military reasons.[34]

Unit 731 was the Japanese army's principal bacteriological warfare research and experimentation organization, led by Army Medical Lieutenant General Ishii Shiro, officially designated as a 'Water Purification Unit'. Established near the Manchurian city of Harbin in 1932, the facility and its work were classified top secret by the military. Between 1932 and 1945, it is estimated that 5000 Japanese military, medical and civilian personnel were employed in the base. Unit 731 was the site of experiments aimed at developing and testing bacteriological agents and means of delivering them as weapons of war. This entailed the use of live human beings as experimental animals by exposing them to diseases such as bubonic and pneumonic plague, anthrax, epidemic haemorrhagic fever, typhoid and syphilis, to mustard gas, to scorching heat and subzero cold, and to a pressure chamber. Their endurance was tested until death. At open-air testing grounds, prisoners were chained and bombarded with bacterial weapons. Victims were subjected to vivisection. At least 3000 prisoners of war, mostly Chinese and Russian, but also Korean, and a few British and Dutch, were slowly tortured and murdered in unbearable suffering, and then incinerated. According to recent research, this estimate may be increased to at least 12 000 murdered in the Unit itself, and more in clandestine field tests, such as poisoned water wells. The interview of Tamura Yoshio, a 'chemical-weapon handler', directed like those of his colleagues by bacteriological scholars – most of them former senior professors at prestigious universities – is revealing and frightening.[35] He recognized that he was a war criminal because of the things he did. However, at the time, he had no feelings of pity: 'We disparaged all other races. That kind of racism. If we didn't have a feeling of racial superiority, we couldn't have done it ... hatred was there, but I simply had to ignore it. In other words, they [the victims] were valuable experimental animals'. As in Nazi Germany, total secrecy was imposed.

Following the entry into war of the USSR (8 August), all installations were destroyed between 10 and 13 August 1945 and 400 prisoners executed. In 1947, in a secret 'pact with the devil', the

US authorities gave immunity from prosecution to Ishii Shiro and all those who participated in the experiments with a guarantee of secrecy, in exchange for the results of their 'research work', perhaps also fearing that the information would fall into Soviet hands. The case was not submitted to the Tokyo Tribunal. Neither the Japanese authorities nor the Japanese Medical Association have initiated any official investigation on the Unit. In 1982, the Japanese Ministry of Health recognized that Unit 731 had existed, but said that they had no proof of the experimentation, although public reports and other publications have revealed in detail the reality of the Unit's activities. In 1993–4, an exhibition on Unit 731 was travelling in Japan, and a number of its former members have given public testimonies on their work in the Unit as an act of repentance.

Breaking the official secret, in December 1996, the US Justice Department's Office of Special Investigations announced that it had added sixteen Japanese World War II veterans to its 'watch list of war criminals who are banned from entering the USA. This list includes surviving members of Unit 731.

CONCLUSION

It is clear that the Tokyo Trial suffered from many flaws, some common with Nuremberg, some of its own. Among the common flaws was the creation and running of both Tribunals by the victors, while trial and punishment was strictly reserved for the vanquished. The open domination of the Tokyo Tribunal by the American government and occupation forces tainted even more than in Nuremberg its 'international' label. In substance, the same criticisms were addressed to both Tribunals on the application of *ex post facto* international law regarding crimes against peace and crimes against humanity. Procedural flaws were more apparent in Tokyo and the final division of the judges into a majority judgment and separate or dissenting opinions seriously weakened the value and impact of the Tribunal's findings and sentences. Under the *tu quoque* argument, the US use of atomic bombs continues to weigh heavily, particularly in the minds of the Japanese people, as a blatant, unacknowledged and unpunished war crime. Finally, the later discovery that the USA had secretly bargained with and granted immunity to the leaders of Unit 731 could only be taken as an affront to any human rights concern, besides making the USA a belated accomplice to a particularly odious war crime and crime against humanity.

The judgment of the Tribunal as a whole, including the majority judgment, the separate, dissenting and concurring opinions and the Official Transcript of the Proceedings, were only published in 1977, at the initiative of former Justice Röling and C. F. Rüter, Professor of Criminal Law at the University of Amsterdam. Was the American decision not to publish the Tribunal's judgment due to the fear that publication might have attracted too many and too public legal challenges as well as potentially embarassing political and moral questions? In contrast, the 42 volumes of the Nuremberg Tribunal's records were promptly published in 1947.

The decision to grant immunity to the Emperor, a political decision with valid reasons for the maintenance of the constitutional Japanese order and as a basis for a progressive democratization of the country, faulted the equity of the trial: there was evidence that the Emperor was not only a figurehead, but that he had approved the decision to declare war in the Pacific as well as the final decision to surrender. The Emperor's immunity could not but affect the assessment of criminal responsibility on to the defendants, in spite of their loyal and constant determination to protect him. One may also wonder whether the reluctance of the Japanese government and people to acknowledge their aggressive expansionism since the 1930s and the concurrent war crimes committed by their armed forces – their apparent amnesia – is not due at least in part to the Emperor's immunity, which may have appeared as a declaration of innocence for the country, while the few real villains, those who had lost the war, were being punished by the Allies. History books have not been revised, in contrast with the attitude adopted by the German governments after World War II: most of the Japanese believe that Japan's advance in other Asian countries was an understandable reaction to Western colonialism and expansionism, to the benefit of their populations.[36] Furthermore, the use of atomic bombs has allowed the Japanese to transfer any possible feelings of war guilt to the Americans and to show themselves as victims.

In Asia, countries that were conquered and occupied by the Japanese during the Asia–Pacific War have long pressed for a formal apology for Japan's wartime aggressions and atrocities. After a long public and political debate, the Japanese government adopted, on 6 June 1995, a formal declaration expressing what was translated as 'deep remorse' for its wartime aggression. A group of former 'comfort women' also want formal apologies and government-paid compensation for the surviving victims. Finally, in August 1996, Prime Minister Ryutaro Hashimoto expressed his 'sincere apologies and remorse' and stated that Japan was 'painfully aware of its moral responsibility in the affair'.

In spite of its faults, the Tokyo Trial confirmed and reinforced the Nuremberg precedent in recognizing the individual criminal responsibility of high-level officials for launching an aggressive war, for conventional war crimes and for crimes against humanity. Tokyo made an additional, albeit controversial, contribution to international criminal law in establishing criminal liability for omission. The Tokyo Judgment concluded 'the atrocities were either secretly ordered or wilfully permitted by the Japanese Government or individual members thereof and by the leaders of the armed forces'. Count 55 of the Judgment alleges that the accused mentioned 'deliberately and recklessly disregarded their legal duty to take adequate steps to secure the observance and prevent breaches' of the laws of the war. Seven accused were sentenced under this count. When he published the Judgment of the Tokyo Tribunal, in 1977, Röling expected that recognized liability for omission could have an important function in the prevention and termination of what is called 'systemic war criminality'.[37]

One of the purposes of both the Nuremberg and the Tokyo trials was to individualize punishment in order to avoid German or Japanese collective criminal responsibility. Has this aim succeeded too well in the case of the Japanese?

4 The Hidden, Denied and Unpunished Mass Crimes

The Nuremberg and Tokyo trials were followed by a number of national trials by criminal or military courts: they tried both Germans and Japanese, and, in Europe, nationals of occupied countries who had collaborated with the Nazis, alleged to have committed violations against traditional international humanitarian law, to which the innovations brought in by the Nuremberg precedent were added progressively. On 11 December 1946, the UN General Assembly affirmed the principles of international law recognized by the Charter of the Nuremberg Tribunal (Res. 95 (1)). As a direct consequence of Nuremberg, the Convention on the Prevention and Punishment of the Crime of Genocide was approved by the UN General Assembly on 9 December 1948, one month after the Tokyo judges rendered their majority judgment. The UN Economic and Social Council urged all states in 1965 to ensure that war criminals and persons who had committed crimes against humanity were traced, apprehended and equitably punished. The General Assembly adopted on 26 November 1968 the Convention on the Non-Applicability of Statutory Limitations to War Crimes and Crimes against Humanity. In 1971, the Assembly expressed its conviction that the effective punishment of war crimes and crimes against humanity was important for ending such crimes and for promoting peace and international security (Res. 2840 (XXVI)). In 1973, it proclaimed certain principles of international co-operation in the detection, arrest, extradition and punishment of persons guilty of war crimes and crimes against humanity (Res. 3074 (XXVIII)).

Although 122 states had ratified or acceded to the Genocide Convention as of 31 August 1996, there is no evidence that either the Nuremberg jurisprudence, or the Convention, or the Geneva Conventions of 1949 and the 1977 Protocols, have had any deterring effect on those who have planned or carried out genocides, other mass slaughters, war crimes or crimes against humanity, in relation to international or civil wars, or internal rebellions against established governments, whether these were caused by territorial disputes, ethnic or racial hatred, political opposition, ideological

imposition and repression, economic or social claims and griev-
ances. Some of these grave breaches of international humanitarian
law have been hidden and, when discovered, denied, as if the perpetrators well realized that their acts had flagrantly disregarded all
established standards of humane conduct in times of war and peace.
The policy of secrecy and the later denial were a recognition of
their guilt, a guilt that perpetrators often tried to share with, or
transfer to, their own victims, accused of provocations and criminal acts. The international community or, more specifically, the five
permanent members of the Security Council, have proved incapable or unwilling to prevent or stop the Cambodian genocide, the
ethnic cleansing carried out in ex-Yugoslavia, the Rwanda genocide of the Tutsis, and the later massacre of Hutu refugees in ex-
Zaïre. The Somalia episode and the humiliations to which the Blue
Helmets in ex-Yugoslavia were exposed have shown the difficulties
of 'international humanitarian interventions' in countries torn by a
civil war caused by political or ethnic rivalries or by competing
territorial claims in a country divided into several states. In such
cases, competing presidents or warlords claiming more power and
more territories show no interest in civil peace, but deliberately
exacerbate ethnic or racial hatred to fuel the conflict.

External and internal wars inevitably cause crimes and other
exactions, as combatants are led to violate international law norms
by their political and military leaders, by orders to kill, destroy or
maim the enemy as well as all civilians suspected of supporting the
enemy, in the knowledge that killing, wounding and torturing are
condoned, if not encouraged, and certainly not punished. Their
exactions may be 'justified' as a retaliation against similar crimes
committed, or allegedly committed, by their opponents. In many
cases, combatants of regular armies or guerrillas have not been
instructed by their chiefs that humanitarian norms exist and should
be respected. Failing prevention of war, and if humanitarian rules
are not known or respected, the last remaining option is to punish
the perpetrators, provided that they can be identified, arrested and
tried by an independent and impartial court of justice.

Persons accused of grave violations of international humanitarian law should normally be tried by a national court, either in
their own country, or in the country where they are detained.
However, it is unlikely that a government that has ordered, authorized or permitted those abuses will allow its courts to judge
and punish the perpetrators, who have only followed their orders,

while the responsible deciders, the senior politicians, military and police officials, remain immune from any accusation and prosecution. When a more democratic government comes to power, political and military authorities who have initiated or covered crimes against humanity (against their own people) have generally demanded that the new democratic government declares an amnesty, in the premature interest of a 'national reconciliation', thus ensuring the impunity of all the criminals at all levels. In other cases, national justice is purposefully delayed for years, sometimes decades, so that eventual sanctions are less severe, witnesses and proof have disappeared, or the defendants are too old to be judged, if not already dead. In some cases, the new government may be or may become as authoritarian, corrupt and criminal as the previous one, leaving no chance for the creation of independent justice. In a number of countries, there is such a scarcity of well-trained judges and lawyers that national justice is often ineffective and unreliable.

As a result, except for Nuremberg and Tokyo, the leaders and officials responsible for many genocides and other mass crimes committed in the 20th century have granted to themselves total impunity. Whether the International War Crimes Tribunals for ex-Yugoslavia and Rwanda are effective will be discussed in Chapters 8 and 9. Whether the possible future creation of a permanent International Criminal Court may have a deterring effect, besides its judiciary functions, is an open question (see Chapter 10). The few examples of massive exactions which follow are not intended to cover systematically all genocides and other mass crimes: they have been selected only as illustrative examples of planned crimes followed by impunity at the national and international levels. While all these cases concern specific countries, they have implications at the international level in so far as they include gross and repeated violations of internationally recognized human rights and grave breaches of conventional and customary international humanitarian law. No attempt is made to restrict this list to only 'genocides', as defined in the 1948 Convention, which refers to 'acts committed with intent to destroy, in whole or in part, a national, ethnical, racial or religious group'. Political groups should be added to this list, and mass killings that may not be strictly labelled as 'genocides' are also included here, without joining the theoretical debates on the issue of the appropriate definition for a genocide.

Building on Chalk and Jonassohn's typology,[1] the objectives of genocides may include one or several of the following:

1. To eliminate a real or potential threat against the perpetrators' population, their institutions, their religion, their lives, their property, their ambitions, in a self-proclaimed preventive self-defence exercise.
2. To acquire economic wealth or territory, in an effort to augment the country's power and wealth.
3. To implement a belief, a theory, or an ideology, or to eliminate a belief, a theory or an ideology considered hostile to the perpetrators' beliefs or objectives. The ultimate purpose is to enforce conformity and social equality, to purify the race, to strengthen a new political regime in eliminating all potential, imagined or real political opponents, or, more drastically, in eliminating all social classes which do not conform with the new regime's theories and objectives.

Genocides and other mass killings require the designing and implementation of a systematic plan, usually ordered and organized by the state's authorities, a plan which is usually kept more or less secret from the outside world, or from part of its own population, in parts of, or in all of, its development. They require that future victims be identified either as a foreign enemy, or as a part of the perpetrator's society that is to be rejected. In the latter case, the target group has to be clearly identified, isolated and segregated. In all cases, the future victims have to be dehumanized, considered at best as soulless animals, and accused of the worst real or imagined crimes or intentions against the perpetrators' population.The genociders will then arouse hatred among that population, insist that the danger caused by the future victims requires immediate and drastic action, and take all measures to spread terror in the target group, which will be either deported and exterminated, or simply murdered in their villages and houses. The leaders will ensure impunity to the perpetrators.

The Armenian genocide, during World War I, and massacres in the USSR from 1917 until the 1950s, will first be recalled. Among the many mass exactions committed since World War II, we have included a few notes on the mass killings in Indonesia and brief statistics on China, followed by a more detailed description of the exemplary and infamous Cambodian Genocide.

THE HIDDEN AND DENIED ARMENIAN GENOCIDE

Between April 1915 and July 1916, an estimated 1.0–1.5 million Turkish Armenians, approximately two-thirds of the Armenian population in the Ottoman Empire, were killed by the Turkish authorities, the army, the gendarmerie and Moslem members of the population.[2] A few more hundreds of thousands died during the Turkish attempt to conquer Russian, then Soviet, Armenia in 1918 and in 1920. An estimated 500 000 managed to survive the deportations and massacres and dispersed across the globe.

Armenian resistance to Turkish domination, including the creation of armed terrorist groups, had been severely repressed in the past. In 1895–6, Sultan Abdul Hamid II organized the slaughter of approximately 200 000 Armenians. In 1909, the Young Turks of the Union and Progress Party (Ittihad) replaced Sultan Abdul Hamid by Mehmet V. The Young Turks soon abandoned their liberal programme for an ultra-nationalist pan-Turkism. In the same year, they carried out the killing of approximately 30 000 Armenians in Adana. In 1911, the Council of the Party decided that 'the Ottomanisation of all Turkish citizens, which never succeeded through persuasion, had to be done by the force of arms'.[3] In 1914, the Armenians were the main ethnic minority under an oppressive Ottoman domination. The ideology of the Young Turks was not only nationalist but also racist: their mission was to achieve and maintain their country's national independence and to restore its original racial purity. They were convinced that the Armenians represented a mortal danger for pan-Turkism. World War I gave them an opportunity to liquidate the internal enemy. Male Armenians, from age 20 to 60, were mobilized in three age groups following the mobilization that became effective on 3 August 1914. On 6 September 1914, the Interior Ministry had instructed the provincial authorities, through a cipher circular, to keep Armenian political and community leaders under surveillance. Following requisitions of Armenian goods and governmental provocations and harassment, there were clashes between Armenians and gendarmes and soldiers, and sporadic isolated acts of sabotage. In November 1914, Turkey joined the Central Powers against the Allies. The Third Turkish Army was totally defeated at Sarikamish in January 1915 by stronger Russian troops. As Russian Armenians were serving in four Russian legions, Turks attributed their defeat to the Armenians and not to their own faulty strategy.

The plan for genocide was initiated by a cipher telegram dated 27 February 1915 from the Minister of War, Enver Pasha, which instructed all the military commanders in Turkey to take part in the extermination of the Armenians: all Ottoman subjects of Armenian origin over five years of age were to be arrested and killed. All Armenians serving in the army were to be separated from their divisions and shot.[4] On 24 April 1915, Turkey's Ministry of the Interior issued an order authorizing the arrest of all Armenian political and community leaders suspected of anti-Ittihad or nationalistic sentiments. Thousands of Armenians were seized and incarcerated. None of them were tried and found guilty of wartime sabotage, espionage or other crime. In a memorandum dated 26 May 1915, the Interior Ministry requested from the Grand Vezir the enactment through the Cabinet of a special law authorizing deportations. The new emergency law, called the Temporary Law of Deportation, was approved by the Cabinet on 30 May and announced in the press. Without referring to the Armenians, the law authorized the commanders of the armies, army corps and divisions, and the commanders of local garrisons, to order the deportation of population clusters on suspicion of espionage, treason and on military necessity. The law resulted in the deportation of the bulk of the Armenian population. The Deportation Law had not been promulgated by the Ottoman Parliament as required by Article 36 of the Constitution. It was repealed on account of its unconstitutionality on 4 November 1918 by the Parliament, in a session during which the Armenian massacres, the scope of the victims and the responsibility of the government were debated. Two supplementary laws enacted on 10 June and 26 September 1915 authorized the expropriation and confiscation of the deportees' goods and assets. On 24 May 1915, the Allies issued a joint declaration condemning 'the connivance and often assistance of Ottoman authorities' in the massacres. 'In view of these new crimes of Turkey against humanity and civilization, the Allied governments announce publicly . . . that they will hold personally responsible . . . all members of the Ottoman government and those of their agents who are implicated in such massacres'.[5]

On 7 October 1918, the Young Turk government of Talaat Pasha fell. Criticisms of the Young Turks became the main theme in the Turkish press. On 13 December, the Ottoman Parliament voted a resolution demanding that the organizers and the executioners of the massacres should be tried by a single court. A Supreme Military

Tribunal was formed for the trial of the perpetrators of the Armenian massacres.

In January 1919, the Preliminary Peace Conference in Paris established the Commission on Responsibilities and Sanctions. The Commission's final report, dated 29 March 1919, spoke of 'the clear dictates of humanity' which were abused 'by the Central Empires together with their Allies, Turkey and Bulgaria, by barbarous or illegitimate methods' including 'the violation of ... the laws of humanity'. The report concluded that 'all persons belonging to enemy countries ... who have been guilty of offenses against the laws and customs of war or the laws of humanity, are liable to criminal prosecution'. The report included the crimes that Turkey was accused of having perpetrated against its Armenian citizens.[6]

On 8 March 1919, the Supreme Military Tribunal

> ... proved the Committee for Union and Progress (at present dissolved) to be guilty of multiple crimes, and its leaders as the authors of those crimes, thus they should face punishment.
>
> ... The court stated that of all non-Muslim nations the Armenians were the most outraged, and realizing how wrong they had been to believe in promised justice, had returned to their former wish for independence. Thus, the Ittihad was to blame for the wrong done to the integrity of the Ottoman Empire.

Three defendants were present, while the main culprits, Talaat Pasha – leader of the Young Turks and Minister of the Interior – Enver Pasha and others, had fled the country and were judged *in absentia*. The Tribunal found guilty and sentenced to death *in absentia* Talaat, Enver, Jemal, Nazim and several other leaders of Union and Progress. Dr Behaeddin Shakir, the chief perpetrator of the crimes, was sentenced to death, and Nazim Bey to 15 years of hard labour: both fled from their punishment. Only Governor Kemal Bey, the chief perpetrator of the deportation and massacre of Armenians in the Yozgad district, was hanged publicly in Constantinople. Talaat, who planned and carried out the Armenian genocide, is considered by the Turks as a hero: he was murdered by an Armenian on 15 March 1921. The Turkish authorities had thus acknowledged that massacres had been committed against the Armenians, and themselves tried and condemned the Young Turks' deeds. However, the Tribunal only tried Ittihad's high officials, most of whom escaped punishment. Thousands of Young Turks were neither judged nor punished.[7]

On 11 June 1919, the Ottoman Prime Minister, Damad Ferid Pasha, recognized before the Peace Conference the crimes committed by the Turks during the war and identified those responsible for these crimes: the leaders of Ittihad, who had created a secret, parallel organization to carry out deportations and executions. On the same lines as Articles 228, 229 and 230 of the Treaty of Versailles, Article 226 of the Treaty of Sèvres of 10 August 1920 stated:

> The Turkish government recognizes the right of the Allied Powers to bring before military tribunals persons accused of having committed acts in violation of the laws and customs of war. Such persons shall, if found guilty, be sentenced to punishments laid down by law. This provision will apply notwithstanding any proceedings or prosecution before a tribunal in Turkey or in the territory of her allies.

Turkey was obliged to hand over to the Allied Powers 'all persons accused of having committed an act in violation of the laws and customs of war . . .' Under Article 230 of the Treaty, Turkey was further obliged

> to hand over to the Allied Powers the persons whose surrender may be required by the latter as being responsible for the massacres committed during the continuance of the state of war on territory which formed part of the Turkish Empire on August 1, 1914. The Allied powers reserve to themselves the right to designate the tribunal which shall try the persons so accused, and the Turkish government undertakes to recognize such tribunal.

The prospect that the League of Nations might create a tribunal competent to deal with these massacres was also mentioned in Article 230. Under Section VI of the Treaty, Turkey recognized Armenia as a free and independent state. The reformist leader Mustafa Kemal (Kemal Ataturk) rejected the terms of this Treaty and, in November 1922, he abolished the sultanate in order to prevent the Sultan from participating in the Lausanne Conference. In 1923, the Turkish Republic replaced the Ottoman Empire.

Justice was not applied by the League of Nations, nor by the Allied Powers because of political dissension between the latter and strong nationalistic reactions in Turkey. The Treaty of Lausanne of 24 July 1923, which replaced that of Sèvres, omitted any mention of violations of the laws and customs of war and of massacres. Its Article 138 prescribed that all judicial decisions, orders and measures issued in Turkey as from 30 October 1918 until the coming into force of the Treaty were to be regarded as definitive, without prejudice to the terms of paragraphs IV and VI of the Amnesty Declaration of 24 July 1923. The Lausanne Treaty did not include the recognition of an independent state of Armenia.

Turkey's Denial

Turkey's official position is that no genocide occurred: 'The events of 1915 are best described as a civil war within a global war.'[8] The Turkish version, endorsed by a number of American historians, emphasizes the 'manner in which Armenian revolutionaries sought to foment rebellion against the state in the 40 years preceding the First World War'. It reduces the deportation and execution orders to a decision of the then-ruling government

> to relocate the Armenian population from the path of the invading Russian armies they were actively supporting by undermining the Ottoman defense effort. This relocation also stemmed from the necessity to forestall further bloodshed resulting from the rapidly escalating fighting between Armenian and Moslem civilian populations.

While the suffering of the Armenians is acknowledged, the Turkish version recalls that 2.5 million Turks and others perished during the period. The Turkish position is that 'there certainly was no government-planned-and-executed scheme to exterminate the Empire's Armenian population', an anti-Turkish historical calumny. Another argument, which the end of the Cold War has made less effective, was directed principally to the American Congress and government: the adoption of a resolution by the US Congress endorsing the Armenian allegations would harm the spirit and foundation of NATO and hurt irreparably the friendly relations between Turkey and the USA. By itself, this argument does not challenge the historical reality of the Armenian genocide: it only suggests that its public revelation would have unfortunate political consequences.

The main Turkish argument is to equalize the position of the unarmed Armenian minority with that of the Ottoman government, its army and police, and to consider that any Armenian 'suffering' was caused by their own provocation and rebellion. Clearly, the political and military power was exclusively in Turkish hands, and wholesale massacres of men, women and children allied to cruel deportation orders and spoliation of Armenian homes, assets and belongings cannot be considered an acceptable response to Armenian discontent and claims. The deportation and execution orders are rhetorically replaced by an innocuous 'relocation', contrary to all historical evidence. Finally, the threat to US–Turkish friendship and to NATO is an obvious act of blackmail, the object of which is only to reject and forget an unpleasant historical episode in the higher interests of US–Turkish friendship. That the present Turkish government is no more responsible for the Armenian genocide than the present German government is responsible for the Jewish genocide has not prevented the post-Nazi German authorities from presenting apologies and assuming moral and financial responsibility for the Nazi crimes. The genocide may be explained, but not justified, by the nationalist ideology of the Young Turks and their clear intent to 'ottomanize' Turkey – to carry out the ethnic cleansing of the country by eliminating the last remaining minority, the Christian Armenians, a turbulent, and at times, rebel group. As in other genocides, the target group had to be exposed as a threat rather than as a victim. The progressive decline of the Ottoman Empire, military defeats and wartime conditions reinforced the resolve of the government and party, who designed the overall plan and ensured its implementation through administrative channels.

Condemnations

The Armenian genocide corresponds to the definition given in Article II of the 1948 Convention on the Prevention and Punishment of the Crime of Genocide:

> ... any of the following acts committed with intent to destroy, in whole or in part, a national, ethnical, racial or religious group, as such:
> (a) Killing members of the group;
> (b) Causing serious bodily or mental harm to members of the group:
> (c) Deliberately inflicting on the group conditions of life calculated to bring about its physical destruction in whole or in part;
> ...

Armenians in the Ottoman Empire were an identified ethnical and religious group. Their claim for a national identity added a political element to the definition of the victimized group. In April

1984, an International People's Tribunal, composed of 13 persons including three Nobel Prize laureates, conducted hearings on the events of 1915–17 (see also Chapter 7). In its final report, the Tribunal affirmed, in part, that the 'Armenian people, rightfully insist and seek formal recognition by legal authorities for crimes and injustices found to have been committed at their expense'. On the other hand, the Tribunal noted with regret that the frustration arising from the denial of the fact of the genocide had led to terrorist actions against Turkish diplomats and others. In its verdict, the Tribunal found that the extermination of the Armenian population through deportation and massacre constituted a crime of genocide not subject to statutory limitations. The government of the Young Turks was guilty of this genocide with regard to the acts perpetrated between 1915 and 1917. The Armenian genocide was also an 'international crime' for which the Turkish state must accept responsibility, without using the pretext of any discontinuity in the existence of the state to elude that responsibility. This responsibility implies first and foremost the obligation to recognize the reality of this genocide and the consequent damages suffered by the Armenian people.[9]

On 2 July 1985, the Whitaker report[10] referred, among other genocides, to the 'Ottoman massacre of Armenians in 1915–1916'. According to the report, at least one million, and possibly well over half of the Armenian population, are reliably estimated to have been killed or death-marched by independent authorities and eye-witnesses. This was corroborated by a list of reports and books. In August 1985, the UN Sub-Commission on Prevention of Discrimination and Protection of Minorities noted, by a 14 to one vote, with four abstentions, the historical fact of the Armenian genocide. The UN Commission on Human Rights endorsed this resolution in 1986. On 18 June 1987, the European Parliament approved a fair and equitable resolution 'On the Political Solution of the Armenian Question'. It stated, in part, that

the tragic events in 1915–1917 involving the Armenians living in the territory of the Ottoman Empire constitute genocide within the meaning of the convention on the prevention and the punishment of the crime of genocide adopted by the UN General Assembly on 9 December 1948; recognizes, however, that the present Turkey cannot be held responsible for the tragedy experienced by the Armenians of the Ottoman Empire and stresses that neither political nor legal or material claims against present-day Turkey can be derived from the recognition of this historical event as an act of genocide;

... Believes that the refusal by the present Turkish Government to acknowledge the genocide against the Armenian people committed by the Young Turk government, its reluctance to apply the principles of international law to its differences with Greece, the maintenance of Turkish occupation forces in Cyprus and the denial of the existence of the Kurdish question, together with the lack of true parliamentary democracy and the failure to respect individual and collective freedoms, in particular freedom of religion, in that country, are insurmountable obstacles to consideration of the possibility of Turkey's accession to the Community.[11]

Turkey acceded to the Convention on the Prevention and Punishment of the Crime of Genocide on 31 July 1950. In 1997, Turkey was still denying that there had been an Armenian genocide and was still rejecting any responsibility for this 'non-event'.

THE UNPUNISHED SOVIET MASSACRES

The number of Soviet victims who died as a result of decisions and orders given by Lenin and Stalin is estimated at 20 million. The Bolsheviks created a totalitarian one-party system, without institutional counter-powers, which effectively prevented the exercise of most individual rights and freedoms. A regime of terror subjected all Soviet citizens to the arbitrary decision-making power of the supreme Communist leader and his close associates in the name of the people. The Marxist-Leninist utopia was to create a new egalitarian society, which implied the destruction of the former social order, of the former elites, of 'counter-revolutionaries' and of 'enemies of the people', an ill-defined group that could include whoever the new power had decided to eliminate. The creation of a new Socialist world, a world of political and social progress which was to replace decadent and corrupt capitalist and social-democrat countries, justified all human sacrifices. Most of the reality – political repression, famines, deportation to concentration camps (the gulags), executions without judgment, forced confessions and condemnations

in well-scripted trials, torture and forced conformity with the official dogma – was carefully hidden from the Soviet population and
from the outside world through propaganda and disinformation,
with the loyal support, in foreign countries, of local Communist
Party leaders and members and convinced fellow-travellers.[12]

For its apologists, the first Red Terror was initiated by Lenin in
order to save the October 1917 Revolution from internal counter-
revolutionaries and external attacks against the Soviet Union. From
1918 to 1922, the Tcheka, the political police, was granted, and
used, all powers to search private homes, and to arrest and shoot
– individually or in groups – all persons suspected of opposition to
the new regime, with or without judgment. In the case of judgment, the sentence is almost always the death penalty, labelled as
the 'supreme measure of social protection'. The repression caused
hundreds of thousands of deaths. The Red Terror and the civil
war were in part 'natural' measures of self-defence against counter-
revolutionary violence and external intervention. According to
Medvedev:[13]

> the terror was also intimately connected with serious errors on
> the part of the first Soviet government in the implementation of
> important economic and political measures. Government actions
> provoked opposition and resistance among an overwhelming ma-
> jority of the petty bourgeois masses of Russia, bringing Soviet
> power to the brink of catastrophe and compelling those in charge
> to resort to mass terror.

Medvedev adds that the excesses of this terror were without any
justification, although it is 'inevitably misleading to judge a revolutionary epoch or wartime situation by the laws and customs normally applicable to peacetime'.

Stalin admitted to Churchill, in August 1942, that 10 million
peasants had been killed or deported during the forced collectivization of the early 1930s. The well-to-do peasants, the kulaks, were
class enemies who had to be eliminated through killings or
deportations. Stalin was responsible for the Ukrainian famine genocide.[14] The nationalist Ukrainians were subjected to harsh de-
kulakization and collectivization: their social base, the individual
land-holdings, had to be destroyed. Grain quotas and levels of
requisition were set at impossible levels. Outside help was prevented.
Conquest estimates that, from 1928 to 1932, 1.5–2.0 million Ukrainians

were deported and 500 000 killed locally as kulaks. From the spring of 1932, at the beginning of the famine, until February 1933, when Stalin stopped the requisitions, out of 20–5 million Ukrainian peasants, approximately 5 million died of famine. The Soviet authorities denied to their own people and to the West that any famine was taking or had taken place. The overall death toll of peasants in the USSR in the period 1930–7 has been estimated by Conquest at 14.5 million.

The Great Purge of 1936–8 adds millions of victims to previous counts. The number of arrests of innocent victims is estimated at 7 million, including about half a million death sentences. For the period 1936–50, an estimated average of 8 million detained in camps, with a 10% death rate per annum, produces a total casualty figure of 12 million dead.[15] The 'gulags' were maintained until 1987. Whole nations were deported without any military or other justification:

- in August 1941, approximately 1 225 000 ethnic Germans living in the USSR were deported to Siberia and Kazakhstan;
- in December 1943, all the Karachai and Kalmyk peoples were deported – the autonomous Kalmyk Republic was liquidated;
- in March 1944, all the Chechen and Ingush peoples were deported and the Chechen–Ingush Autonomous Republic was abolished;
- in April 1944, all Balkars were deported;
- in May 1944, 194 000 Tatars are deported from the Crimea and 86 000 from Georgia.

Of the 2.3 million Soviet prisoners of war detained in Germany and repatriated to the USSR, 80% were deported, exiled or killed.[16]

Stalin's Crimes Disclosed

Stalin's crimes were finally officially disclosed by Nikita Khrushchev in his secret speech to the Twentieth Communist Party Congress on 24 and 25 February 1956. Khrushchev blamed Stalin for having used extreme methods and mass repressions when the Revolution was already victorious. Stalin sanctioned the 'most brutal violation of socialist legality, torture and oppression, which led ... to the slandering and self-accusation of innocent people'. He had annihilated many military commanders and political workers during 1937–41 because of his suspiciousness and through slanderous accusations. The mass deportations from their native places of whole nations initiated by Stalin were 'rude violations of the basic Leninist principles of the nationality policy of the Soviet state'. Stalin himself had encouraged the cult of personality.

Khrushchev's revelations had a considerable impact on world public opinion and on national Communist parties in many countries. Soviet crimes had long been denied, and regarded as slanderous inventions of the bourgeois press. For instance, in France, many writers and artists had adhered to the French Communist Party or were faithful fellow-travellers. When André Gide, who had adhered to the party line in the 1930s, reflected his disappointment with the Soviet regime after a trip to the USSR, he was denounced as an impostor and a traitor. Victor Kravchenko's book *I Chose Freedom*, published in English in 1946, denounced the Stalin regime for its failure to grant political and civil liberties to the Russian people. A former senior Soviet official, Kravchenko had defected to the West in 1944. His book referred *inter alia* to the liquidation of the kulaks as a class, to the famine in southern Russia and Central Asia, to the working of the Purge Commissions, to the magnitude of child labour, slave labour, concentration camps, pervasive oppression and human degradation in the USSR, to the practice of torture, to Stalin's totalitarian tyranny, and to its political regime of lawlessness and violence.

A French Communist periodical, *Les Lettres Françaises*, said in 1947 that Mr Kravchenko had not written the book because he was not intellectually capable of doing so, that instead the American secret service had written it, and that Mr Kravchenko was a drunkard, an embezzler and a traitor to the Soviet Union. Kravchenko sued the periodical for libel. During the trial in Paris in 1949, he was verbally and physically abused by French Communists and fellow-travellers, and by Soviet officials: he was again called a traitor and a liar. He won his suit.[17]

Many books and articles were published in the USSR and abroad in the 1960s which confirmed that the 'anti-Soviet rumors' had in fact described the realities of Soviet life and some of the consequences of Lenin's and Stalin's reigns of terror. Among these publications, Solzhenitsyn's *One Day in the Life of Ivan Denisovich* and *The Gulag Archipelago* – published in English in 1970 and 1973 respectively – were particularly significant and influential in the West.

Khrushchev's 1956 speech was approved by the Twentieth Congress, which instructed the Central Committee 'consistently to carry out measures with the object of fully overcoming the cult of personality, which is alien to the principles of Marxism–Leninism, and eliminating the consequences in every aspect of Party, state and ideological activity'.[18] After Stalin's death in March 1953, Beria – former chief of the political police and vice-President of the Council of Ministers – had been arrested and executed after a secret trial in the same year. After his execution, his closest associates were put on trial in various cities, but Stalin's name was never mentioned in these trials, and the entire responsibility for lawlessness was attributed to the NKVD.

Khrushchev himself and many other senior members of the Central Committee and the Presidium shared responsibility in the implementation of Stalin's policies and decisions, if not in the decision-making process itself, decisions which caused massive losses of life and great suffering. However, no systematic investigations or organized prosecutions of those responsible at various levels for the violations of human rights were ever initiated. In fact, Khrushchev's speech had only attacked Stalin's deviations from Marxism-Leninism, not the Soviet ideology that was at the root of these deviations. The Party's structure and its officials, who had benefited from privileges linked to their status and who undoubtedly also shared responsibility in the implementation of Stalin's decisions, were still in power and would have resisted any attempt to probe and reveal unpleasant facts, without even speaking of prosecutions and punishment.

On the more positive side, by the autumn of 1956 several millions of political prisoners were liberated. Most of those who had died in the camps and prisons in the period 1935–55 were rehabilitated. On the other hand, there was no Party rehabilitation for members of the Opposition of the 1920s. No formal reconsideration was given to the sham political trials of 1928–31 or 1936–8. In a recent interview with a French periodical, Tatiana Dmitrieva, Minister of Health of Russia since August 1996 and Director of the Serbski Institute, declared that, in her personal view, most of the dissidents, interned against their will for political reasons, were suffering from psychiatric disorders, of varying degrees: 'The diagnoses were justified, in their overwhelming majority.' She added that investigations would be too expensive and that the archives of the Institute are closed 'by respect for the private life of the former patients'.[19] In other words, there is no need for an independent investigation of the political and psychiatric persecution of political dissidents – no prosecution is warranted. This unfortunate support for past abuses is untenable: many dissidents were submitted to abusive psychiatric treatment in the Serbski Institute during the Soviet era for holding unorthodox political views. The Soviet officials who ordered the psychiatric internments of dissidents, and the doctors who gave them unwarranted and harmful physical and chemical treatment, are enjoying total impunity.

As seen in many other countries, the investigation of old crimes and opening of old wounds is a particularly difficult task: it may be an impossible task in Russia when the demise of the USSR has essentially left, in positions of political, military and economic power, the same persons who held important positions in the Soviet Union Communist hierarchy. It is therefore unlikely that the main senior Soviet officials responsible for genocide, other massacres and exactions inflicted on their own population, if still alive, will ever be prosecuted, judged and punished.

By reference to the Genocide Convention, the Ukrainian famine, initiated and planned by Stalin, carried out and finally stopped under his orders, may be classified as a genocide with intent to destroy, in whole or in part, a national or ethnic group. The other enormous losses of population may be considered as political 'class' genocides, in view of their ideological motivation, linked, in some cases, to ignorance of the economic consequences of political decisions, or voluntary neglect of such considerations.[20]

INDONESIA: THE 1965 MASSACRE

The former Dutch Indies became independent in 1949 as Indonesia, under the leadership of Sukarno, its first President and one of the leaders of the Thirld World. It is composed of more than 3000 islands, with a population of over 185 million and a large diversity of languages (more than 250), ethnic groups (3% are Chinese) and – religions 90% Muslim, 3.5% Christian, 2% Buddhist and the remainder being Hindu and animists.[21] By 1957, efforts to establish parliamentary rule had collapsed, and there was widespread rebellion. The army took power, and in 1959 Sukarno re-emerged as head of state in alliance with the Indonesian Communist Party (PKI) and the army under the banner of 'Guided Democracy'. With 10 million members in 1965, the Communist Party began to push for radical land reform and rent reduction, alarming many traditional elites. The

army was opposed to the Party because of its influence with Sukarno
and because of its penetration of part of the airforce and the navy.
The Communist Party was also perceived as a threat to landowners
because of its collectivist plans, to Muslims because of its atheist
and anti-religious doctrine, and to the USA, concerned about Communist designs for assuming power in Southeast Asian countries.

On the night of 30 September/1 October 1965, a group of junior
officers murdered six senior generals in an attempted coup, claiming to overthrow Sukarno's leadership. The failed coup was officially
interpreted as a Communist plot to seize power, although the purpose and sponsorship of the coup have not been clarified. The army,
under the direction of General Suharto and with the support of
the CIA, then took power. It initiated and encouraged the savage
killing of Communist Party leaders, members and supporters, with
the aid of bands of youths and of the local population. In a holy
war, fanatical Muslims slaughtered atheists. The victims included
many thousands of Chinese, suspected because China had become
Communist, but also targets of long-standing ethnic resentment in
view of their domination of commerce and trade. Possessions were
looted and houses burned. Eventually, the army re-established order.
The number killed is estimated at about 500 000 for the period
December 1965 to mid-1966, and the number of those arrested
also at 500 000. Most were detained without judgment and were
only released in 1978. The massacres had first an internal political
motivation: to eliminate the Communist threat from Indonesian
politics, within the context of the East–West confrontation that
provided US support to the Indonesian political and military leaders. As noted above, ethnic, religious and economic factors also
contributed to the hatred and violence. The primary political motivation should identify the massacres as a genocide, even if the
present terms of the Convention do not include this category. The
secondary and perhaps accidental destruction of members of ethnic, racial and religious groups was genocidal, although not intended
as a total extermination of these groups and limited in time.

General Suharto became President in 1968 and was still Chief of
State in 1997. Indonesia is a police state, which suppresses free
expression, and jails and tortures political opponents. Those who
initiated and condoned the massacres in 1965 are still in power.
Failing a democratic revolution, the perpetrators of the massacres
will not be prosecuted or sanctioned.

CHINA

According to Rummel,[22] the number of deaths caused by the Chinese Communist regime amongst its own population may be estimated as follows:

The Totalization Period:	8 427 000
Collectivization and 'The Great Leap Forward'	7 474 000
The Great Famine and Retrenchment Period	10 729 000
The 'Cultural Revolution'	7 731 000
Liberalization	874 000
TOTAL	35 235 000

These human losses were related to, and caused by, an ideological drive aimed at transforming the traditional Chinese political and social system into a Communist society, initially on the Soviet model. The first enemies were the counter-revolutionaries, nationalist sympathizers and other political opponents. Then, landlords, rich peasants, the gentry and the bourgeoisie as class enemies were to be re-educated or exterminated. The Communist Party and the army were periodically purged. The collectivization of the peasants and the 'Great Leap Forward' caused the world's greatest recorded famine. Unlike the Ukraine famine willed by Stalin, the Chinese famine was 'only' the result of erroneous decisions by the Great Helmsman. The succession of massacres, either intentional or accidental, was caused by political leaders intent on creating a 'new society' and a 'new (Communist) man' without any consideration for the human consequences. Notwithstanding its political motivation, the extent of human losses and suffering should justify the charge of genocide, even if the present text of the Convention has excluded this category.

China is still a one-party Communist dictatorship, in absolute power, in spite of its economic evolution. Only dissidents are punished: none of the past or present Communist leadership is liable to be considered responsible and accountable for the criminal consequences of their political and economic decisions.

THE KHMER ROUGE GENOCIDE

Even if terror cannot be rated in numbers of victims, types of atrocities or the duration of a genocide or massacres, the killings, torture and associated suffering inflicted by the Khmer Rouge upon their own population in a small country between 1975 and 1978 appear particularly monstrous. The Marxist real-life (or real-death) 'scientific' social experiment resulted in approximately 1.7 million deaths amongst its eight million people. A despotic, dogmatic group made use of the worst sadistic instincts of indoctrinated youths to destroy a traditional society, eliminate the elites and ethnic groups, break up families, condemn the masses to hard labour under starvation conditions and transform a country into a prison camp under high security, an immediate death sentence being applied to any suspected deviations from the orthodox ideology.

Brief Historical Sequence

Cambodia gained independence from France in 1953 under the leadership of Prince Norodom Sihanouk, and the 1954 Geneva Conference on Indochina recognized its neutrality. American bombing over Cambodia started in 1969, on Vietnamese Communist camps in the border areas of the country. In March 1970, Sihanouk was deposed while abroad and power was seized by the General Lon Nol, with US support. Sihanouk formed a National United Front with his former enemies, the Khmer Rouge, to fight against Lon Nol. In January 1973, the Paris Agreement on ending the war in Vietnam was signed: it included the withdrawal of foreign troops from Cambodia. Massive US air bombing carried out on Cambodia from February to August 1973 caused deaths, suffering and a strong hate of the Americans, which played into Pol Pot's hands.

Following armed offensives in January 1974 and January 1975, the Khmer Rouge entered the capital, Phnom Penh, on 17 April 1975 and took over the country. Lon Nol had left Cambodia on 1 April. In December 1978, the Vietnamese army intervened, meeting no resistance except from the retreating Khmer Rouge forces, which took shelter in forest sanctuaries along the Thai border. A pro-Vietnamese government was installed in Phnom Penh as the People's Republic of Kampuchea, and was soon recognized by Vietnam, Laos and the USSR and her allies.

The USA, China and Thailand, all enemies of Vietnam, recognized, supported and continued to send arms to the Khmer Rouge and their chief, Pol Pot. The Khmer Rouge continued to represent Kampuchea in the United Nations, the Vietnamese intervention being condemned as 'aggression'. In 1991, the Paris Conference on Cambodia adopted the 'Agreements on a Comprehensive Political Settlement of the Cambodia Conflict' which created the UN Transitional Authority in Cambodia (UNTAC). UNTAC was to deal with the four competing factions of Cambodia, including the genocidal Khmer Rouge's Party of Democratic Kampuchea. In spite of Khmer Rouge harassment, refusal to disarm and refusal to participate in the UN-organized elections, these were held in May 1993 with a high voter participation (approximately 90% of the registered voters). This was the beginning of the final loss of power and influence of the Khmer Rouge, which accelerated with defections from the Pol Pot core group in 1996 and the final capture of Pol Pot himself in 1997.

The Khmer Rouge Revolution

In Kiernan's words:[23]

> In the first few days after Cambodia became Democratic Kampuchea, all cities were evacuated, hospitals cleared, schools closed, factories emptied, money abolished, monasteries shut, libraries shattered. For nearly four years, freedom of the press, of movement, of worship, of organization, and of association, and of discussion all completely disappeared. So did every day family life . . . Democratic Kampuchea was a prison camp state, and the eight million prisoners served most of their time in solitary confinement.

The systematic evacuation of the cities caused a gigantic exodus of more than 2 million people, with thousands of deaths. Then followed the identification of persons belonging to condemned groups, deportations and massacres, hard labour, starvation and uncared-for diseases, leading to more deaths. The 'old society', the foreign-educated professionals, the bourgeoisie, the 'corrupt city-dwellers' and educated people, had to be eliminated to leave only a young fanatic class of revolutionaries. Chiefs of co-operatives and soldiers had full powers to punish and kill. Children were separated from their parents at the age of seven. They lived in children's units, where they were submitted to political training without any other education, used as spies and then enrolled in the army.

The revolution also attempted to destroy Buddhist roots: members of the high clergy were murdered, and bonzes were either killed or grouped into special villages. This sociopolitical cleansing was accompanied by ethnic cleansing, i.e. genocide against minority groups: against the hereditary enemy, the Vietnamese living in the country, and an ethnic-religious group, the Chams. The country's authorities and its orders were hidden under the name of 'Angkar', which was only revealed to be the Central Committee of the Communist Party in 1977. Cambodia was sealed from the rest of the world. The borders were closed, foreign embassies (except those of nine Communist countries), press agencies and foreigners expelled, newspapers and television stations shut down, radios confiscated, mail and telephone use suppressed, and the speaking of foreign languages punished.

The Khmer Rouge leaders' dogmatic barbary was a product of ill-conceived Marxism and Maoism, on a basis of national pride, independence and economic self-sufficiency, rejection of foreign imperialism, hate of the Vietnamese, and a spirit of revolutionary violence.

A Reluctant Discovery

The geographical, diplomatic and communications closing of Cambodia and the usual Communist propaganda were the first reasons why the criminal nature of the Khmer Rouge revolution was not revealed and condemned publicly while it was in progress. A second reason was the reluctance of Western intellectuals and leftists in Western Europe and North America to have to condemn yet another Communist regime, following their shattered naive admiration for Lenin, Stalin and Mao, and their 'social conquests'. The new Kampuchea, with its re-creation of a new man, its return to nature and its rejection of Western political, economic and cultural givens, appeared as a worthy experiment that should be defended against false accusations.

As recalled by Ternon,[24] the first revelations were made in France by Father Ponchaud in *Le Monde* in 1976 and in a book in 1977, *Cambodge, année zéro* (Paris, Julliard). In the USA, John Barron and Anthony Paul wrote articles in the *Readers' Digest*, then published in a book in 1977. Leftist intellectuals, fellow-travellers and revisionist historians protested and denied the existence of any genocide, in spite of more revelations of more atrocities. On 30 January 1979, evidence presented to the UN Commission on Human Rights showed that gross and persistent violations of human rights had occurred in Democratic Kampuchea since mid-1975, which, according to several members of the Sub-Commission, had brought about the deaths of hundreds of thousands if not millions of people from all walks of life – men, women and children. The Commission had received submissions from the governments of Canada, Norway, the UK, the USA and Australia, and from Amnesty International and the International Commission of Jurists.

The expected response from the government of Democratic Kampuchea was to ignore or reject these allegations. In a note of 22 April 1978, the government rejected these charges as 'the slander and calumny of hoodlums, traitors and stateless persons'. The submission of the Sub-Commission report to the UN Commission on Human Rights was labelled as an 'impudent interference' in the country's internal affairs.[25] Mixed political alliances and supports during the Cold War led to more confusion and prevented the genocide from being brought formally to the United Nations Security Council. China was supporting the Khmer Rouge for ideological reasons and as a counterweight to Vietnam, the assertive regional power with the hegemonic ambition of recreating an Indochinese federation. The USA kept their own support for the Khmer Rouge after the Vietnamese intervention out of their own humiliation after having lost the Vietnam war. The USSR was supporting Socialist Vietnam. Any draft resolution condemning the Khmer Rouge government would have been vetoed in the Security Council. No military intervention by Western countries could have been envisaged: France had not yet recovered from its own Vietnamese colonial defeat, and the USA was clearly not ready for another Asian intervention.

National Justice and Denial

Following the Vietnamese intervention, the People's Revolutionary Tribunal, sitting in Phnom Penh in August 1979, pronounced the two Khmer Rouge leaders, Pol Pot, former Prime Minister, and Ieng Sary, former Deputy Prime Minister, guilty of the crime of genocide and condemned them to death *in absentia*.[26] All their properties were to be confiscated. The defendants had been defended by three lawyers, two Cambodian and one American, who admitted that the charges against Pol Pot and Ieng Sary were well grounded. They had been found guilty on the following counts:

(a) Planned massacre of innocent people: systematic massacre of many strata of the population, indiscriminate extermination of nearly all the officers and soldiers of the former regime, liquidation of the intelligentsia, repression and massacre of individuals and organizations suspected of opposition to the regime, including purges of their own supporters as from April 1978.
(b) Forced evacuation of people from towns and villages.
(c) Concentrating people (herding people into 'communes') and forcing them into hard labour in physically and morally exhausting conditions.
(d) Abolition of religion (Buddhism and Islam) and destruction of economic and cultural structures and family and social relations: massacre of priests and believers, systematic extermination of national minorities, extermination of foreign residents, undermining the national economy, abolition of culture, education and health services.

The Tribunal recognized that the crime of genocide committed by this clique, and without precedent in world history, was far graver that the definition featured in the Convention of 9 December 1948.

At the June 1986 ASEAN Foreign Ministers' meeting in Manila, William Hayden, Australia's new Foreign Minister, proposed the establishment of an international tribunal to try the Pol Pot leadership for its crimes. The proposal was supported in principle by the Malaysian Foreign Minister, and a few weeks later by the Indonesian Foreign Minister. However, the US Secretary of State George Shultz opposed it, as did Australia's Prime Minister.[27] A Commission of documentation on Cambodia directed by David Hawk, and composed of refugees, human rights specialists and jurists, has been working since 1982 on the Khmer Rouge crimes. Witnesses' testimonies have been recorded from survivors in Thailand, the USA and Canada. Photographs of torture and execution centres, of charnel-houses and of destroyed temples, official archives and records of ideological propaganda from Radio Phnom Penh are being collected.[28]

In 1994, the US Congress adopted the Cambodian Genocide Justice Act, which expresses the American government's commitment to the pursuit of justice for the victims of the genocide. In the same year, the Cambodian Genocide Program at Yale University began the work of documenting the mass killings in Cambodia during the Democratic Kampuchea regime headed by Pol Pot between 1975 and 1979. The Program's aims are (a) to collect and study all extant information about this period in Cambodian history, (b) to make this information available to a court or tribunal willing to prosecute Cambodian war criminals, and (c) to generate a critical analytical understanding of genocide which can be marshalled in the prevention of political violence against populations elsewhere in the world. The Program is advancing these goals through a variety of activities, including documentation, preservation, research and training.[29]

In an effort to split the remaining Khmer Rouge forces, in September 1996, King Norodom Sihanouk granted an amnesty to Ieng Sary, who had broken, with his 3000 troops, from Pol Pot. Ieng Sary had been the number three of the Khmer Rouge régime, after Pol Pot and Nuon Chea. He had pleaded for a massive 'cleansing' of the old population. He was one of those mainly responsible for the genocide. In public declarations, he said that he had neither remorse not regrets, as the massacres were not his responsibility. To a French journalist, he said that Pol Pot, Nuon Chea and Son Sen determined the fate of the intellectuals and other exactions, not him. He opposed Pol Pot on the question of the evacuation of the cities. He was no longer a Communist.[30]

A show trial of Pol Pot by the Khmer Rouge, held in Anlong Veng in the North of Cambodia on 23 July 1997, was witnessed by Nate Thayer, the correspondent for the Far Eastern Economic Review. The aged and sickly Pol Pot was publicly humiliated by a small, disciplined group and condemned to life imprisonment. The intent of this 'hoax', in the words of a French historian of the movement, Christophe Peschoud, was probably to distance the remaining Khmer Rouge from their genocidal past. In an interview with Thayer on 15 October 1997, Pol Pot said that he had no regrets; his conscience was clear.[31]

The massacres ordered and implemented by the Khmer Rouge on their own people were essentially based on a ruthless, cruel, utopian ideology, which rejected all societal and humane considerations, in total ignorance of economic realities. The condemnation to death of Pol Pot and Ieng Sary by a Vietnamese-inspired Tribunal, although more than justified in substance, suffered from procedural weaknesses, and has not been carried out. His recent condemnation by his own group to life imprisonment, in an even more imperfect trial, does not satisfy the continuing need for a full, documented exposure of the Khmer Rouge genocide and for a public trial of its leaders by an independent and impartial tribunal.

On 21 June 1997, Prince Norodom Ranariddh and Hun Sen, respectively First and Second Prime Ministers, asked for the assistance of the UN and the international community in bringing to justice those persons responsible for the genocide and crimes against humanity during the rule of the Khmer Rouge from 1975 to 1979. As Cambodia did not have the resources or expertise to conduct this procedure, UN assistance was necessary on the basis of similar efforts to respond to the genocide and crimes against humanity in Rwanda and the former Yugoslavia.[32] It is, however, unlikely that the UN and the international community will respond positively to this request by creating another *ad hoc* International Tribunal. It is also clear that the present Cambodian government, headed by a former Khmer Rouge member, is both unwilling and incapable of holding a fair and well-documented trial of Pol Pot and his main associates. There is as yet no international criminal court to investigate and prosecute the Khmer Rouge atrocities. Stanton[33] has proposed that the Cambodian genocide case be submitted to the International Court of Justice under Article 9 of the Genocide Convention: however, no government has agreed to take the case to the Court (see Chapter 8).

In view of the lack of political will on the part of governments to bring the Khmer Rouge to national or international justice, the last 'weak' but feasible alternative would be that the (non-governmental) International Peoples' Tribunal hold a session on the Cambodian genocide: proposals have been made, but have failed because of internal divergencies of the initiators and lack of funds (see Chapter 7).

CONCLUSION

From this short, selective, possibly biased and necessarily incomplete review of a few cases of genocides and massacres, a first observation is that one of the major reasons for violent conflicts triggering mass killings is the political urge to gain power, or to retain power, or to impose a chosen ideology, or forcefully to change a society according to pre-established revolutionary norms through the physical destruction of any political opposition, or counter-revolutionaries, or 'enemies of the people', or unwanted segments of the society. This corresponds to the third category of objectives defined in Chalk and Jonassohn's typology, 'to implement a belief, a theory, or an ideology, or to eliminate a belief, a theory or an ideology considered hostile to the perpetrators' beliefs or objectives'. Massive crimes committed by the USSR, China and Cambodia fall into this category. This not unexpected finding would require a re-examination of Article II of the Genocide Convention, in order to add 'political' groups to those listed, i.e. national, ethnical, racial or religious, in spite of the expected opposition of those countries that have, or intend to, persecuted their population on political/ideological grounds.

With regard to Chalk and Jonassohn's typology, one could consider a fourth category, or a subcategory of the third category, which could be defined as 'involuntary genocide' by miscalculation, error through ill-conceived and ill-applied political and economic ideology. This would also apply to the same countries; the USSR, China and Cambodia. The Armenian genocide and the Indonesian massacres would fall under the first category of the same typology: to eliminate a real or potential threat against the perpetrators' population, their institutions, their religion, their lives, their property, their ambitions, in a self-proclaimed preventive self-defence exercise. Acquiring wealth for the government and the Moslem majority (the second category in the typology) may have been one element, among others, in the Armenian genocide.

As a second and also well-shared observation, a major and minimal requirement for genocidal excesses is a dictatorial and totalitarian political regime, which does not tolerate any counter-powers. Communist regimes, based on an ideological utopia, a revolutionary drive and the fiction of people's power building a new democracy, easily fall into this model. The recipe for disaster for their population is having an all-powerful party holding all of the reins of power – government, the legislative, the judiciary, the army, the police and the media – at all levels and in all parts of the country. Authoritarian, non-Communist, countries benefiting from 'Presidents-for life' and corrupt elections are also likely to indulge in human rights abuses, persecutions of minorities and hidden and denied exactions.

A third observation is the major importance given by the authorities (the perpetrators) to hide their plans and their exactions from their own populations and from the world at large. Once discovered, their reaction is to deny their crimes or to reduce them to occasional, insignificant incidents, or to show them as reasonable responses to inexcusable provocations. This 'homage of vice to virtue' (in the French formula) is in fact a recognition that they knew that their exactions were grave breaches of international humanitarian law and violations of all human rights and fundamental freedoms. Such regimes do not recognize their faults, and their perpetrators, still in power, continue to benefit from long-term impunity from any national judiciary prosecution.

Current history shows that, even if denounced and exposed by the media, genocides and massacres are still carried out in various parts of the world. The 'intervention fatigue' of the big powers leaves those killings and counter-killings to proceed at their own pace. At the intergovernmental level, external interventions are now limited to diplomatic expressions of 'concern' or 'grave concern', or even 'condemnations' and possible requests for international enquiries by governmental, intergovernmental or non-governmental teams. Only the latter may provide the necessary independence from national and international politics. Hence, the importance of the independent role of human rights NGOs such as Amnesty International, Human Rights Watch, the International Commission of Jurists and others as witnesses, analysts and public advocates for action and/or repression cannot be underestimated. The need for scientific fact-finding by independent teams working in the field, and by independent researchers and historians, is also essential, in order to establish and document historical facts on an objective basis.

Within countries, there is no hope for a change of heart of those in absolute power which will lead them to give up that power willingly. Only strong international pressure, and a strong internal political and social movement, may lead a country to adopt democratic institutions and practices – a long and difficult transition under the best circumstances. The creation of effective representative counter-powers, including an independent judiciary, is an essential requirement, among others, to establish basic conditions for an effective national justice. In the following chapter, the impact of Truth and Reconciliation Commissions, as a substitute or a complement to national or international justice, will be reviewed.

5 Truth and Reconciliation

Victims, survivors and their families deserve respect and need reparation, but, first, they have a right to know the truth. The perpetrators usually take great pains to hide their crimes, to deny that they have been committed, and, if the crimes are discovered, to deny that they have any degree of responsibility for them. Corpses are burned, buried or dropped into lakes or seas, evidence is tampered with, dispersed or destroyed, witnesses are threatened or killed, massacres are changed into isolated or unfortunate incidents, propaganda disguises exactions under a veil of patriotism or ideology, history is carefully revised to distort the reality and protect the leaders. Confident that they will not be prosecuted in their country, nor extradited from another country where they took refuge, the perpetrators often live a peaceful, comfortable life, without remorse.

Their peace may be disturbed when their country shifts from a totalitarian regime backed by military force to a form of democracy. The most difficult question, for the freely elected new leaders and parliament, is to decide how to deal with past grave breaches of human rights and fundamental freedoms committed, or allowed to be committed by the former leaders, including senior military and police officials, when the main perpetrators still have formal power or informal influence and are still supported by the armed forces. Will the truth be allowed to be divulged through proper investigation? Will the main offenders be prosecuted and judged? Should there be an amnesty, and for whom and under what conditions? Should some compromises be accepted in the interest of national reconciliation?

In his final report on the 'Question of the impunity of perpetrators of violations of human rights (civil and political rights)' submitted in June 1997 to the Sub-Commission on Prevention of Discrimination and Protection of Minorities of the UN Commission on Human Rights, the Special Rapporteur, Louis Joinet, set principles resting on three fundamental rights of victims: the right to know, the right to justice and the right to reparation. Under the 'right to know', he set out the inalienable right to the truth and the duty to remember. Two proposals followed: the prompt creation of extrajudicial commissions of inquiry as a preliminary stage in establishing the truth, particularly when it has previously been denied, and urgent steps to be taken with regard to the preservation of, and access to, archives of the reference period.

The report sets out the following principles in relation to the Extrajudicial Commissions of Inquiry. The task of commissions is to establish the facts. Their investigations should secure recognition of the truth, in order to restore the dignity of the victims, families and human rights defenders. The legitimacy of commissions should be founded upon guarantees of independence and impartiality. They should not have authority to act as substitutes for the courts. Their investigations should relate to all persons cited in allegations of human rights violations. Priority should be given to violations appearing to constitute a consistent pattern of gross violations. Legal guarantees should be given to persons implicated, while the security and protection of victims and witnesses should be guaranteed. Commissions' recommendations should encourage, *inter alia*, the perpetrators to admit their guilt. Recommendations should also set out legislative or other measures to put these principles into effect and to prevent further violations. These measures should primarily concern the army, police and justice system and the strengthening of democratic institutions. The commissions' inquiry may be kept confidential, but the final report should be made public and widely disseminated.

The former Special Rapporteur of the Sub-Commission, Theo van Boven, submitted to the UN Commission on Human Rights, in January 1997, a Note of the 'Basic Principles and Guidelines on the Right to Reparation for Victims of [Gross] Violations of Human Rights and International Humanitarian Law'. The Note included the following, non-exhaustive forms of reparation, to be provided in accordance with the law of every state:

- restitution requiring, *inter alia*, restoration of liberty, family life, citizenship, return to one's place of residence, and restoration of employment or property;
- compensation for physical or mental harm, lost opportunities, material damages and loss of earnings, harm to reputation or dignity, legal or expert costs;
- rehabilitation;
- satisfaction and guarantees of non-repetition.[1]

In addition to the clear principles set out in the Joinet and van Boven reports, other questions would have to be negotiated by the parties concerned and agreed upon. Should the commission be composed of national or international members? An international commission would, in principle, have more credibility than a national one: it would be more free in its research and in its identification of perpetrators, less open to internal pressures and manoeuvres. The creation of an international commission either by the UN Security Council or General Assembly, a regional group or an *ad hoc* group of countries, or as part of a bilateral or multilateral treaty, would give the commission international support and give its report and recommendations more visibility. However, the findings of an international commission may be rejected by part of the population as the biased work of hostile foreigners who should not meddle in 'our' own affairs.

Another question is that of the duration of the mandate given to a commission: a short period of a few months would not allow the commission to carry out its task in depth, while an extended period of time might periodically re-open old wounds and possibly damage the reconciliation process. It is generally agreed that the ultimate purpose of truth commissions is to facilitate the healing of a bruised society and to help promote national reconciliation. They should provide an objective and detailed record of the history of the violations, so that events are not later viewed as fabricated, exaggerated or distorted. They are seeking justice for the victims through a public recognition that specific crimes have been committed and a public condemnation of those who have committed those crimes. They should act as a deterrent to prevent further violations and abuses. They will be seen as promoting a culture of human rights and a respect for the rule of law and thereby reinforce the country's transition to democracy. Truth will permit mourning for the victims' relatives. A public declaration of their crimes by the perpetrators, hopefully accompanied by sincere repentance, may help to put the past behind and focus the country's energy on building up or strengthening democracy. For Scharf, a truth commission may serve as 'historical group therapy sessions'.[2] Truth commissions may also support concurrent or later judicial action by providing to prosecutions and courts an historical record of crimes, victims and perpetrators.

A number of truth commissions have been established since World War II, the purpose of which was or is not only the search for

truth, but which were also asked to make general recommendations on constitutional and legislative matters, and were to search
for reconciliation. Commissions only concerned with fact-finding
are not considered here. Hayner has made a comparative study of
15 truth commissions in the period 1974 to 1994.[3] The United Nations
has recently established truth commissions for El Salvador and
Guatemala. Our review will be limited to the experiences of three
Latin American countries – Chile, El Salvador and Guatemala –
experiences which underline the dilemma between the research of
truth and the impunity provided by forced and hasty amnesties. As
another model, the complex and more sophisticated South African
experiment should eventually provide rich information on the costs
and benefits to be expected from such a process.

LATIN AMERICAN COMMISSIONS

The first Latin American truth commission was established in Bolivia in October 1982: it had a limited mandate and impact. The
Argentina Commission attracted wide international attention. Its
1986 report, *Nunca Mas*, documented the cases of almost 9000
persons and became a national bestseller. An 'Investigative Commission on the Situation of "Disappeared" People and its Causes'
established by the Uruguayan parliament in 1985 only reported on
164 disappearances and had a limited impact.[4]

Chile

In April 1990, President Aylwin created the National Commission
for Truth and Reconciliation (the Rettig Commission, by the name
of its chairman). The presidential decree creating the Commission
assigned it four tasks: to establish as complete a picture as possible 'of the most serious human rights violations'; 'to gather evidence that may make it possible to identify the victims by name
and their fate and whereabouts'; to recommend reparations for the
families of the victims; and to recommend legal and administrative
measures designed to ensure that such violations would never occur again.[5]

In December 1989, Aylwin had won the presidency, although the
1980 Constitution allowed the former Head of State, General Augusto
Pinochet, to remain commander of the army. Pinochet had taken

dictatorial power in a *coup d'état* in 1973. The UN General Assembly had expressed its concern about human rights in Chile at each session since 1974. In 1990, the Special Rapporteur of the UN Commission on Human Rights, Fernando Volio of Costa Rica, noted in his report on Chile among 'continuing problems' the existence of torture, abuses by military courts, the lack of independence of the judiciary, and the lack of appropriate judicial measures against persons involved in some of the notorious cases of killing, disappearance, and burning over recent years.[6]

The Rettig Commission worked for nine months to investigate the 3400 cases brought to it: 2920 of these were determined to fit within its mandate. Each case was thoroughly investigated. Released on 4 March 1991, the Commission's report implicated the military and secret police at the highest levels in the death or disappearance of 2279 people between September 1973 and March 1990. However, the Commission limited its investigation to those cases involving death, with the result that tens of thousands of cases of torture, forced exile and other grave human rights violations were not investigated. Furthermore, the Commission's mandate prevented the naming of alleged perpetrators, directing the Commission to submit any evidence of criminal action to the courts. In presenting the report to the public, President Aylwin formally apologized to the victims and their families on behalf of the state, and asked the army to acknowledge its role in the violence.

The Commission had recommended the creation of a Corporation for Reparation and Reconciliation to continue the search for the disappeared and oversee reparations to victims, and a human rights ombudsman to denounce future violations. The National Corporation was created in 1992 and its mandate was extended until the end of 1995. By the end of 1994, the total number of people who had been killed or had disappeared under the military government was officially acknowledged to be more than 3000. As a result of the protection provided by an amnesty law for all political crimes issued by the Pinochet government in 1978, only a few perpetrators were judged and sentenced by civilian courts for human rights violations committed under the military government.[7]

El Salvador

A Commission on the Truth was established under the Mexico Agreements of 27 April 1991 between the Government of El Salvador and the Frente Farabundo Marti para la Liberacion Nacional (FMLN). The reasons for its creation were similar to those which led to the establishment of the Chilean Commission: revealing the truth about some of the worst exactions committed during a military regime was expected to assist in achieving civil peace, national reconciliation and a successful transition to democracy: it is estimated that more than 75 000 victims were killed in El Salvador during the military dictatorship period, 1979–92. In both Chile and El Salvador, the Commission was created at the end of a long and bitter civil war, which had left the population of each country bruised, angry and divided. In both countries, the military applied effective pressures to ensure that the Commission's conclusions and recommendations were applied only in part, or delayed, and that an amnesty which afforded impunity to the military and civilian perpetrators neutralized most of its findings on individual cases.

However, several of the characteristics of the El Salvador Commission differentiate it from the previous case. The main difference was that the Chilean Commission was essentially the result of a national initiative, while the creation of the El Salvador Commission was part of a comprehensive peace settlement brokered by the United Nations, within the context of a regional peace process also sponsored by the UN and involving five Central American countries, a peace dividend of the end of the Cold War.[8]

The Truth Commission in El Salvador was the first such commission sponsored by, paid for and staffed by the UN, although its concept was based on the experiences of the purely national commissions set up in Argentina and Chile. The then UN Secretary-General, the Peruvian Javier Perez de Cuellar, had taken an active and direct interest in promoting the regional peace process and, more particularly, the conclusion of agreements between the El Salvador government and the FMLN, with the explicit support of the Security Council, of the USA and of the then USSR. The 'Group of Four Friends of the Secretary-General' – Columbia, Mexico, Spain and Venezuela – had also actively supported the negotiations. A UN Mission, ONUSAL, was set up in El Salvador to oversee the demobilization of forces, the elections and, through one of its Divisions, to monitor the implementation of a human rights agreement signed by the two parties in July 1990 (the San Jose Agreement). The three members of the Commission were appointed by the UN Secretary-General after consultation with the parties. The Commission's report was to be transmitted to the parties and to the

Secretary-General 'who shall make it public and shall take the decisions or initiatives that he deems appropriate'.[9] The role of the UN was therefore that of an active intermediary between the parties, in the interest of regional and national peace and democracy, although it did not exclude diplomatic caution.

In this international context, both parties in El Salvador were periodically subject to open or discreet pressures aimed at promoting progress of the peace process through compromises. Peace agreements were also to be promoted and strengthened by international guarantees.[10] Finally, the international composition of the Commission gave its members more independence than would have been possible for a purely national body. Unlike the more cautious Rettig Commission, the El Salvador Commission's report publicly named individuals about whom it developed incontrovertible evidence that they had committed crimes according to international humanitarian law and international human rights law. The latter's mandate did not provide explicitly for such a power, but it 'urgently required that the complete truth be made known': complete truth cannot name only victims and ignore perpetrators.

The peace process between the government and the FMLN started in April 1990 with the Geneva Agreement with the purpose of ending the armed conflict by political means as soon as possible. The Mexico City Agreements of 27 April 1991 established the Commission on the Truth as a 'political agreement': the Commission would not function as a judicial body, although it could refer cases to the Attorney-General of the Republic.The Commission was entrusted with the task of investigating serious acts of violence that had occurred since 1980 and 'whose impact on society urgently required that the public should know the truth'. The parties undertook to carry out the Commission's recommendations. The Commission was to complete its work in six months.

In July 1991, the 101 members of the UN Observer Mission in El Salvador (ONUSAL) started work in the country. Following UN-sponsored negotiations, the New York Agreement of September 1991 established a National Commission for the Consolidation of the Peace (COPAZ) with members from the government and from the FMLN. On 10 December 1991, the UN Secretary-General announced the appointment of the three members of the Commission on the Truth: Belisario Betancur, former President of Colombia, Thomas Buergenthal, Professor of Law at George Washington University and Reinaldo Figueredo, former Foreign Minister of

Venezuela – three eminent personalities, with a supporting team of 57 advisers, researchers, experts and administrative personnel. On 31 December 1991, definitive agreements were announced by both parties in New York, and a Law of National Reconciliation was approved in January 1992 granting a limited amnesty. A cease-fire took effect on 1 February 1992. In January 1993, the UN Secretary-General revealed that the Ad Hoc Commission on the Purification of the Armed Forces had recommended the dismissal or transfer of 103 officers. The government delayed action on these recommendations, which were applied only 'broadly'.

The Commission on the Truth submitted its report on 15 March 1993, with the appropriate title of 'From madness to hope – the 12 year war in El Salvador'.[11] Of the 18 000 victims on which the Commission had gathered information, 60% were found to have been killed, abducted or made to 'disappear' by army personnel, 25% by the security forces affiliated with the army, 10% by right-wing death squads with army participation, and 5% by members of the FMLN. The report contained both recommendations concerning individuals, and general policy recommendations. It recommended the dismissal from their posts and discharge from the armed forces of more than 40 senior officers, who were personally implicated in the perpetration or cover-up of serious acts of violence, or who did not fulfil their professional obligation to initiate or co-operate in the investigation and punishment of such acts. A number of civilian officials in the civil service and the judiciary, who covered up serious acts of violence or failed to discharge their responsibilities in the investigation of such acts, were to be dismissed from their posts. All those implicated in acts of violence should be disqualified from holding any public post or office for at least ten years. They should be disqualified permanently from any activity related to public security or national defence. On judicial reform, the report attributed 'tremendous responsibility' to the judiciary for the impunity with which serious acts of violence occurred. It denounced the glaring inability of the judicial system either to investigate crimes or to enforce the law, especially when it came to crimes committed with the direct or indirect support of state institutions: El Salvador had no system for the administration of justice which meets the minimum requirements of objectivity and impartiality so that justice can be rendered reliably. However, the Commission had no easy remedy for this situation within its mandate except to stress the need for restructuring the system of justice. A more specific recommendation was that the new procedure for the election of judges to the Supreme Court of Justice approved as part of the peace process should be applied immediately – currrent members should resign. The dismissal of members of the National Council of the Judiciary should be possible only for precise legal causes. The Career Judicial Service Act should establish that only those judges who have demonstrated judicial aptitude, efficiency and concern for human rights and offer every guarantee of independence, judicial discretion, honesty and impartiality may remain in the career judicial service.

As part of the eradication of structural causes linked directly to the exactions, the Commission mentioned the need for reforms in the armed forces, the demilitarization of the police. Private armed groups should be disbanded and investigated. On 20 March 1993, five days after the release of the Commission's report, the National Assembly approved a government-backed amnesty, as a direct blow against the hopes created by the Commission's report. The UN Secretary-General admitted that the amnesty was 'strictly speaking' an internal affair, but requested the government to inform him how and when it proposed to implement the recommendations of the Commission in light of developments. The military had already responded to the Commission's report with a televised statement presented by the Defence Minister, calling the Commission's actions illegal and out of line with its mandate.[12]

In April 1994, the UN Human Rights Committee noted that most of the recommendations of the Truth Commission had not yet been implemented. The Committee expressed

> grave concern over the adoption of the Amnesty Law, which prevents relevant investigation and punishment of perpetrators of past human rights violations and consequently precludes relevant compensation. It also seriously undermines efforts to re-establish respect for human rights in El Salvador and to prevent a recurrence of the massive human rights violations experienced in the past.

In July 1994, new members were elected to the Supreme Court of Justice and the evaluation of all judicial personnel was being carried out. However, also in July 1994, a report of ONUSAL's human rights division reported on the progress of judicial investigations into 75 cases of violations of the right to life since 1992. In not one case had those responsible been brought to justice. In a quarter of the cases no judicial proceedings whatsoever had been initiated. The impunity of the perpetrators was still the main cause of human rights violations in the country. The failure of the authorities to carry out effective investigations into political killings and other human rights violations had been repeatedly criticized by ONUSAL.

In July 1996, the UN Secretary-General welcomed the approval by the National Assembly of a package of constitutional reforms recommended by the Commission on the Truth and of the Police Career Law.[13]

Guatemala

One of the five countries which were parties to the regional peace process, Guatemala has had the longest on-going civil war, for more than three and a half decades at a cost of human lives estimated at 150 000 in a country of 10.5 million inhabitants. At least 100 000 people have been killed, mostly by the army and paramilitary forces; 40 000 are listed as having 'disappeared', thousands more have been raped, tortured or illegally detained, and more than a million have been forced into exile or displaced from their homes.

As in El Salvador, the Guatemalan peace process has benefited from UN support, while the USA was deemed to have less leverage on the Guatemalan military than in other Central American countries. Negotiations between the government and the Unidad Revolucionaria Nacional Guatemalteca (URNG) started in April 1990 and only approved a Framework Agreement, with a UN Moderator of the negotiations, on 29 March 1994 at Mexico City. The Agreement included a Comprehensive Agreement on Human Rights, an Agreement on a Timetable for the Negotiation of a Firm and Lasting Peace in Guatemala and a joint statement of the two parties. Article III.3 prescribed that 'No special law or exclusive jurisdiction may be invoked to uphold impunity in respect of human rights violations.' As part of the Agreements, the parties requested the UN to establish a mission to verify the implementation of the human rights agreement. The creation of the UN Mission for the Verification of Human Rights and of Compliance with the Commitments of the Comprehensive Agreement on Human Rights in Guatemala (MINUGUA) was approved by the General Assembly on 19 September 1994.[14]

The position of both parties had evolved over time. Before signing any cease-fire or peace agreement, the guerrilla leaders insisted on the establishment of a truth commission, operating under UN auspices, to investigate human rights violations and the implementation of measures to prevent such occurrences in the future. The government then rejected UN involvement as unconstitutional and unnecessary, in view of the prior creation of an office of human rights ombudsman. On 18 December 1996, the Guatemalan Congress adopted a Law of National Reconciliation providing for an amnesty, endorsed by the two combatant groups, the Guatemalan Armed Forces and the Guatemalan National Revolutionary Unity, but criticized by national and international human rights groups. The law calls for courts to rule on petitions for amnesty by soldiers and guerrillas on a case-by-case basis. The law, the result of a negotiated compromise, was in breach of the 1994 Agreement on Human Rights, as it gave impunity to some categories of perpetrators. The text of the law prescribes that 'This law will not be applicable to the crimes of genocide, torture and forced disappearance'. Human rights groups had sought to add 'extrajudicial killings' and 'illegal detention' to the list. They had also tried unsuccessfully to prohibit immunity specifically not only for those who took part in such activities, but also for those who ordered them or covered them up, including senior military officers and guerrilla commanders. At the end of December 1996, the government and rebels signed a final peace agreement that includes establishment of a Commission for Historical Clarification entrusted to produce a final, definitive account of the abuses committed during the war. The Commission is composed of three members and should complete its work in six months. It will not assign individual responsibility for crimes. Otilia Lux de Coti, one its members, a prominent Maya educator, said 'We are neither judges nor hangmen ... We are not ready for that [naming names]; we need more maturity, and at this juncture I do not see the point of sowing more bitterness'.

Critics of the Commission's mandate reply that bitterness will remain until surviving victims and their relatives see justice done, whether formal or symbolic. An Alliance Against Impunity has challenged the constitutionality of the amnesty law in courts on grounds of vagueness and contradictory language. An earlier private initiative, the Project to Recover Historical Memory, was established by the Catholic Church in 1995, in order to compile a comprehensive record. It is financed by donations from Scandinavian countries. The coordinator of the Project, Edgar Gutierez, intends to name the names of perpetrators in the Project report. The Project has documented 483 mass killings and has received information about the locations of more than 300 clandestine cemeteries, which has led to exhumations. Between 1995 and 1997, some 800 volunteer workers have interviewed more than 5000 people, mostly in small Indian villages scattered across the country. In addition, the group has been approached by about 200 former soldiers or civil patrol members who took part in killings or torture and wanted to clear their conscience. At the same time, a coalition of 27 human rights groups is pooling files from some 10 000 cases of executions, forced disappearance and torture collected over twenty years. It plans to publish the information after making it available to the official Commission.[15]

SOUTH AFRICA

While every country has its own history, South Africa, when it abolished the *apartheid* system, faced some of the same problems faced by other countries in a different transition to democracy: how to deal with a legacy of oppression, how to restore the rule of law and establish a culture of respect for human rights, how to democratize the institutions of the country, and how to establish firmly and durably a freely elected parliament, an accountable government, an independent justice, a disciplined army and police under government control. In all these countries, the government and other parties have had to decide how the truth on a violent past would be investigated and revealed, whether the main perpetrators would be publicly identified, prosecuted and sanctioned, or whether a total or partial amnesty would be decreed, whether the victims, the survivors and their relatives would obtain some type of reparation. In South Africa, as in other countries, the terms of the transition had to be negotiated between the parties – military-supported government versus armed rebels, or, in South Africa, the *apartheid* government versus the African National Congress (ANC). The stakes were somewhat similar: the threat of civil war, or renewed civil war or the hope of peace. The same methods were used: a negotiation process between the parties, sometimes mediated or prodded by the international community, which demands give and take and political compromises, with the aim of restoring peace, law and order. The same dilemma between the demand for truth, retribution and reparation, and the counter-pleas that past excesses should be forgotten or forgiven in the interest of civil peace and national reconciliation, had to be faced and resolved.

However, the South African situation is on its own in view of the extraordinary success achieved by Nelson Mandela, together with the *apartheid* government leaders, in a peaceful transition from a minority government to free elections with universal suffrage, an assembly and a government representative of the whole population. Although the UN applied recurrent pressure on South Africa to end *apartheid*, through resolutions and sanctions, and sent a small mission to observe the first legislative elections by universal suffrage, it had no role in setting up the Truth and Reconciliation Commission (TRC), nor in monitoring its work. South Africa is also set apart in granting this Commission the power to grant amnesty to individuals: the danger of a blanket amnesty leading to total impunity was thus set aside.

Another South African exception was the previous creation of truth commissions by the rebel movement, ANC, before the end of *apartheid*, the only example of an armed resistance group to establish a commission to investigate and publicly report on its own past human rights abuses.[16] Their experience was a useful precedent and experiment for the later TRC. Following reports of abuses in ANC detention camps, Nelson Mandela appointed in March 1992 the 'Commission of Enquiry into Complaints by Former African National Congress Prisoners and Detainees'. The Commission's report documented 'staggering brutality' in ANC camps over the past years. It did not name the perpetrators but recommended that ANC 'clean its own ranks'. The report was issued to the press and the public. Mandela accepted collective responsibility for the leadership of the ANC for the 'serious abuses and irregularities' that had occurred, but insisted that individuals should not be named or held personally accountable. This Commission was criticized for its composition, as two of its members were ANC members and for not providing sufficient opportunity for accused individuals to defend themselves.

Mandela then named a second Commission, the 'Commission of Enquiry into Certain Allegations of Cruelty and Human Rights Abuses Against ANC Prisoners and Detainees by ANC Members', composed of three commissioners from the USA, Zimbabwe and South Africa, who adopted a formal approach with legal representation for both complainants and defendants. The Commission's report, submitted in August 1993, included a description of each case submitted to it with a list of specific individuals who violated the rights of each complainant: names were named. The ANC accepted the Commission's general conclusions and called for a truth commission to be set up to cover abuses on both sides of the conflict in South Africa since 1948.

The Truth and Reconciliation Commission (TRC) was created by an act of the South African Parliament promulgated in December 1995, the 'Promotion of National Unity and Reconciliation Act', following debates in conferences, workshops and review by a parliamentary standing committee on justice.[17] In other countries, the creation and mandate of the truth commission were negotiated between government and the rebellion, while the role of the National Assembly, still dominated by government forces, was generally limited to voting an amnesty. The Commission has 17 members serving full-time, appointed by President Mandela in consultation with his cabinet, following a selection process by a representative committee and public hearings, which reduced a list of 299 names to a shortlist of 25. Additional committee members are allowed for, plus professional and administrative staff and an Investigative Unit. It is a national, not an international, body. The Commission has to complete its work in two years, plus three months for the final report to be completed.

The Commission deals with gross human rights violations that took place between 1 March 1960 and 5 December 1993. It is not seeking vengeance or retaliation, but is rather trying to bring about national unity and reconciliation. Its ultimate aim is to help develop a culture of human rights in South Africa, so that the suffering and injustices of the past never occur again. Its objectives are to:

- give a complete picture of the gross violations of human rights which took place and which came from conflicts of the past;
- restore to victims their human and civil dignity by letting them tell their stories and recommending how they can be assisted; and
- consider granting amnesty to those 'perpetrators' who carried out the abuses for political reasons, and who give full details of their actions to the Commission.

The Commission is composed of three separate committees: a Human Rights Violations Committee which conducts public hearings for victims of gross human rights violations and their survivors, i.e. people who were killed, abducted, tortured or severely ill-treated; an Amnesty Committee which hears, and decides on, applications for amnesty; and a Committee on Reparation and Rehabilitation which provides emotional support services to victims and witnesses, makes recommendations to the President and Parliament in cases where immediate relief is needed, recommendations on ways to prevent similar human rights violations in the future and recommendations on guidelines to assist in the formulation of the policy on reparation. Hearings are open to the media and to the public: this transparency should provide an educative opportunity – particularly for the whites who reject all guilt – and may assist in the healing process. As for the El Salvador Commission, the TRC publishes the names of perpetrators but ensures conditions of due process. Another difference with other commissions, is that the TRC has powers of subpoena and of search and seizure. The Commission may sanction those who defy a subpoena or refuse to answer questions satisfactorily by a jail term.

However, the main innovation is the Commission's power to grant amnesty on an individual basis under specific conditions: applicants for amnesty must complete a prescribed form which is published in the *Government Gazette*: detailed information must be given on specific human rights violations; applicants must make a 'full disclosure' of their human rights violations in order to qualify for amnesty; in most instances, applicants will appear before the Amnesty Committee in hearings open to the public; only those gross human rights violations committed between 1960 to 1993 will be considered for amnesty; amnesty applications must have been made before 14 December 1996. Finally, a list of criteria laid down in the Act will determine whether or not the applicant for amnesty may be successful: the list is shown in Presentation 5.1. However, even if applicants satisfy these criteria, they will not automatically be granted amnesty.

The Commission, presided over by Desmond Tutu, the respected retired Anglican archbishop, started work in April 1996 and, by August 1997, 11 519 statements had been submitted to the Committee on Human Rights Violations: out of approximately 7000 applications for amnesty, forty-seven had been approved.[18] On 28 January 1997, five former security policemen confessed, in an application for amnesty, to having killed Stephen Biko, leader of the Black Consciousness Movement, who died in police detention

PRESENTATION 5.1
The South African Truth and Reconciliation Commission Committee on
Amnesty – Criteria for Granting Amnesty

Where a particular act, omission or offence is an act associated with a
political objective, amnesty shall be decided with reference to the following criteria:

1. the motive of the person who committed the act, omission, or offence;
2. the context in which the act, omission or offence took place, and in
   particular, whether the act, omission or offence was committed in the
   course of or as part of a political uprising, disturbance or event, or in
   reaction thereto;
3. the legal and factual nature of the act, omission or offence, including
   the gravity of the act, omission or offence;
4. the object or objective of the act, omission or offence and in particular
   whether the act, omission or offence was primarily directed at a political opponent of State property or personnel or against private property or individuals;
5. whether the act, omission or offence was committed in the execution
   of an order of, or on behalf of, or with the approval of, the organization, institution, liberation movement or body of which the person who
   committed the act was a member, an agent or a supporter; and
6. the relationship between the act, omission or offence and the political
   objective pursued, and in particular the directness and proximity of
   the relationship and the proportionality of the act, omission or offence
   to the objective pursued.

The following criteria are not included:

1. for personal gain: provided that an act, omission or offence by any
   person who acted and received money or anything of value as an in-
   former of the State or a former State, political organization or liberation movement, shall not be excluded only on the grounds of that person
   having received money or anything of value for his or her information;
2. out of personal malice, ill-will or spite, directed against the victim of
   the acts committed.

Source: A. Boraine, Vice Chairperson, South African Truth and Reconciliation Commission, 'Alternatives and Adjuncts to Criminal Prosecutions',
Brussels Conference, 20–21 July 1996 (by permission).

on 12 September 1977. This crime had long been covered up as an accident, or a suicide. Biko had become the hero of a generation of anti-*apartheid* activists. His family has opposed the expected amnesty of his murderers, while, in other cases, victims, survivors or relatives may accept the confessions of applicants as a relief and not demand punishment.

The confessions of lower-level operators led to more applications for amnesty from higher-level officials, in an attempt to avoid prosecution for themselves, and to show that they were not acting on their own, but that policy and instructions came from the government, Prime Minister, ministers and other senior officials. In October 1996, Johan van der Merwe, a police commissioner during the 1980s, admitted that he gave the order for the police to blow up the Johannesburg headquarters of the South African Council of Churches in 1988. He said that Adriaan Vlok, the former Law and Order Minister, instructed him to arrange the blast, in which 23 persons were wounded, and that Vlok said that the instruction came from President Pieter Botha. In September 1996, a senior official indicted on six counts of murder and 83 other charges and facing multiple life sentences, confessed to the many exactions committed under his direction. Eugene de Kock, former head of Vlakplaas, South Africa's secret counter-insurgency police unit, stated before the Pretoria Supreme Court that Vlakplaas actions had been sanctioned by former President and Nobel Prize co-winner Frederick W. de Klerk, his predecessor, P. W. Botha, and more than 20 other high-ranking police and political officials. By denouncing the collusion of high officials, from whom he was taking orders, he was hoping that the court would be more lenient.

F. W. de Klerk had formally apologized to the Commission in August 1996 for the pain and suffering caused by his National Party's *apartheid* policies, which lasted from 1948 to 1994. However, he did not detail these abuses and refused to take the blame for them. One day later, Deputy President Thabo Mbeki admitted to the Commission that the ANC tortured and executed renegade cadres in its anti-*apartheid* war. He submitted a detailed document on these exactions. He said that the ANC was sorry for the human rights abuses that it committed during an otherwise 'just war' of liberation. The Commission issued its first summonses compelling former guerrillas of the ANC to testify about attacks during the liberation war in April 1997.

The Commission is not a substitute for criminal justice, although those granted amnesty will avoid prosecution. Seventeen former military generals were on trial for murder. However, Magnus Malan, former South African Defence Minister, and 15 other defendants were acquitted in October 1996 of murder and conspiracy charges in connection with the 1987 massacre of 13 blacks in Durban, due to insufficient evidence.[19]

Although it is too early to assess the Commission's work and impact, it is already the target of controversies and accusations. Blacks are calling it a whitewash, whites call it a witch hunt. Whites would rather leave the past behind and forget their own active or passive role in supporting *apartheid* and its exactions. Some of the victims, survivors and families do not want to be reconciled with their torturers and killers – they feel that perpetrators should not be amnestied but prosecuted and punished. According to the Trauma Center for Victims of Violence and Torture, 50–60% of the victims they talked to said they suffered psychological difficulties after testifying before the Commission, or expressed regret at having testified. Some observers felt that testifying made some victims more embittered. The perpetrators are amnestied while the victims receive no concrete help, such as pensions, or job training or other assistance.[20] Individual material reparations are needed. On a more positive note, the Commission is playing a necessary role in documenting the crimes committed during the *apartheid* era for all South African citizens and, more particularly, for the whites.

Regarding charges that granting amnesty is unfair, Dr Boraine, Vice Chairperson of the TRC, recalls that the peaceful transition was essentially determined by a political compromise. He argues that it is morally defensible to argue that amnesty was the price to pay for peace and stability. As another argument, without the carrot of amnesty, the truth could have remained hidden, corrupting the country's future.[21] Finally, it was hoped that the non-judicial Commission would help to heal the wounds of the past, and would be a substitute, in a number of cases, for costly and politically divisive criminal trials.

CONCLUSION

Truth and reconciliation commissions can play a useful role in those unstable and sensitive situations where a country is moving from dictatorship and repression to a more open, accountable democratic regime. While building for the future, accounts must be made for the past and those commissions may give some moral relief to victims, survivors and families in establishing objectively what happened and why, where mass or individual exactions were committed: they may assist in ending or easing mourning. Lies will be cleared, distorted history restored, myths replaced by unpleasant and unwanted facts: the country's collective memory will have to accept the dark and bloody parts of its own history. Perpetrators' denials or cover-ups are challenged, crimes are publicly exposed and their authors may be prosecuted.

The establishment of commissions should satisfy a number of requirements, as recommended in the Joinet report. They should be independent from political forces and have access to reliable expertise and information. Their mandate should include the review of exactions committed by the main actors (government, army, police and rebel groups) focusing on violations that appear to constitute a consistent pattern of gross violations, or serious acts of violence 'whose impact on society urgently demands that the public should know the truth', in the words of the Mexico Agreement.[22] As noted by Hayner,[23] there is no one best model on which to pattern a truth commission, nor a set of universal rules or recommendations to guarantee its success. Characteristics may vary according to current political circumstances, economic and social factors, history, culture, religion etc. In practice, the establishment of a commission is generally the outcome of political negotiations between the main parties involved, aiming at civil peace and reconciliation. Based on the balance of power and expected benefits for both parties and for the population at large, a political compromise will be required in order to defuse potential threats from extremists on both sides. As stated by Boraine, 'the central tension is between the politics of compromise and the radical notion of justice'.[24] Bronkhorst agrees that there is no model for the reconciliation process which would apply to all, or most countries. However, he sets the following minimum requirements: the establishment of the truth; reconciliation must contribute to a strengthening of the rule of law, in a manner compatible with international law and with social justice; reconciliation must be a democratic, verifiable process; and victims must be granted the right to compensation and reparation, at least morally, and where possible, materially.[25]

Should the commission be composed of national or international members, or a mix of national and international members? This question has received different answers in different countries. It would seem preferable, in principle, that it should be composed of national members, on a fair political representation basis, in order to avoid any charge of foreign interference in the domestic affairs of the country. However, as in El Salvador, an international commission is less sensitive to the pressures of national politics, and may be more objective and detached from historical and local considerations than a national commission. As another compromise, a mixed national–international commission would respond to most criticisms.

The commission should have a time-limited mandate. In spite of the substantive results obtained by the El Salvador Commission, a six-month term appears too short for any careful and extensive work programme. A one- to two-year term would appear more appropriate. While the South African model may not be transferrable to any country or situation, it contains a number of very positive elements: parliamentary debates and approval of the commission's mandate by parliament, public hearings, naming the alleged perpetrators with due process provisions. Among the major problems identified in the above cases, two call for special mention.

1. First, should perpetrators be identified by name during the commission's work, and in its report? It is difficult to escape from the conclusion that truth requires total disclosure, and that naming only crimes and victims would show a very incomplete and unsatisfactory picture of past events. Perpetrators should be named, with a priority for those mainly responsible for the policies which caused a pattern of grave violations of humanitarian and human rights law, and those mainly responsible, by commission or omission, for the worst crimes, subject to due process provisions.
2. The second problem concerns the implementation of the commission's recommendations on general issues (reform of institutions) and on individual cases. On the latter point, this is directly related to decisions on amnesty. A broad amnesty may nullify the commission's work of identification of perpetrators.

Here again, the South African solution of case-by-case amnesty under prescribed conditions may provide a reasonable answer to this problem. Victims need respect and moral reparation.[26] Public rituals of atonement may help individuals to heal: public recognition by top officials of the state's responsibility for repression and public apologies, monuments to the victims, scholarships in the name of victims. Victims also need material reparation. The reactions of victims who testified before the South African Commission show that the expected relief that they should have experienced was followed by tensions, regrets and a sense of frustration and neglect. Emotional support, moral, symbolic reparation are not enough: concrete support, in the form of pensions, job training, indemnification, assistance to housing conditions, among others, should be seriously considered.

Will a Truth Commission bring reconciliation; will it facilitate healing? There is no hard evidence that such a result will automatically follow a commission's work, but it is a fair assumption that an ailing country needs to know the truth about its past as one of the conditions for its recovery. A Truth Commission is a good instrument to search and find the truth, but it is only one of the elements leading to a successful democratic construction or rehabilitation. Other key elements include the legal recognition of a plurality of political parties, free elections, institutional reform, the reform of the judiciary, the army and the police, the rule of law, respect for human rights and fundamental freedoms, equitable economic and social development. Hearings and amnesty will not suffice: fair justice will also have to be applied. Finally, time is needed: new generations may find it easier to look forward to the future rather than to keep on crying for the past.

In summary, one should not place excessive expectations on a truth commission: the commission cannot change people nor institutions by itself. It can recommend change, hoping that those parties which created it and committed themselves to accept its recommendations will implement them fairly and in time. The reform process should be promoted by internal and international monitoring and pressures. However, no truth and reconciliation commission could be usefully created in countries and situations where hates and massacres are still prevalent: fact-finding commissions are needed in ex-Yugoslavia, Rwanda, Burundi and the Congo (ex-Zaire), but no reconciliation is likely, in the near future, between Serbs, Croats and Bosnian Moslems, nor betweeen Tutsis and Hutus.

Finally, truth commissions should not be a substitute for criminal prosecution: there cannot be civil peace without justice.

6 Impunity, National Justice and Foreign Courts

Truth and reconciliation commissions cannot act as substitutes for the courts, which alone have jurisdiction to establish individual criminal responsibility, assess guilt and, as appropriate, pass a sentence. Cherif Bassiouni, the former UN chief investigator in ex-Yugoslavia, said 'There cannot be peace without justice. When people feel aggrieved, they cannot reconcile'.[1] The Joinet report recalled the primacy, in principle, of national justice, subject to some conditions:

> It shall remain the rule that national courts normally have jurisdiction, particularly when the offence as defined in domestic law does not fall within the terms of the international court. International criminal courts shall have concurrent jurisdiction where national courts cannot yet offer satisfactory guarantees of independence and impartiality, or are physically unable to function.[2]

States have an obligation under international law to investigate violations of international humanitarian law or human rights law, to take appropriate measures in respect of the perpetrators, to ensure that they are prosecuted, tried and sentenced, and to provide the victims with effective remedies. Impunity is therefore a failure of states to meet these obligations.

In spite of these principles, a number of states, under the pressure of their military and police forces, have often had recourse to amnesty, as seen in the previous chapter, which ensures the impunity of most or all perpetrators. For instance, on 14 June 1995, the Peruvian Congress proclaimed a general amnesty to all the members of the military and police who had been the object of a complaint, of an inquiry, of an indictment, of a trial, of a condemnation. This one-sided amnesty, which does not apply to the rebels and is not even linked with the creation of a Truth Commission, has been condemned by the opposition and human rights observers.[3] Such impunity cannot lead to reconciliation and civil peace: it only threatens the people's belief in a democratic society, creates disrespect for laws, promotes collective rebellion against the leaders and individual revenge.

Impunity does not always require the voting of a law: implicit amnesty may be given to perpetrators when governments and dependent courts wilfully delay investigations, prosecutions and judgments. The primary jurisdiction of national courts requires first that these are 'physically able to function', that they have the necessary physical, financial and manpower resources to render justice. Secondly, their functioning should respond to the standards established by the International Covenant on Civil and Political Rights: no arbitrary arrest or detention, any person arrested or detained on a criminal charge to be brought promptly before a judge, everyone entitled to a 'fair and public hearing by a competent, independent and impartial tribunal established by law', the right to be presumed innocent, the right to be informed promptly of the charge against the accused, and to have adequate time and facilities for the preparation of his (her) defence and to communicate with counsel of his own choosing, to be tried without undue delay, to be tried in his presence and to defend himself in person or through legal assistance of his own choosing, to examine witnesses, not to be compelled to testify against himself or to confess guilt, and the right that his conviction and sentence may be reviewed by a higher tribunal. Anyone charged with a criminal offence should benefit from the principle of non-retroactivity of national and international laws, except that a person may be tried and punished 'for any act or omission which, at the time when it was committed, was criminal according to the general principles of law recognized by the community of nations'.[4]

These requirements are not always satisfied. The independence of the judiciary at all levels may not be guaranteed by legislation, or the guarantees provided by legislation are not respected; criminal codes do not provide the required safeguards of due process, or these are not respected; there may be a lack of trained and experienced judges, prosecutors and lawyers, a lack of resources for the conduct of investigations, the hearing of witnesses and victims and the setting-up and maintaining of records; amnesty or prescription may hamper prosecution; alleged criminals may be unduly protected by the right of asylum or by the refusal of granting extradition on the grounds of 'political offences'; and military personnel may be unduly protected by dependent military courts. In some countries, new governments engage in 'victor's justice' as a judicial revenge against the former political, military and administrative leaders.

Even countries with a long democratic tradition have delayed rendering justice in cases of war crimes and crimes against humanity committed by their own nationals, or have conveniently 'forgotten' these crimes. Alleged war crimes committed by the French Army in Vietnam and in Algeria have not been investigated or sanctions applied: amnesty was granted in both cases. War crimes committed by the US military in Vietnam were sparingly sanctioned. Alleged war crimes committed by British soldiers during the Falklands War have not been publicly investigated. The abuses allegedly committed by Canadian peacekeepers in Somalia were attributed by a national Commission as only reflecting 'systemic, organizational and leadership failures'. The Canadian Defence Minister criticized the report as 'insulting', in a reaction typical of defence and military officials in most countries. Two Belgian paratroopers accused of torturing a Somali boy during the same UN peacekeeping mission were acquitted on 30 June 1997 by a military court.[5] In France, many years passed before a French national was prosecuted for crimes against humanity committed during World War II. Slow national criminal justice towards a country's own nationals was in contrast with the expeditious international 'victors' justice' of Nuremberg and Tokyo rendered over vanquished enemies.

THE LONG-DELAYED FRENCH TRIALS

Resolution 170 (II), approved by the UN General Assembly on 31 October 1947, recommended that member states 'continue with unabated energy to carry out their responsibilities as regards the surrender and trial of war criminals': this resolution was aimed mainly at German and Japanese war criminals. Following the first Nuremberg trial, legal prosecution against German defendants was waged by the military tribunals of the occupation authorities in their respective zones. Several liberated countries were prompt in trying and sentencing their own nationals accused of collaboration with the Germans, but slow or ineffective in bringing proceedings against their own nationals accused of crimes against humanity. The first trial waged in France on charges of crimes against humanity was the trial of Klaus Barbie, a former Gestapo head for Lyon and its region. Barbie was convicted and sentenced to life in prison in July 1987.

Charges of crimes against humanity committed against the Jews during World War II were only brought against four ageing Frenchmen in the 1980s. Even then, the highest political and judicial authorities deliberately delayed their trials, partly in the belief that these crimes should be forgotten in the interest of a final reconciliation between Vichy and De Gaulle supporters, partly on account of a connivance among senior members of the establishment. The first Frenchman to be tried and sentenced on the grounds of crimes against humanity was Paul Touvier, at the age of 81, almost 50 years after he ordered the execution of seven Jews when serving in a pro-Nazi militia. He had been twice condemned to death *in absentia* and had been pardoned by President Pompidou in 1971 at the behest of senior Catholic Church officials. He had hidden for 45 years with the help of church sympathizers. Three more senior Vichy officials were to be tried, but two died before their trials could be held. In January 1997, the third one, Maurice Papon, aged 86, was finally ordered to stand trial for the deportation and deaths of 1690 French Jews between 1942 and 1944. On 2 April 1998 Papon was sentenced to 10 years' criminal imprisonment for complicity with crimes against humanity.

The legislative process that finally allowed for such trials was as slow and reticent as the judiciary one. It was only in 1992 that war crimes, crimes against humanity and the crime of genocide were included in the French penal code. A judgment rendered by the Cour de Cassation in 1985 had first given a restrictive definition of crimes against humanity: the two necessary elements of this crime were the systematic commission of inhuman acts or persecutions and their implementation at the service of an hegemonic policy of a totalitarian state. In consequence, a crime against humanity can only be prosecuted in France for acts committed by the Axis Powers and their accomplices[6]. The bringing to French justice of Barbie and Papon was made possible and unavoidable mainly through the persistent efforts of Serge Klarsfeld, a French activist lawyer and historian, following the publications of an American historian, Robert O. Paxton, on Vichy's France, and the evolution of French collective memory on the war period which finally demanded to know the truth as a basic condition for reconciliation.

These delays or opposition in applying national justice to nationals of the same country charged with crimes against humanity are typical of a resistance on the part of political, military and judiciary authorities found in old democracies as well as in countries in transition to democracy. Can national justice be rendered fairly against the leaders of an overthrown Communist regime in a country still run by another autocratic government?

THE ETHIOPIAN TRIALS

The principal leaders and officials of the former Communist dictatorship of Lieutenant Colonel Mengistu Haile Mariam have been indicted, individually and collectively, on charges of genocide, crimes against humanity, summary or arbitrary executions, detentions, disappearances and forcible resettlement, before a national court of three judges in Addis Ababa. Mengistu fled to Zimbabwe into a comfortable exile in May 1991: he will be judged *in absentia.* His regime, the Dergue, ruled Ethiopia from 1974 until 1991, when it was overthrown by the Ethiopian Peoples' Revolutionary Democratic Front. The new leader is President Meles Zenawi. Emperor Haile Selassie and 59 of his ministers and officers were killed by the Marxist regime. Hundreds of thousands of young people were expelled from Addis Ababa and sent to rural zones for a Marxist re-education. During the Red Terror from 1976 to 1978, tens of thousands of Ethiopians were killed, mostly young victims. During that era, state-run radio regularly broadcast long lists of people that the government had executed as 'counter-revolutionaries', 'feudalists' or 'reactionaries', in typical Communist terminology. In 1984–5, one million Ethiopians starved in the northern province of Tigre during a famine intensified by the government in order to depopulate rebel areas. The number of deaths is estimated at between 40 000 and 100 000.[7]

The new government established the Special Prosecutor's Office (SPO) in August 1992 with a mandate to create a historical record of the alleged abuses of human rights committed by the former military regime, and to bring to justice those who may be criminally liable for gross human rights violations and/or corruption. The trials commenced in March 1994 before the three judges of the First Division of the Central Supreme Court of the Transitional Government of Ethiopia, and the first hearings were in December 1994. They were open to the press, the public, international and national monitoring bodies. The Trial Observation and Information Project (TOIP) followed and reported on the proceedings as from October 1995.[8]

The SPO has charged 73 Dergue members, including Mengistu, with the following charges.

1. *Genocide; crimes against humanity* in violation of Article 281 of the Ethiopian Penal Code of 1957 which states:

> Whosoever, with intent to destroy, in whole or in part, a national, ethnic, social, religious or political group, organizes, orders or engages in, be it in time of war or in time of peace;
> (a) killings, bodily harm or serious injury to the physical or mental health of members of the group, in any way whatsoever; or
> (b) measures to prevent the propagation or continued survival of its members or their progeny; or
> (c) the compulsory movement or dispersion of peoples or children, or their placing under living conditions calculated to result in their death or disappearance, is punishable with rigorous imprisonment from five years to life, or, in cases of exceptional gravity, with death.

The Ethiopian Penal Code had added 'political' groups to the incomplete list of the 1948 Genocide Convention.

In its charges, the SPO listed victims of the alleged genocide:

- identified killings, 1823;
- identified bodily harm, 99; and
- identified enforced disappearances, 194.

It was also stated that the victims were people from the diversified political, ideological, and social sectors of the Ethiopian communities.

2. *Alternative charge: homicide in the first degree*. Approximately half of the charges were allegations of genocide, most of the other charges, were homicides, and a few concerned misappropriation of property.[9] In March 1994, the counsels for all the defendants submitted to the Court comprehensive written objections to the SPO charges, asking the Court to drop the charges against the defendants on various grounds. On 8 October 1995, the Court ruled as follows on the issues raised:

(a) The alleged 'immunity of the Head of State': there is no immunity for the crime of genocide.
(b) 'A demand for an International Tribunal, as the Domestic Court does not have jurisdiction or mandate to try crimes of geno-

cide': under the principle of territorial jurisdiction, Ethiopian
Courts may judge offences committed on Ethiopian territory.
Furthermore, the crime of genocide has been included in the
Ethiopian Penal Code.

(c) 'Where there is no law there cannot be guilt': all offences are
specified in the Ethiopian Penal Code.

(d) 'The defendants complied with a legal duty': genocide, crimes
against humanity, homicide are acts prohibited under both international and national law.

(e) 'As the trials and the resulting punishment do not serve any
purpose, earlier crimes ought to be forgiven in the interest of
national reconciliation': the argument was rejected as an extra-
legal issue.

The Court rejected all objections and asked the SPO to amend the
charges in accordance with the Penal Code's requirements. On
28 November 1995, all the defendants pleaded 'not guilty'.

The prosecution has collected a considerable amount of evidence,
including documents recording execution orders, films of torture
sessions, forensic evidence from mass graves and the testimony of
more than 2500 witnesses. All the defendants have counsels.

The case for the prosecution against 46 defendants, present in
person, started on 4 April 1996. Earlier, the prosecutor had said
that more than 1000 detainees were awaiting charges. The Court
decided that, in order to preserve the neutrality and independence
of the Court and do justice to the defendants, no reporting of the
witnesses' testimonies would be allowed.[10] In spite of this ill-advised
order, the TOIP regularly issues summaries of the testimonies in
its 'Trial Updates'. By March 1997, 182 witnesses for the prosecution had given testimony, followed by an occasional cross-examina-
tion by defendants' counsels, and by a few questions from the Court.
Witnesses testified about arbitrary detention – the first witness, heard
on 9 April 1996, remained in jail for more than six years after
being acquitted by a military tribunal; the second witness, heard
on 23 April 1996, spent nine years in jail without a court hearing –
summary executions, confiscation of property, the use of a 'military
tribunal' as a legal guise in the name of which mass murders were
committed, and torture of detainees. Details were given on the 'major
political decision' taken on 22 November 1974 by Dergue members, under the chairmanship of Mengistu, to execute 59 imprisoned officials of the Emperor's regime. The extra-judiciary decision
was taken by the group by simple majority vote. Oral evidence was

also given on Haile Selassie's murder, carried out on 26 August 1975: he had been designated as an oppressor, a reactionary and the head of a feudal system.[11]

As the trials are still going on (in 1997) and may go on for months or years more, a thorough assessment is premature. At the present stage, the positive element is that the trials appear to be carried out in a fair way, with adequate legal representation of the defendants, respect for due process under international supervision and monitoring. The slow pace of the trials is justified by the large number of defendants and witnesses, by the abundant documentation and by the relatively limited or uneven legal and judiciary experience of the court, prosecutors and lawyers. The trials have been hailed, perhaps with some excess, as a 'turning point in the history of the country and the continent'. For the TOIP, 'the act of bringing public officials before a court of law for crimes committed against their own citizens is without precedent in Ethiopia and, indeed, in Africa'. While Amin Dada and other African despots have not been judged for their exactions, former 'Emperor' and President for life Jean Bedel Bokassa was judged and condemned to death by a Central African court in March 1986 for assassinations and embezzlement. He served seven years in prison before he was finally pardoned by his successor, General André Kolingba.[12]

On the negative side, one wonders whether fair justice may be rendered in a country where neither democracy nor the rule of law are firmly embedded. According to Amnesty International, several thousands of suspected opponents were detained during 1994, many of whom, including several journalists and party activists, were tried and imprisoned for political offences. There were widespread accusations of torture and reports of 'diappearances' and extrajudicial executions of political opponents.[13]

On balance, the initiation and conduct of the Ethiopian trials represent a significant judiciary advance in that country. Victims and survivors are allowed to present evidence of their suffering, evidence of coercive action by the previous government is given, such as forceful resettlement and the withholding of relief food for populations exposed to famine, evidence of killings. Alleged perpetrators are assured of legal advice and representation. The ultimate purpose is to show that the grave violations of humanitarian and human rights law committed by senior government officials will not be protected by impunity. This message should be understood in Ethiopia itself, and in other countries as well.

FOREIGN COURTS

According to Principle 23 of the Joinet report, 'The subsidiary jurisdiction of foreign courts shall be exercised by virtue either of a provision on universal jurisdiction set forth in a treaty in force or of a provision of internal law establishing a rule of extraterritorial jurisdiction for serious crimes under international law'. Principle 25 recommends that 'States may for efficiency's sake take measures in their internal legislation to establish extraterritorial jurisdiction over serious crimes under international law committed outside their territory which by their nature are within the purview not only of internal criminal law but also of an international punitive system to which the concept of frontiers is alien'.

Recent examples of effective jurisdiction by a foreign court over grave humanitarian or human rights violations by nationals of another country are rare but significant. In February 1994, a US Federal Judge declared that General Prosper Avril, who led the country between 1988 and 1990, was responsible for acts of torture committed in Port-au-Prince over six Haitian democracy activists. In April 1995, another Federal Judge found Guatemalan General Hector Gramajo Morales liable for acts of torture and genocide committed under his command. However, these were civil suits, not criminal cases, unable to result in sentences other than pecuniary ones.

In March 1996, a Spanish High Court judge started a criminal investigation into the torture, disappearance and murder of 600 Spanish citizens in Argentina. The investigators in Spain have charged 110 former and active Argentine military and police officers, including army commanders, intelligence chiefs and even doctors, who are said to have supervised torture sessions during the dictatorship (1976–83). Argentine contended that Spain has no jurisdiction over events in Argentina and that the leaders of its security forces were tried in 1985 and 1986, imprisoned and finally pardoned in 1989 by President Carlos Saul Menem. The Spanish judge ruled that he had jurisdiction, as crimes against humanity enjoy universal jurisdiction and have no statute of limitations. On 10 October 1997, the former Navy Captain Adolfo Scilingo was indicted in Madrid of genocide and imprisoned in preventive custody. A Canadian court recognized in July 1996 the participation of a Rwanda official, Léon Mugesera, in the preparation of the genocide, through a public appeal to kill Tutsis. The court considered that the appeal was a violation of the 1948 Genocide Convention, as 'a direct and public incitation to commit the crime of genocide'.

On 23 May 1997, Novislav Djajic, a Bosnian Serb, was found guilty and sentenced by a German court to five years in jail for taking part in a massacre of 14 Muslims in Bosnia in April 1992. German federal prosecutors took on the case because of an overload at the Hague War Crimes Tribunal. However, the first reason was that the authorities in the ex-Yugoslavia states cannot be relied upon to try members of their own forces. Most of the trials have involved members of opposing forces, where the defendants' right to due process had been violated and the victim's right to fair justice had not been respected (see also Chapter 11). In contrast with these courageous decisions, French courts declined to accept jurisdiction in a number of cases. A judgment of the Paris Appeal Court of 24 November 1994 refused to admit complaints from Bosnian nationals against Radovan Karadzic, on the grounds that there was no provision of international law directly applicable in French law which would allow French courts to hear such complaints. In a judgment of 20 March 1996, the 'Chambre d'accusation de la Cour d'appel de Nimes' considered that the charges against a Rwandan priest exiled in France, Wenceslas Munyeshyaka, were allegations of torture and other cruel, inhuman or degrading treatment or punishment which, according to the 1984 Convention, gave universal jurisdiction to national courts. However, these crimes constituted also crimes of genocide, crimes graver than torture to which the Court should give priority. As the Genocide Convention did not provide for universal jurisdiction, the Court conveniently declared that it was not competent to judge this case.[14]

These decisions amount to a denial of justice: they constitute a guarantee of impunity for perpetrators. In the French context, two reasons may explain, but not justify, these judgments. First the French judiciary system is unusually, and at times illegally, reticent in applying the provisions of international treaties and conventions, or the judgments of international courts of justice. The second reason is political: state prosecutors and judges are likely to be influenced by the government, which, in the case of Rwanda, did not want any public exposure on the French political and military support to the Hutus.

The case of Lithuania is another, more extreme and graver case of much-delayed national justice. During the Nazi occupation, approximately 220 000 Jews lived in Lithuania, 94% of whom were murdered during the years 1941–4. Most were killed locally, in many cases by local, willing executioners. The Soviet occupation prevented any acknowledgement of the crimes and prosecution of the main perpetrators. A law passed by the Lithuanian parliament on 2 May 1990, before the 1991 independence, enabled 'the rehabilitation of those repressed for resistance to the occupying regime' which dealt almost exclusively with Lithuanians convicted by the Soviets. Finally, in 1997, following US and Israeli pressures, the Lithuanian Prime Minister announced that he would propose legislation to permit the indictment of Aleksandras Lileikis and other Nazi collaborators who allegedly participated in acts of genocide.[15]

CONCLUSION

Even if national courts should, as a rule, have jurisdiction on serious humanitarian or human rights crimes under international law, this jurisdiction may be long-delayed, or even denied on legal and/or political grounds, their impartiality may be challenged and their judgments labelled as victors' justice. National justice is often influenced by political considerations leading to both extremes of too harsh or too lenient sentences, or even to impunity. The basic requirement of fair national justice is the establishment of an independent judiciary and the training of competent judicial personnel. In addition, the Joinet report has recommended a number of restrictive measures in order to combat impunity at the national level. These are related to prescription, amnesty, the right of asylum, extradition, the exclusion of *in absentia* procedure, the principle of due obedience and the effects of legislation on repentance, the principle of the jurisdiction of military courts and the irremovability of judges. The Joinet report has also proposed to set forth supplementary procedural rules to enable any victim to institute proceedings on his or her own behalf where the authorities fail to do so, or to become an associated party. This option should be extended to NGOs able to show proof of long-standing activities for the protection of the victims concerned.[16] These principles should be integrated by countries in their national legislations, including the provisions of the 1968 Convention on the Non-Applicability of Statutory Limitations to War Crimes and Crimes against Humanity.

The independence and impartiality of national courts and judges and the holding of national criminal trials are usefully and effectively monitored and assessed by independent human rights bodies such as the International Federation of Human Rights Leagues and the International Commission of Jurists, with the support of the media. If national justice does not respond to the requirements of a constitutional, democratic State or is physically unable to function, or if a country's current leaders oppose the holding of a fair trial, or if amnesty has been declared, other countries should assume their responsibility as a subsidiary jurisdiction. If both national justice and foreign courts are ineffective, the case should be referred to an international court as the only remaining judicial remedy.

The next questions are: What international court and under what conditions?

7 International Peoples' Tribunals

On 29 February 1992, an International War Crimes Tribunal found US President George H. W. Bush, Vice-President J. Danforth Quayle, Secretary of Defense Richard Cheney, General Norman Schwarzkopf, Commander of the Allied Forces in the Persian Gulf, and others named in an initial complaint, guilty of 19 crimes having been 'established beyond a reasonable doubt'. Among others, these included crime against peace through leading Iraq into provocations justifying US military action against Iraq; war crimes: violation of Article 51.4 of the 1977 Protocol I Additional to the Geneva Conventions of 1949, indiscriminate bombing and use of excessive force, use of prohibited weapons capable of mass destruction; violation of Article 56 of the same Protocol, intentional attack of installations in Iraq containing dangerous substances and forces; and crimes against humanity, by intentionally depriving the Iraqi people of essential medicines, potable water, food and other necessities. These findings did not include any 'sentence' to be applied to the individuals named in the 'Judgment', except that the Tribunal's members 'condemned in the strongest possible terms' those found guilty of the charges.

The Judgment urged the immediate revocation of all embargoes, sanctions and penalties against Iraq 'because they constitute a continuing crime against humanity', and urged that the 'power of the UN Security Council, which was blatantly manipulated by the USA to authorize illegal military action and sanctions, be vested in the General Assembly, that all permanent members be removed and that the right of veto be eliminated as undemocratic and contrary to the basic principles of the UN Charter'.[1] This Tribunal was a self-appointed body created by individuals to review and assess the specific issue of alleged 'US War Crimes Against Iraq' and make general recommendations. As it was not created by governments, it had no coercive powers and could not issue enforceable sanctions.

The 22 members of the Tribunal included distinguished personalities: Sheik Mohamed Rashid, former Deputy Prime Minister of Pakistan, Britain's Lord Tony Gifford, Member of Parliament, who

voted in the House of Lords against his country's participation in
the Gulf War, judges and other jurists, and human rights activists
from Panama, Turkey and the USA. The Tribunal met in New York
in February 1992 to hear evidence gathered in ten months of hearings from some 3000 witnesses worldwide. The nineteen charges
were drawn up by a Commission of Inquiry headed by former US
Attorney-General Ramsey Clark. They were based on violations of
the Nuremberg law, of the UN Charter, and of the Hague and
Geneva Conventions signed by the USA. The Tribunal was not
impartial, nor was it meant to be impartial. Its Judgment ignored
the fact that Iraq's annexation of Kuwait was an act of aggression
under Article 39 of the UN Charter, and that the UN Security
Council had acted within its rights in authorizing enforcement action against Iraq under Article 42. The Tribunal had also ignored
Iraq's own war crimes. In February 1991, the Parliamentary Assembly of the Council of Europe adopted a resolution proposing
the creation of a War Crimes Tribunal to judge the many crimes
committed by Iraqi authorities. In April 1993, the USA transmitted their report on Iraqi war crimes to the UN. In January 1997,
UK Prime Minister John Major and (then) opposition leader Tony
Blair expressed their support for an NGO's campaign to arraign
Saddam Hussein and other leading Iraqis on charges of war crimes,
crimes against humanity and genocide against Kurds and marsh
Arabs in Southern Iraq in 1987–8.[2]

Why initiate this extensive research focusing on alleged US crimes
only, and set up a powerless Tribunal? Its initiators felt that it was
the only way to bring out the 'whole truth', a balanced perspective
and impartiality, against the overriding media presentation of a victory
for a 'new world order', the successful use of the collective security measures contained in the UN Charter against an aggressor,
the only villain, Saddam Hussein. Their aim was to publicize the
other, hidden side to the Gulf War, to denounce US 'provocations
and exactions', to mobilize world public opinion and possibly to
'prevent new aggressions by the USA'. This quixotic venture had
been inspired by the Russell Tribunals of the late 1960s.

THE RUSSELL TRIBUNALS

The first Russell 'International War Crimes Tribunal' was set up
on an *ad hoc* basis to fill the institutional void left after the demise

of the Nuremberg and Tokyo Tribunals. The Tribunal accused the US government of aggression, bombardment of civilians, the use of experimental weapons, the torture and mutilation of prisoners and genocide involving forced labour, mass burial, concentration camps and saturation bombing. It showed the systematic destruction of hospitals, schools, sanatoria, dams, dykes, churches and pagodas. The investigators – surgeons, biochemists, radiologists, doctors, agronomists, lawyers, sociologists and historians – were of many nationalities. The Tribunal's inspirer, Bertrand Russell, the famed philosopher and mathematician, was its Honorary President, and Jean-Paul Sartre, the French philosopher and writer, its Executive President. Vladimir Dedijer, Doctor of Jurisprudence and historian, was the Chairman and President of Sessions, attended by 21 other members, including parliamentarians, jurists, writers, pacifists and liberation fighters. It was held in Stockholm 2–10 May 1967 and in Roskilde (Denmark) from 20 November to 1 December 1967.

The Tribunal found that the US government had committed acts of aggression against Vietnam under the terms of international law; that there had been deliberate, systematic and large-scale bombardment of civilian targets; that the US government was guilty of repeated violations of the sovereignty, neutrality and territoriality of Cambodia, and that it was guilty of attacks against the civilian population of a number of Cambodian towns and villages; that the US government committed aggression against the people of Laos; that the US armed forces used or experimented with weapons prohibited by the laws of war; that prisoners of war captured by the US armed forces had been subjected to treatment prohibited by the laws of war; that the US armed forces had subjected the civilian population to inhuman treatment prohibited by international law; that the US government was guilty of genocide against the people of Vietnam; and that the governments of Australia, Japan, New Zealand, Philippines, South Korea and Thailand had been accomplices of the USA in the aggression against Vietnam, in violation of international law.[3] In his messages to the Tribunal, Russell abusively compared US behaviour in Vietnam to Nazism and to Hitler's behaviour in Eastern Europe, with the same aim of crushing the revolution. He wrote that the Tribunal was 'defying the powerful rulers who bully and butcher with abandon . . . The Tribunal must begin a new morality in the West'.

The Tribunal was ignored or rebuffed by US and UK leaders. General de Gaulle opposed the Tribunal's meeting in France on the grounds that the USA remained a traditional friend of France in spite of differences of opinion between the two countries. He criticized the Tribunal's proceedings as 'exceeding the limits of international law and custom' by intending to give a juridical form to its investigations and the 'semblance of a verdict to [its] conclusions'. He recalled that justice of any sort, in principle as in execution, emanates from the State. He added that some of Russell's friends would not add to their moral value 'by assuming robes borrowed for the occasion'. For other critics, the Tribunal was a 'kangaroo court' in which the evidence offered led to a predetermined judgment, with no right of defence, a self-appointed body lacking legal standing, impartiality and objectivity. Its supporters replied that it was a Tribunal, not a Court, and that it functioned as a commission of inquiry, or like a US Grand Jury. On the basis of an overwhelming mass of *prima facie* data, derived largely from the Western media, the Tribunal brought in an indictment and investigated exhaustively all aspects of this indictment. For Sartre, the Tribunal's legitimacy derived 'equally from its total powerlessness and from its universality'. The Tribunal, an international jury of conscience, was to encourage the mobilization of the peoples of the world, including the American people, through its investigations, findings and judgment. Its mandate and orientation were openly political: its inspiration was anti-imperialist, anti-capitalist and pro-oppressed peoples of the Third World.

Between 1974 and 1976, the Russell Tribunal II held three sessions in Brussels on the deterioration of democratic rights in Latin America. The Russell Tribunal III was convened in 1978 to inquire into the more narrow issue of civil rights violations in West Germany. The Russell Tribunal IV focused on the indigenous peoples of America, and the Delgado Tribunal judged crimes committed by the PIDE in Portugal during the regimes of Salazar and Caetano. Following those *ad hoc* Tribunals, the Permanent Peoples' Tribunal was created in 1979 in Bologna, Italy by the Lelio Basso International Foundation for the Rights and Liberation of the Peoples.[4]

THE PERMANENT PEOPLES' TRIBUNAL

The Tribunal bases its activity in part on human rights instruments such as the Universal Declaration of Human Rights and regional

Human Rights Conventions, the 1948 Genocide Convention and other UN Declarations and Conventions, UN General Assembly Resolutions, the Hague and the Geneva law, and the Statute of the Nuremberg Tribunal. More fundamentally, it refers to the 'Universal Declaration of the Rights of the Peoples' which was proclaimed by a non-governmental assembly of international law experts and activists at Algiers on 4 July 1976. The symbolic date was chosen to underscore the shift of the US role from the status of an oppressed colony to that of 'chief imperial actor'. The Declaration was meant to complement the UN Universal Declaration on Human Rights by affirming that the effective respect for (individual) human rights necessarily implies respect for the rights of people. It attacks the domination of imperialism and neo-colonialism through military regimes and multinational enterprises, and promotes liberation struggles, which may, in the last resort, use force. It affirms peoples' right to the respect of their national and cultural identity, to political self-determination, their exclusive right over their natural wealth and resources, their right to the protection of their environment, and the rights of minorities. While these 'rights' are mostly of a collective nature, individual human rights are referred to in Article 4 but only in reference to peoples' identity or integrity: 'None shall be subjected, because of his national or cultural identity, to massacre, torture, persecution, deportation, expulsion or living conditions such as may compromise the identity or integrity of the people to which he belongs.'

The Tribunal declared itself competent for all international crimes, especially crimes against peace and humanity, for all infringements of the fundamental rights of peoples and minorities and for all serious and systematic violations of the rights and freedoms of individuals. However, the Tribunal will not pronounce itself on particular violations of individual rights unless these are connected with a violation of the rights of peoples. The Tribunal organizes its sessions 'at the request of groups which are publicly neutral in political matters or political groups united in a common programme sufficiently broad to be able to guarantee the greatest possible representation': in reality, these requests are generally complaints from human rights or other groups against their government, 'the accused entity', groups which can hardly be considered neutral nor broadly representative.

The Tribunal is composed of 35 to 75 members, who should enjoy the highest moral consideration and fulfill the conditions required for holding high judiciary functions, or be eminent scholars, jurists, or eminent political, religious or moral personalities. Members have included several Nobel Prize winners. For each session, a minimum of 11 members is convened. The seat of the Tribunal is in Rome, but sessions may be held in other locations. The list of the Tribunal's sessions held between 1979 and 1995 is shown in Table 7.1.

Table 7.1
List of Sessions of the Permanent Peoples' Tribunal
1979–95

1979	Brussels	Western Sahara
1980	Geneva	Argentine
1980	Milan	Erythrea
1980	Antwerp	The Philippines and the Bangsa Moro people
1981	Mexico	El Salvador
1981	Stockholm	Afghanistan I
1981	Lisbon	East Timor
1982	Rotterdam	Zaire
1982	Paris	Afghanistan II
1983	Madrid	Guatemala
1984	Paris	Armenia
1984	Brussels	Nicaragua (US intervention)
1988	Berlin	The policies of the International Monetary Fund and World Bank
1989	Barcelona	Puerto Rico
1990	Paris	Brazilian Amazonia
1991	Bogota	Impunity of crimes against humanity in Latin America
1992	Padua-Venice	The Conquest of America and international law
1992	Strasbourg	Tibet
1994	Madrid	The policies of the International Monetary Fund and World Bank
1994	London	The damage caused by wild industrialization to human rights and the environment ('Bhopal')
1994	Berlin	The right of asylum in Europe
1995	Bern	Crimes against humanity in ex-Yugoslavia I
1995	Naples	Violations of the rights of children and minors
1995	Barcelona	Crimes against humanity in ex-Yugoslavia II

Source: Lelio Basso International Foundation for the Rights and Liberation of Peoples (Translated from the French by the author)

Starting with the first Russell Tribunal, and including the 1992 International War Crimes Tribunal mentioned earlier (organized independently from, and not sponsored by, the Permanent Peoples' Tribunal), these sessions of the Peoples' Tribunals show the US government and policies as favourite targets. The USA is either shown as directly responsible for crimes against peace, crimes against humanity and war crimes (Vietnam, Iraq), or the USA is guilty of crimes committed by other governments because of its determining intervention in supporting those governments in Latin American countries as instigator and accomplice (Guatemala, Nicaragua and others), or in occupying militarily a territory as a colonial possession and denying its people's rights to self-determination (Puerto Rico). In balance, the USSR was only taken to task twice for its intervention in Afghanistan, and China for its annexation of Tibet. In spite of its pro-Third-World attitude, the Tribunal has defended peoples' rights of Western Sahara versus Morocco, Erythrea versus Ethiopia, East Timor versus Indonesia, and of native people in the Philippines and in Brazil. The Tribunal has declared (former) President Mobutu guilty of systematic and massive violations of elementary human rights on the people of Zaire. In 1995, in its sessions on ex-Yugoslavia, the Tribunal found ample evidence of preplanned and systematic perpetration of the crime of genocide against the Muslim population of Bosnia-Herzegovina, evidence implicating all the fighting forces of all sides in the commission of massive violations of the rights of ethnic and religious communities, evidence of the wanton and brutal utilization of women as a weapon of war, including rape, mutilation, murder and traumatization of children, girls and women, directed principally against Muslim women. But why hold these sessions in 1995 when the International Criminal Tribunal for the Former Yugoslavia had been created in 1993?

Other sessions are concerned with the policies of the financial institutions and other general topics show the interest of the Tribunal's organizers in international economics and environmental issues, which are beyond the scope of the present review, as they do not relate to violations of international humanitarian and human rights law.

CONCLUSION

Peoples' Tribunals are not a legitimate substitute for *ad hoc* inter-governmental War Crimes Tribunals, nor for a permanent International Criminal Court. They do not have the legitimacy or the powers of a body created by governments or by an international treaty – they do not create international law, and their judgments are not binding on states or on individuals. Peoples' Tribunals are created by self-appointed individuals, whatever their moral, social or scientific renown. The use of the word 'Tribunal' has been criticized as a misnomer. Their 'sentences' generally condemn governments or other entities, and only rarely specific individuals. Their choice of targets is considered biased against the 'imperialist' and 'neo-colonialist' powers. None of the Peoples' Tribunals has reviewed Stalin's crimes against the Ukrainian people, nor Red China's long list of massacres of its own people, nor the Khmer Rouge genocide. By their reference to 'peoples' rights', they tend to focus on collective rather than on individual human rights. Their scope has extended well beyond crimes against peace, crimes against humanity and war crimes: their founders' battle against an unfair world economic order has led them to institute proceedings against the financial institutions and multinational enterprises. One session of the Permanent Peoples' Tribunal has shown its concern for the environment, a cause not always shared by developing countries. Another Tribunal, the 'International Peoples' Tribunal on Human Rights and the Environment', has been created by a coalition of NGOs and its first session was held in New York in June 1997. It affirmed that the environment and development are human rights issues.[5]

With the end of the Cold War, and following the creation by the UN of the Tribunals for ex-Yugoslavia and Rwanda and the proposed creation of a permanent International Criminal Court, the disappearance of the Peoples' Tribunal could have been expected. On the contrary, as shown in Table 7.1, ten sessions of the Permanent Peoples' Tribunal have been held since 1990, plus the 1992 meeting of the International War Crimes Tribunal (US War Crimes against Iraq) and the creation of an International Peoples Tribunal on Human Rights and the Environment in 1997. This renewed interest in Peoples' Tribunals seems to respond to a need, that of the expression of a populist counter-power versus the power of governments. This is linked to the extraordinary growth of the NGO movement in the last two decades, and to the NGOs' often successful attempt to exert influence at both national and international levels.

Peoples' Tribunals are not a substitute for national and international criminal courts but they may play an auxiliary role, including that of a provocative 'irritant' to established institutions and leaders. Peoples' Tribunals may take up cases of grave violations of humanitarian and human rights law if these are not prosecuted and judged by national or international courts, in order to mobilize international public opinion against the responsible governments, but not only against collective authorities. They should choose their targets more carefully by focusing on the most serious and extensive crimes against humanity and their individual perpetrators. They should not duplicate the work of established Tribunals, provided that these are independent and impartial. They should develop a wider scope of investigations with the support of specialized NGOs, in order to produce reliable data, which could be used later by the prosecutors of national and international courts. While they only have a limited power of influence, they should be included as one of several tools to combat impunity at the international level, subject to the above qualifications and recommendations.

8 The International Tribunal for Crimes in the Former Yugoslavia

On 25 May 1993, the UN Security Council unanimously confirmed its decision of 22 February 1993 to establish an International Tribunal for the Prosecution of Persons Responsible for Serious Violations of International Humanitarian Law Committed in the Territory of the former Yugoslavia since 1991.[1] This decision, taken 47 years after the Nuremberg Tribunal completed its mandate, was apparently a significant success in the long road leading to international criminal justice, although the immediate motivation of its authors was to appease an international public opinion shocked by the reports of atrocities in the former Yugoslavia. The Tribunal was a convenient substitute for a military intervention rejected by the main Powers.

For a European observer, the conflict in the former Yugoslavia and its revolting humanitarian exactions had revealed the incapacity and/or unwillingness of members of the European Union to prevent or stop the conflict and its abuses, and their division. Neither the pro-Serb French, nor the British, nor the pro-Croat Germans were willing to intervene militarily in the Yugoslav quagmire. In the UN Security Council, the USA had no intention to send the 'boys' into combat, and the pro-Serb Russians were against any identification of the Serbs as aggressors and perpetrators of exactions. The first alibi found to justify the lack of any serious and determined intervention to stop the Serb aggression was to authorize the UN to provide humanitarian assistance to the victims, which led to the public humiliation of UN peacekeepers in the hands of the Serb military. While feeble diplomatic efforts failed one after the other, the second alibi for the big powers' ineffectiveness was to create an international Tribunal to punish crimes which they had been unable to prevent. However, the Tribunal was to take second place to further diplomatic attempts to stop the carnage, and for some of its founders (France and the UK) it was not to become effective. The Dayton Agreement of December 1995 finally

146

brought the fighting to an end but did not compel the Yugoslav, Croat and Bosnian governments fully to co-operate with the Tribunal, while NATO refrained from arresting the major indicted war criminals.

Leaving aside these political and diplomatic considerations, the creation of the Tribunal was more than justified by the extent of atrocities committed by the combatants of all sides, but mainly by the Serbs, during a conflict initiated and carried out under the leadership of Slobovan Milosevic, the Communist leader in Serbia, intent on creating a Greater Serbia reserved for Serbs only.

THE ATROCITIES

The war caused approximately 3.5 million refugees and internally displaced persons, as a result of planned and systematic 'ethnic cleansing' intended to create 'pure' territories by initially expelling Moslems and Croats from towns and houses in which they had lived for centuries. This was carried out through systematic forced expulsions, terror and massacre, as well as rape and torture in detention camps. In May 1992, the UN Secretary-General had already reported that ethnic cleansing was not the effect of the conflict, but its actual goal. By the summer of 1992, widespread and credible reports of atrocities prompted the Security Council to condemn atrocities publicly as violations of international humanitarian law. Resolution 764, adopted on 13 July 1992, stressed 'that persons who commit or order the commission of grave breaches of the [1949 Geneva] Conventions are individually responsible in respect of such breaches'. On 6 October 1992, the Council established a Commission of Experts to investigate and collect evidence on 'grave breaches of the Geneva Conventions and other violations of international humanitarian law' in the conflict in the former Yugoslavia (Res. 780). The Commission was to be modelled on the Allied War Crimes Commission, which had gathered evidence of Nazi atrocities during World War II, evidence then referred to the Nuremberg prosecutors. While the UN Commission was originally expected to submit similar evidence to the Tribunal which was established in 1993, it was not given adequate staff, sufficient financial resources or political support to enable it to build prosecutable cases, and its work was abruptly stopped on 30 April 1994, even though the Prosecutor's post was not filled until July.[2] The main reason for the lack of political support was that priority was then to achieve a political settlement between the fighting parties, and that the collection of reliable evidence, possibly followed by prosecution, could only be detrimental to the success of the on-going but fruitless diplomatic negotiations. The first chairman of the Commission, Professor Frits Kalshoven, who resigned in September 1993, said in an interview that the real problem was the lack of support by important UN members 'such as France and Britain' and also 'bureaucratic entanglements at the UN'.[3]

In spite of these obstacles, the Commission produced some significant results. The Commission stated in its Final Report of May 1994 that of a population of 6 million, 1.5–2.0 million were refugees abroad after being deported or forced to flee their homes. Civilian and military casualties exceeded 200 000. A total of 187 mass graves had been discovered. In addition, 960 places of detention, including 700 prison camps, were reported, where violations such as rape and torture occurred. Following its investigation of ethnic cleansing in Opstina Prijedor, the Commission concluded that events in that area since April 1992 constituted crimes against humanity and possibly genocide. Altogether, the cases revealed that massive and brutal victimization, affecting thousands of individuals, had taken place in the former Yugoslavia. The majority of alleged violations involved murder, torture, kidnapping/hostage taking, forced eviction and imprisonment. All parties to the conflict appeared to have committed these violations of international humanitarian law. However, the database contained substantially more allegations of violations committed by Serbian and Bosnian Serb forces against Bosnian Moslem civilians than by or against any other ethnic or religious group.[4]

The reality of the atrocities was confirmed in another, separate investigation carried out by Tadeusz Mazowiecki, former Polish Prime Minister, appointed by the UN Human Rights Commission in August 1992 as a Special Rapporteur. Following a request by the USA, the Commission had met in an unprecedented exceptional session on 13–14 August 1992, to discuss reports of detention camps, arbitrary imprisonments and executions, and destruction of homes and villages in the former Yugoslavia. The Commission voted a resolution by consensus condemning the practice of ethnic cleansing and authorizing the appointment of a Special Rapporteur. He would gather credible information and visit 'areas of interest'. The information thus obtained, including that which might constitute war crimes, could be of use in prosecuting violators of international humanitarian law. His report would be made available to the Security Council. The Yugoslav representative told the Commission that he denied all allegations of the existence of concentration camps for civilians in the 'Serbian Republic of Bosnia–Herzegovina' or anywhere else in Yugoslavia.

The Special Rapporteur reported in June 1994 that Bosnian Serb forces had committed massive human rights violations during their March/April offensive on Goradze. Civilian targets had been deliberately targeted and there had been interference with attempts to bring care to the wounded. Bosnian government forces had also committed human rights violations, but not on the same scale as the Bosnian Serbs. Perpetrators should be brought to justice. The Rapporteur had been deeply shocked by his visit to the civilian detention camp in Velika Kladusa. The very existence of the detention camp, as well as the appalling conditions therein, were wholly unacceptable. In August 1994, the Rapporteur told the Commission of the serious difficulties he had faced in his efforts to implement his mandate, due to the uncooperative attitude of the Government of the Federal Republic of Yugoslavia. All requests to undertake missions to the Republic in order to collect first-hand information and to investigate allegations of human rights abuses had been rejected. The Government had 'justified' its decision by referring to the work of the Rapporteur as 'one-sided, full of prejudice and above all politicized'. In November 1994, the Rapporteur stated that the Bosnian-Serb Forces were responsible for a 'pattern of terrorization' that had been particularly evident in Banja Luka, Prijedor and Bijeljina. Ethnic cleansing was continuing in 1995.[5]

On 11 July 1995, General Mladic's forces took over Srebrenica, a UN safe haven, where they carried out the worst war crime in Europe since World War II. In a few days, all the Moslem population, about 40 000 persons, was eliminated from the area: some fled, some were deported, and from 4000 to 10 000 were systematically killed by the Serb forces. On 27 July, Mazowiecki resigned from his position in protest against the UN having allowed the Srebrenica and Zepa 'safe areas' to fall to abusive forces. He deplored the lack of consistency and courage displayed by the international community and its leaders: 'Crimes have been committed with swiftness and brutality and by contrast the response of the international community has been slow and ineffectual.'[6]

According to David Rohde, Christian Science Monitor staff writer, the vast majority of Serbs he talked to were convinced that the Srebrenica massacres did not happen.[7] The Serbs' reaction to the vast evidence of war crimes and crimes against humanity committed by their forces was first to deny the crimes, to prevent access of investigators to sites such as mass graves (an involuntary admission of guilt), then to blame the other parties and finally to label the work of independent investigators as prejudiced and politicized.

THE ESTABLISHMENT OF THE TRIBUNAL

Both resolutions 808 and 827 of the Security Council determined that the continuing reports of widespread violations of international humanitarian law in the former Yugoslavia, including reports of mass killings and the continuance of the practice of ethnic cleansing constituted a threat to international peace and security. Resolution 827, adopted unanimously by its members on 25 May 1993, expressed the conviction of the Council that the establishment as an *ad hoc* measure of an international tribunal and the prosecution of persons responsible for serious violations of international humanitarian law would contribute to the restoration and maintenance of peace and would contribute to ensuring that such violations were halted and effectively redressed.

Acting under Chapter VII of the UN Charter, the Council decided to establish the Tribunal to prosecute persons responsible for serious violations of international humanitarian law committed in the territory of ex-Yugoslavia since 1991 and adopted its Statute.[8]

The Innovative Decision of the Security Council

For the first time, the Council has created a judiciary body as a means to maintain or restore peace and security. Measures decided upon by the Council under Chapter VII, Article 41 of the Charter have included arms, air travel and oil embargoes, economic, financial, cultural and sport sanctions. Under Article 42, it has authorized the creation of multinational forces to combat aggression. Creating a tribunal for the trial of individuals to maintain or restore peace was indeed an innovative move for the Council and a broadening of its mandate. The International Court of Justice was set up in 1945 under the UN Charter and its basic instrument, the

Statute of the Court, forms an integral part of the Charter, an international treaty which member states have to ratify. The creation of the Tribunal for the Former Yugoslavia only required the approval of nine members of the Council, including the five permanent members. Using the Council's powers for the creation of the Tribunal, rather than initiating the traditional process of an international treaty, has raised questions about the legitimacy of the Tribunal and its potential lack of independence, as a subsidiary organ of the Council. In his report to the Security Council of 3 May 1993 (Doc. S/25704), the Secretary-General affirmed that the Tribunal would have to perform its functions independently of political considerations. It would not be subject to the authority or control of the Council with regard to the performance of its judicial functions. The Secretary-General added this ominous, albeit legally correct, qualification: 'As an enforcement measure under Chapter VII, however, the life span of the international tribunal would be linked to the restoration and maintenance of international peace and security in the territory of the former Yugoslavia, and Security Council decisions related thereto.'[9] Would the international community readily accept that on-going and uncompleted prosecutions and judgments would be stopped abruptly and the Tribunal disbanded when the Council decides that international peace and security have been restored in that territory? Could international justice be dispensed with at the will of the Security Council? Was the Tribunal established in a valid manner by the Council as an 'enforcement measure'? The Secretary-General has admitted that expediency or 'urgency' was behind his decision to bypass the normal treaty route, or to involve the General Assembly in the drafting or the review of the Statute of the Tribunal, and use the Council's powers under Chapter VII. The treaty process would probably have taken years, if not decades, and might have been derailed through the opposition of a number of governments. States most closely involved with the conflict would probably decline to become parties to the treaty. On the other hand, Article 25 of the Charter binds all UN Members to accept and carry out the decisions of the Security Council. The General Assembly is associated with the Tribunal insofar as it elects the judges and approves its budget, which provides for the *post facto* consent of its members. The Assembly welcomed the establishment of the Tribunal in December 1993 (Res. 48/88 and Res. 48/143) and encouraged the provision of all necessary resources to the Tribunal in December

1994 (Res. 49/10 and Res. 49/205). In the Tadic Case, the Appeals Chamber of the Tribunal has rejected a motion that the Tribunal had not been validly established, which settles this legal point in relation to cases submitted to it (see below, under 'Indictments and judgments').

The Statute of the Tribunal and Nuremberg

The Nuremberg and Tokyo tribunals (shortened to 'Nuremberg' hereunder) were set up by the victors in order to try and punish the most senior German and Japanese officials responsible for crimes against peace, war crimes and crimes against humanity. It was hoped that the Tribunals' judgments would prevent further crimes. The new Tribunal also has the purpose of bringing alleged criminals to justice and halting and redressing violations, and is to act as a deterrent. While Nuremberg took place after hostilities had ended, the new Tribunal was created in the midst of fighting. Its creation was also meant to contribute to the restoration and maintenance of peace.

Nuremberg had jurisdiction over crimes against peace, war crimes and crimes against humanity, in so far as the latter were related to crimes against peace. The new Tribunal does not have jurisdiction over crimes against peace, but over grave breaches of the Geneva Conventions of 1949, violations of the laws or customs of war, genocide and crimes against humanity. In addition to murder, extermination, enslavement, deportation and persecution on political, racial and religious grounds committed against any civilian population, the Statute of the new Tribunal includes imprisonment, torture and rape under 'crimes against humanity'. Nuremberg judged individuals and organizations; the new Tribunal will only judge individuals. As in Nuremberg, the official position of any accused person, whether as Head of State or Government or as a responsible government official, will not relieve such person of criminal responsibility, nor mitigate punishment. The fact that an accused person acted pursuant to an order of a government or of a superior does not relieve him of criminal responsibility but may be considered in mitigation of punishment if the Tribunal determines that justice so requires. The new Tribunal has primacy over national courts. The new Tribunal has an international composition, significant progress over Nuremberg, whose judges and prosecutors were only citizens of the victorious countries. The new Tribunal is composed of 11 independent judges, of 11 different nationalities, elected by the UN

General Assembly from a list submitted by the Security Council. The President is elected by the judges. The Prosecutor acts independently as a separate organ of the Tribunal. He is not to seek or receive instructions from any government or from any other source. He is appointed by the Security Council on nomination by the Secretary-General. The Prosecutor has the independent power to determine if a *prima facie* case exists, and if so, to prepare an indictment and to transmit it to a judge of the Trial Chamber. If satisfied that a *prima facie* has been established, the judge confirms the indictment. If not, the indictment is dismissed. Fair trial guarantees are given to the accused: Article 21, 'Rights of the accused', is modeled on Article 14 of the International Covenant on Civil and Political Rights.

Contrary to Nuremberg, an accused person may not be tried *in absentia.* However, the new Tribunal has found a way to prevent the wilful absence of an accused person from obstructing the course of justice. The Tribunal has created a special procedure, Rule 61, 'Procedure in case of failure to execute a warrant', which allows for the confirmation by the full Trial Chamber of an indictment issued against an accused person who has not been arrested. It provides for a public hearing at which witnesses may be called to give evidence. If the Trial Chamber is satisfied that there are reasonable grounds for believing that the accused has committed any of the crimes charged in the indictment, it makes a public announcement to that effect. An adverse finding will first result in the issue of an international arrest warrant by the Trial Chamber, which is transmitted to all states and may result in the arrest of the accused abroad, or in preventing him from crossing a border in view of the risk of arrest. If the Trial Chamber is satisfied that the failure to execute the warrant was the result of failure by a state to co-operate with the Tribunal, the President notifies the Security Council accordingly, on the expectation that the Council will provide support to the Tribunal.

While the judgment of Nuremberg was final and not subject to review, the new Tribunal has Trial and Appeals Chambers. The new Tribunal may impose a prison sentence, but not the death penalty as in Nuremberg. The seat of the Tribunal is at the Hague. An international jail of 24 individual cells receives indicted prisoners in the Tribunal's Detention Unit. Those sentenced to imprisonment will be sent to jails in states willing to accept convicted persons: by 1997, six states had agreed without reservation to imprison persons convicted by the Tribunal: Bosnia–Herzegovina, Croatia, Iran, Finland, Norway and Pakistan. An additional five states have agreed to accept prisoners only if their own nationals or residents were convicted. Ten states – including France, a permanent member of the Security Council – have indicated that they are not in a position to accept prisoners.[10] The expenses of the Tribunal are to be borne by the regular budget of the UN, to which voluntary contributions may be added. The initial budget for 1994 was $11 million. The USA, which had contributed $800 000 to the Commission of Experts, contributed $3 million for the start-up costs of the Tribunal and sent a number of experienced legal specialists to the Prosecutor's Office, without cost to the Tribunal. For the 1994–5 biennium, the Assembly appropriated $39.1 million (net) and authorized an increase of the staff from 108 to 258. The Assembly appropriated $35.4 million for 1996. In December 1996, the General Assembly appropriated $21 146 000 net for the period 1 January to 30 June 1997 (Res. 51/214). The Tribunal had requested $69 million for 1997: the Secretary-General reduced this to nearly $50 million, and reduced the number of additional posts proposed from 197 to 50.[11]

The Organs of the Tribunal

The Tribunal comprises three organs: its judiciary, consisting of 11 judges assigned to two Trial Chambers and one Appeals Chamber, the Office of the Prosecutor and the Registry. On 20 August 1993, the Security Council nominated 21 men and two women, representing the principal legal systems of the world, as candidate judges to be presented to the General Assembly (Res. 857). On 15 and 17 September, the Assembly elected the 11 judges of the Tribunal (including the two recommended women) by the required absolute majority of the votes of member states and non-member states maintaining permanent observer missions at UN headquarters. The judges, elected for a four-year term of office, were from Egypt, Italy, Canada, Nigeria, France, China, the USA, Costa Rica, Pakistan, Australia and Malaysia. At the inaugural meeting of the Tribunal, on 17 November, the judges made a solemn declaration that they would perform their duties and exercise their powers 'honourably, faithfully, impartially and conscientiously'. On 18 November, Judge Antonio Cassese (Italy) was elected President of the Tribunal by acclamation. Members of Trial and Appeals Chambers were also elected. On 20 May 1997, the General Assembly elected anew 11 judges for another four-year term: judges are now from Italy, France, the UK, the USA, Zambia, Colombia, Egypt, Portugal, Guyana, Malaysia and China, five of whom were re-elected.[12]

On 11 February 1994, the Tribunal adopted its Rules of Procedure and Evidence, on a largely adversarial approach, rather than the inquisitorial approach. The Rules confirm the primacy of the Tribunal over national court proceedings on the same subject matter. The Tribunal may require a state to defer to the Tribunal's jurisdiction, particularly if it appears that the national court proceedings are not impartial or are designed to shield the accused from international criminal responsibility. In May, the Tribunal amended its Rules so that, in sexual assault cases, no corrobation of the victim's testimony would be required. At its Third Session (25 April–5 May 1994), the Tribunal adopted its Rules Governing the Detention of Persons Awaiting Trial or Appeal Before the Tribunal or Otherwise Detained on the Authority of the Tribunal, and Guidelines for the Assignment of Counsel.[13]

The key post of Prosecutor was only filled in July 1994 by South African Judge Richard J. Goldstone. The Secretary-General's first submission was for the appointment of M. Cherif Bassiouni, the former Chairman of the Commission of Experts: however, the Europeans on the Security Council opposed this nomination, as they feared that his competence and his knowledge of the database he compiled might have started the Tribunal's work too soon, at the risk of damaging the on-going peace talks. On 21 October 1993, the Council appointed Ramon Escovar-Salom, Attorney-General of Venezuela to the post. However, Escovar soon resigned, without taking office, in order to assume the position of Minister of the Interior in his country. An Acting Deputy Prosecutor – Graham Blewitt, from Australia – was appointed in February 1994. Richard J. Goldstone established his office and worked vigorously to bring indictments against those accused of crimes in the former Yugoslavia. Upon his resignation, he was succeeded by Canadian Justice Louise Arbour in October 1996. The Secretary-General appointed Theo van Boven (Netherlands) as Acting Registrar in January 1994. The current Registrar is Ms D. de Sampayo Garrido-Nijgh. The Registry is responsible, among other things, for court management functions, management of the legal aid system for indigent accused, and supervision of the Detention Unit and the Victims and Witnesses Unit.[14]

INDICTMENTS AND JUDGMENTS

In its Third Annual Report issued in November 1996, the Tribunal announced that 75 persons had been indicted. Of these, 18 public indictments had been submitted to and confirmed by the Tribunal. In five cases where the Tribunal was unable to obtain custody of an accused, proceedings under Rule 61 of the Rules of Procedure and Evidence were applied: the full Trial Chamber met and confirmed the indictments by determining that evidence established reasonable grounds to believe that the crimes had been committed. As a result, the charges and evidence had been made public and international arrest warrants had been issued. Indictments against Radovan Karadzic and Ratco Mladic were among those confirmed during the Rule 61 proceedings. However, the international arrest warrants were not executed due to the refusal of the Federal Republic of Yugoslavia and Republica Srpska to co-operate. There were only seven indictees in the Detention Unit at the Hague. By the end of 1997, the Tribunal had sentenced two defendants, Drazen Erdemovic, a Croat and Dusan Tadic, a Bosnian Serb, to ten and 20 years in jail respectively.

The First Case: Dusan Tadic

On 26 April 1995, in a pre-trial hearing, Tadic was presented by the Tribunal's prosecutor with an indictment formally charging him with 'genocide, through the policy of ethnic cleansing, and crimes against humanity, such as assault, murder, rape and persecution based on religious grounds'. He pleaded not guilty, claiming that he was a victim of mistaken identity. Tadic was arrested in Germany in February 1994 on a genocide charge, after witnesses asserted that he had killed and maimed Muslim prisoners while serving as a guard at concentration camps run by the Bosnian Serbs and was later extradited to the Hague.[15] In a motion filed with the Trial Chamber in June 1995, Tadic challenged the jurisdiction of the Tribunal under three lines of argument: first, that the Tribunal had not been established in a valid manner, because the Security Council lacked the power to do so; secondly, that the primacy of the Tribunal's jurisdiction over that of national courts, as provided for in the Tribunal's Statute, was unlawful; and thirdly, that the Tribunal lacked subject-matter jurisdiction, because the articles of the Statute named in the indictment (Articles 2, 3 and 5) are applicable only to international armed conflicts, and the alleged crimes, if proven, were committed in an internal armed conflict. The Trial Chamber upheld the jurisdiction of the Tribunal in a judgment on 10 August 1995. On 2 October, the Appeals Chamber decided that the Tribunal had been established in a valid manner and affirmed both its primacy and its subject matter jurisdiction.

On the validity of its establishment, the Appeals Chamber decided that the Security Council had the power in the circumstances to invoke Chapter VII of the Charter, that the establishment of the Tribunal was an appropriate measure in the circumstances under Article 41 of the Charter, and that the Tribunal was established 'in accordance with the rule of law' in that it was 'established in accordance with the appropriate procedures under the UN Charter and provides all the necessary safeguards of a fair trial'. On the issue of primacy, the Appeals Chamber dismissed the defendant's plea on the grounds that this primacy was necessary to prevent forum shopping or fake proceedings designed to shield criminals. On subject-matter jurisdiction, the Appeals Chamber assumed that the Security Council had intended that the Tribunal would punish serious violations of international humanitarian law 'without reference to whether the conflicts in the former Yugoslavia were internal or international' and concluded that both types of conflicts existed in those territories. For the majority of the Appeals Chamber, there has been a convergence of the rules governing international conflicts and those governing internal conflicts, with the result that internal strife is now governed to a large extent by the rules and principles which had traditionally only applied to international conflicts. This convergence was the result of the following factors: (a) the increase in the number of civil conflicts; (b) the increase in the level of cruelty of internal conflicts; (c) the increasing interdependence of states; and (d) the influence of universal human rights standards. These important decisions of substance allowed the Tribunal to proceed with the Tadic and other cases. They will bind the Tribunal in its future work.

The Tadic trial was held from May until November 1996: 125 witnesses were called. On 7 May 1997, the Trial Chamber found the accused not guilty on 20 counts – nine murder counts because of insufficient evidence and 11 counts declared inapplicable – and guilty on 11 counts – six crimes against humanity and five violations of the laws or customs of war (persecution and beatings resulting in death). The charge of rape had been withdrawn earlier

by the prosecution, because of the unwillingness of the victim to
testify. On 14 July 1997, Tadic was sentenced to 20 years' imprisonment. The verdict represents the first judicial condemnation of
the ethnic cleansing policy. Tadic's Defence Counsel appealed against
the Sentencing Judgment on 13 August 1997.[16]

The First Judgment: Drazen Erdemovic

Erdemovic was the first defendant to plead guilty to the Tribunal's
charges of crimes against humanity. A Croat who had joined the
Bosnian Serb army, he said that he had been forced to take part in
the summary execution of hundreds of Muslims who had surrendered to the Serbs in Srebrenica in July 1995. He was arrested in
Serbia in March 1996 and extradited to the Hague after confessing
to his role in the massacre during interviews with the media. He
appeared as a prosecution witness against Karadzic and Mladic in
a hearing in July 1996. As he was not contesting the charges of
having killed between 10 and 100 persons, his case proceeded
directly to sentencing. On 29 November 1996, Erdemovic was
sentenced to ten years in jail. The sentence will be subject to an
appeal.[17]

Other Cases

On 30 January 1996, General Djordje Djukic and Colonel Aleksa
Krsmanovic, both Bosnian Serbs, were arrested by chance by the
Sarajevo authorities, and then transferred to the Hague on 12 February. On 1 March, the Tribunal indicted General Djukic of crimes
against humanity as senior Bosnian Serb army commander in charge
of logistics and weapons supply to the Bosnian Serb army. He was
then allowed to go to Belgrade on provisional leave on health
grounds, where he died on 18 May. Colonel Krsmanovic was sent
back to Sarajevo by the Tribunal on 29 March on the grounds of
lack of sufficient evidence for an indictment. Upon US insistence,
a Croat General, Tihomir Blaskic, surrendered to the Tribunal on
1 April 1996 to answer his indictment for involvement in the destruction of 14 Muslim villages in central Bosnia during the Croat-
Muslim fighting of 1993. He had been promoted from colonel to
general in the regular Croatian army shortly after his indictment
by the Tribunal. His trial started on 24 June 1997. He pleaded not
guilty. He has been allowed by the Tribunal to live in a guarded

apartment provided by the Dutch government during the proceedings, and not in the Tribunal's Detention Centre.

In its first indictment for crimes against Serbs, the Tribunal charged three Bosnian Muslims and a Bosnian Croat with subjecting detainees in a camp in Celebici, in 1992, to 'murder, torture, including rape of female detainees, beatings and inhumane treatment'. The trial started in March 1997. Zdravko Mucik, the former camp commander, was first detained in Vienna, and Zejnic Delalic, a former Bosnian Muslim regional military commander, in Munich. Hazim Delic, deputy camp commander, and Esad Landzo, one of the guards, were arrested in Bosnia and handed over to the Tribunal. All four deny the charges.

The arrest of Slavko Dokmanovic on 27 June 1997 showed three innovations. It was the first operation carried out on the territory of a former warring state without its knowledge or co-operation, i.e. in Eastern Slavonia, a region of Croatia held by the Serbs. Secondly, the arrest was carried out by Tribunal investigators with the support of the UN Transitional Administration for Eastern Slavonia. Thirdly, it revealed the existence of non-public indictments for the first time, a device aimed at facilitating the search and arrest of suspects while the risks of armed resistance would be minimized. The Tribunal had secretly indicted Dokmanovic on 26 March 1996. He was the former mayor of Vukovar in November 1991, when Yugoslav army and Serb paramilitary forces are alleged to have abducted 260 civilian men, mostly Croat, from the city's hospital, who had then been beaten and shot to death, with the accused's participation, according to the indictment. The Yugoslav government strongly protested the arrest, as a 'most serious incident'.

Milan Kovacevic, a Bosnian Serb doctor, was arrested on another secret indictment on 10 July 1997 by SFOR troops in Bosnia, the first suspect to be arrested by NATO forces. He was indicted by the Tribunal for complicity in genocide against the Bosnian Muslims and Croats of the municipality of Prijedor in the period between 29 April and 31 December 1992. In a separate detention action in the vicinity of Prijedor, the indicted war criminal Simo Drljaca, the former police chief in Prijedor, opened fire on SFOR soldiers and was killed when fire was returned in self-defence. The Yugoslav government issued a warning.[18]

THE MAIN PROBLEM

Four years after its creation, the Tribunal has indicted 75 persons, but only has nine suspects in custody in the Hague, and has only sentenced two to imprisonment. The Tribunal issued warrants for the arrest of the leaders of the Bosnian and Croatian Serbs in July 1995, and again in November 1995. Bosnian Serb leader Radovan Karadzic and army commander Ratko Mladic were charged with genocide, crimes against humanity and violations of the laws or customs of war. The initial charges included the persecution, shelling, killing and deportation of civilians throughout Bosnia-Herzegovina, the sniping campaign against civilians in Sarajevo, and the capture of UN peacemakers as hostages and use of them as human shields. Their second indictment alleged that they were individually responsible for the mass executions of Bosnian Muslims in Srebrenica in July 1995. They were criminally responsible as commanders for the acts of their subordinates. Croatian Serb leader Milan Martic was charged in connection with the firing of cluster-bombs into Zagreb in May 1995.[19]

These leaders have not been arrested, and most of the other warrants have not been executed. The reason for this frustrating state of affairs is that the Tribunal is an isolated body without enforcement powers: it has no international police at its disposal. Upon its establishment under Chapter VII, the Tribunal was to be endowed, through the Security Council, with enforcement measures which failing the voluntary co-operation of member states, would ensure compliance with its requests for judicial assistance. The Council has failed to ensure such compliance. The Tribunal's Statute prescribed that states would co-operate with the Tribunal in the investigation and prosecution of persons accused of committing serious violations of international humanitarian law (Article 29). This article prescribes *inter alia* that states

> 'shall comply without undue delay with any request for assistance or an order issued by a Trial Chamber, including ... (d) the arrest or detention of persons; (e) the surrender or the transfer of the accused to the International Tribunal'.

These obligations have only been respected in a few cases. The general rule has been a rejection of the Tribunal's orders, or the lack of effective enforcement of these orders, which revealed all too clearly that the Tribunal had no real political support from the main parties concerned.

Non-co-operation by Governments

It was no surprise that those governments that initiated the war, promoted ethnic cleansing and encouraged the commission of war crimes and crimes against humanity by their combatants rejected any useful co-operation with the Tribunal, or limited this co-operation to the minimum. They protected their war criminals, promoted them to more important functions and ignored the Tribunal's warrants. Their ultimate purpose is to prevent the Tribunal from collecting enough evidence to indict the major responsible leaders for crimes authorized, or allowed to be committed, by different levels of responsible political and military officials. Their degree of responsibility and guilt is demonstrated by their degree of non-co-operation with the Tribunal. Alleged criminals will not facilitate their own prosecution and sentencing. As noted in the Third Annual Report of the Tribunal issued in August 1996, Republika Srpska has failed to execute any of the scores of arrest warrants addressed to it, or to explain its inability or failure to do so, as required by the Tribunal's rules. According to numerous media reports, mass grave sites to which the Tribunal's investigators were given access had been emptied of corpses or otherwise tampered with, which constitutes destruction of evidence. The Federal Republic of Yugoslavia (Serbia and Montenegro) has an almost equally dismal record of co-operation with the Tribunal. The Republic has failed to arrest any indictees in its territory and has allowed prominent indictees, notably Mladic and Sljivancanin, to appear publicly in Belgrade with impunity. The Republic has also failed to take the most elementary step of enacting implementing legislation to enable it to co-operate with the Tribunal, as required by the Tribunal's Statute and international law.

The Tribunal's Report notes that the Republic of Croatia occupies a middle rung in this ladder of co-operation. It arrested only one accused in its territory, Zlatko Aleksovski, and assisted (under US pressure) with the surrender of Blaskic to the Tribunal. However, it failed to exercise its acknowledged authority and influence over other Bosnian Croats with a view to arresting them. It has failed fully to investigate and prosecute serious violations of international humanitarian law allegedly committed by Croatian forces in August 1995 during and after 'Operation Storm'. On the other hand, it is not surprising that the party that was exposed to most exactions and suffered most victims, among the three fighting parties, has been, so far, the most co-operative government. The Republic of Bosnia-Herzegovina has replied to nearly every warrant addressed to it, explaining its inability to execute arrest warrants in Bosnian territories outside its control. It executed warrants against Delic and Landzo.

Leaving aside the countries in which crimes occurred and in which most criminals are given impunity, the lukewarm co-operation given to the Tribunal by those countries that created the Tribunal may sound at the least irrational, unless one believes that this creation was a placebo given to the victims, to international public opinion moved by the horrors exposed by the media, and to those governments which wanted to protect the Bosnian Muslims, or at least to support the imposition of international justice.

Among the five permanent members of the Security Council who voted for the creation of the Tribunal, China's main interests are in Asia, not in Europe, but its leaders are wary of any international intervention in a country's internal affairs, particularly if they relate to human rights. Russia is pro-Serb, as was France under Mitterand's presidency. France, which was at the origin of the creation of the Tribunal, and the UK tried unsuccessfully to find a political solution to the ex-Yugoslavia war, and supported a humanitarian intervention in preference to a military expedition in the Balkan 'quagmire'. France is the only Western country to prevent its former UN peace-keeping commanders from giving testimonies to the Tribunal as witnesses, in violation of its legal obligations.[20] The USA has been the most active supporters of the Tribunal, as they were for Nuremberg and Tokyo, but their Vietnam experience and the Somali syndrome led them to avoid or limit their contribution in US armed forces in the field. NATO's position, until July 1997, was that its troops will arrest indicted war criminals if they encounter them in the course of normal operations, such as during a patrol or at a checkpoint. NATO would, however, not mount specific operations to arrest them, in spite of the international warrants issued by the Tribunal. NATO troops were not trained for police work.[21] However, the real rationale for NATO's refusal to be involved in the arrest of indicted persons was that priority had to be given to the maintenance of peace and to the implementation of the Dayton Agreements: arrests of important indicted personalities might trigger new fighting and ex-

pose NATO troops to reprisals. Western Powers who have negotiated with Milosevic and Tudjman in order to complete the Dayton
Agreements, and still need them to maintain a semblance of peace
in the area, are also reluctant to pursue too aggressively judiciary inquiries and prosecutions which might well reach the top
echelon. The elusive diplomatic search for a political settlement,
accompanied by rare shows of limited force, continues to prevail
over international justice, in spite of the recurrent pleadings of the
Tribunal's President and Prosecutors.

BOSNIA'S APPLICATION TO THE INTERNATIONAL COURT OF JUSTICE

On 20 March 1993, almost one month after the Security Council
had decided to establish the Tribunal, the Government of the Republic of Bosnia–Herzegovina filed an application before the International Court of Justice alleging violations of the 1948 Convention
on the Prevention and Punishment of the Crime of Genocide by
the Government of the Federal Republic of Yugoslavia. Bosnia
requested the Court to first adjuge and declare that Yugoslavia
had breached and continued to breach its legal obligations toward
the people of Bosnia under the Genocide Convention, under the
four Geneva Conventions of 1949, their Additional Protocol I of
1977, the customary international laws of war including the Hague
Regulations on Land Warfare of 1907, and other fundamental principles of international humanitarian law, under the Universal Declaration of Human Rights and under the UN Charter. Bosnia alleged
that Yugoslavia had killed, murdered, wounded, raped, robbed,
tortured, kidnapped, illegally detained and exterminated the citizens of Bosnia, and was continuing to do so. Secondly, Bosnia
demanded that Yugoslavia should desist immediately from its systematic practice of ethnic cleansing, from the murder, summary
execution, torture, rape, kidnapping, mayhem, wounding, physical
and mental abuse, and detention of Bosnia's citizens, from the wanton
destruction of villages, towns and religious institutions, from the
bombardment of civilian population centres, from continuing the
siege of such centres, from the starvation of civilian population,
from the interruption of, or harassment of humanitarian relief sup-
plies, from all use of force and threats of force against Bosnia.
Thirdly, the Court should adjudge and declare that Yugoslavia had

an obligation to pay Bosnia reparations for damages to persons
and property as well as to the Bosnian economy and environment
caused by these violations of international law in a sum to be
determined by the Court.[22]

Yugoslavia raised a number of preliminary objections, arguing
that the Application was not admissible because of the lack of an
international dispute, the lack of authority of the President of Bosnia
at the time the Application was filed, and that the Court lacked
jurisdiction. On 8 April 1993, the Court issued an Order calling
upon Yugoslavia (Serbia and Montenegro) to 'immediately . . . take
all measures within its power to prevent commission of the crime
of genocide'. The Court also held that neither Yugoslavia nor Bosnia
should take any action to aggravate or extend the existing dispute
over the prevention of punishment of the crime of genocide, or
render it more difficult of solution. On 13 August 1993, Bosnia
filed a second request with the Court for provisional measures to
be ordered against Yugoslavia to prevent commission of the crime
of genocide. Among these measures, Bosnia was to be granted the
means, including arms, munitions and equipment, to defend its people
and state 'from acts of genocide and partition and dismemberment
by means of genocide'. On 13 September 1993, the Court issued
an interim Order of provisional measures which reaffirmed its Order
of 8 April: 'the present perilous situation demands not an indication
of provisional measures additional to those indicated by the Court's
Order of 8 April 1993, but immediate and effective implementation
of those measures'. The Court declined to adopt more far-reaching
injunctions requested by Bosnia, as it could order interim measures only within the scope of the jurisdiction conferred on it by
the Genocide Convention. However, the Court recorded that despite its Order of 8 April and many resolutions of the UN Security
Council, 'great suffering and loss of life has been sustained by the
population of Bosnia and Herzegovina in circumstances which shock
the conscience of mankind and flagrantly conflict with moral law'.[23]

On 11 July 1996, the Court rejected by clear majorities the preliminary objections raised by Yugoslavia and found that the Application was admissible, but that its only jurisdiction to entertain the
case was on the basis of Article IX of the Genocide Convention.[24]
The Court determined that Bosnia was a party to the Genocide
Convention on the date of the filing of its Application. On the
basis of the complaints formulated by Bosnia against Yugoslavia
and Yugoslavia's denial of those complaints, the Court found that

a legal dispute existed between the parties. The Court found that the Genocide Convention is applicable without reference to the circumstances linked to the domestic or international nature of the conflict, provided that the criminal acts referred to in Articles II and III of the Convention have been perpetrated. It also found that an international dispute existed. It follows from the object and purpose of the Convention that the rights and obligations enshrined in it are *erga omnes*. Therefore, the obligation each state has to prevent and punish the crime of genocide is not territorially limited by the Convention. Following three years of provisional measures and preliminary objections procedures, the Court will then proceed to deal with the merits of the case.

One may wonder whether Bosnia's recourse to the International Court of Justice served a useful purpose when an international criminal tribunal had been set up to prosecute and judge persons responsible for serious violations of international humanitarian law, including the crime of genocide. Such a recourse should, in principle, be limited to cases where national tribunals are ineffective and no international criminal tribunal has been established, as is the case for Cambodia. Stanton[25] proposed in 1980 that a state that is a party to the Genocide Convention submit a case against Cambodia to the Court. The complaint would contend that the Khmer Rouge government had violated the Convention by failing to punish those responsible for committing genocide. However, he also found that no government was willing to take the case, presumably for diplomatic concern for reciprocity, and in view of previous support given the Khmer Rouge regime by a number of countries. Bosnia's recourse to the Court has, however, produced important legal pronouncements concerning the Genocide Convention. The Court has decided that it had jurisdiction over a dispute between two Contracting Parties relating to the responsibility of a state for genocide or any of the other acts enumerated in Article III, in accordance with Article IX of the Convention. If Bosnia allows the case to be determined on its merits, the Court will legally and publicly assign international responsibility for the violations of the Genocide Convention committed in Bosnia to the government concerned, i.e. Yugoslavia. Other states could avail themselves of this jurisprudence in order to submit to the Court any disputes between Contracting Parties relating to the responsibility of a state for genocide when justice cannot be rendered by competent and independent national tribunals or by an international criminal court. For Bosnia, the Court's proceedings are bound to increase the public international opprobrium which has already tainted Yugoslavia's name.

The limitation of Bosnia's application-to-the-Court approach is that the only practical consequence of the Court's probable determination that Yugoslavia has breached its legal obligations under the Genocide Convention would be the award of financial compensation to Bosnia for the damages and losses caused. As only states may be parties in cases before the Court, its judgment will be addressed to governments and will ignore the individual criminal responsibility of political and military leaders. Even though the Court recorded in its interim Order of 13 September 1993 the great suffering and loss of life of the Bosnian population in 'circumstances which shock the conscience of mankind and flagrantly conflict with moral law', its eventual judgment on the merits of Bosnia's Application will remain in the abstract domain of international law assigning criminal responsibility to the abstract state, and in the more concrete but limited domain of financial compensation. The Court is not competent to identify, judge and sentence those individuals who are responsible for the crime of genocide.

CONCLUSION

Article VI of the Genocide Convention provides that

> Persons charged with genocide or any of the other acts enumerated in Article III shall be tried by a competent tribunal of the State in the territory of which the act was committed, or by such international penal tribunal as may have jurisdiction with respect to those Contracting Parties which shall have accepted its jurisdiction.

In view of the inability and unwillingness of the warring parties in the former Yugoslavia to have alleged war criminals of their nationality tried by competent and independent Tribunals, and as no permanent international criminal court had yet been established, the creation of the International Criminal Tribunal for Former Yugoslavia by the Security Council was a well-justified innovation, in order to give a judicial response to serious violations of international humanitarian law committed in those territories.

It was at first hailed as a significant legal progress in the field of international criminal law, the creation of a successor to the Nurem-

berg and Tokyo Tribunals, more respectful of the requirements of
the composition of an international court, without the 'original sin'
of victors' justice, and without the burden of imposing *ex post facto*
legislation. It has been hailed as a real-life test for the proposed
permanent international criminal court. The Tribunal has been credited with setting up, operating and testing its entire normative and
logistical infrastructure. The Tribunal's provisions regarding detention,
provisional release and sentencing have been applied, and regula-
tory texts regarding the assignment of counsels, handling of exhib-
its have been issued. The Tribunal has strengthened international
humanitarian law, it has further eroded the distinction between the
rules governing international conflicts and those governing internal conflicts. As Meron states,[26] it has affirmed the customary, unwritten law that binds all states to international standards of
behaviour. The Appeals Chamber's rulings on jurisdictional issues
in the Tadic case have been 'the first judicial affirmation of international criminality and individual responsibility for violations of
international humanitarian law since Nuremberg'. At the opening
meeting of the Tribunal in the Hague on 17 November 1993, the
former UN Legal Counsel, Carl-August Fleischhauer, said that few
Security Council decisions in recent years had created such expectations as the establishment of the Tribunal. Through the UN, the
international community had reaffirmed its determination not to
allow mass killings, so-called 'ethnic cleansing', the systematic rape
of women and other crimes to continue unabated, and to hold those
responsible accountable before the law of nations. He added that,
in establishing the Tribunal, the Security Council had three important
aims: to end the crimes being committed in the territory of the
former Yugoslavia; to bring to justice the persons responsible for
them; and to break the seemingly endless cycle of ethnic violence
and retribution by providing for prosecution and judgment under
the rule of law, and thereby contribute to the restoration of peace.

By the end of 1997, the Tribunal has only been able to bring to
justice a small number of accused, and has not been allowed to
take custody of, and judge the major deciders and organizers of
ethnic cleansing and related atrocities, as a result of the lack of
co-operation of the governments concerned. The Srebrenica atrocities
took place in July 1995, when the Tribunal was fully operational.
The Tribunal has had no role in the fragile cessation of hostilities
obtained by the Dayton Peace Agreement of December 1995. In
turn, the Dayton Agreement has not strengthened its authority.

The success or failure of this experiment depends on the political and military will of the Western powers. If they fail to arrest the main perpetrators within the next few months, the Tribunal will fail, damaging the credibility of the UN Security Council, and confirming the arrogant impunity of those responsible for the genocide and other atrocities. It will show to the victims and to the world that international justice without powers of enforcement, or at least, without the firm support of member states, has little value.

9 The International Criminal Tribunal for Rwanda

Following the establishment of the Tribunal for Former Yugoslavia in May 1993, the Security Council created on 8 November 1994 a second *ad hoc* international criminal court, the International Tribunal for the Prosecution of Persons Responsible for Genocide or Other Serious Violations of International Humanitarian Law Committed in the Territory of Rwanda and Rwandan Citizens Responsible for Genocide and Other Such Violations Committed in the Territory of Neighbouring States, Between 1 January 1994 and 31 December 1994 (Res. 955). The Council had expressed its grave concern at the reports indicating that genocide and other systematic, widespread and flagrant violations of international humanitarian law had been committed in Rwanda and determined that this situation continued to constitute a threat to international peace and security. The establishment of the Tribunal would contribute to ensuring that such violations were halted and effectively redressed and would also contribute to the process of national reconciliation and to the restoration and maintenance of peace. The Council decided that 'all States shall cooperate fully with the ... Tribunal ...'.

THE GENOCIDE AND ITS CAUSES

Between April and July 1994, an estimated half a million persons were massacred by soldiers and militias loyal to President Juvénal Habyarimana, who had been killed, together with President Cyprien Ntaryamira of Burundi, when his plane was hit by a rocket. Most of the victims were Tutsi, but Hutus who opposed the killings or supported power sharing between the Hutu majority and the Tutsi minority were also killed. Most of the killers belonged to the Hutu majority ethnic group: they were members of the Rwandan government forces, but in the main they were drawn from the Presidential Guard, the *interhamwe* (the youth militia recruited and formed by the late President's party) and village people who killed their neighbours. The massacres, carried out mostly by machetes and clubs, were systematic, planned and condoned at the highest level. Radio broadcasts, particularly from the *Radio-télévision libre des mille collines* incited the killings of Tutsis across the country. The Tutsis were de-humanized: they were 'cockroaches' that need to be exterminated. This ideology acquired legitimacy among the Christian clergy: Tutsis are devils and it is not against the laws of God to kill a devil.

In May 1994, the UN Secretary-General reported estimates of between 250 000 and 500 000 dead, out of a population of approximately seven million. Displaced persons were in the range of 1.5 million, with an additional 400 000 refugees in neighbouring countries. In October, he revised these figures to one million dead, more than two million refugees, and between 800 000 and two million internally displaced persons.[1] On 7 April, the Tutsi-led Rwandan Patriotic Front (RPF) launched an offensive to end the genocide. At the end of June, the RPF took Kigali and set up an interim government of 'national unity'. About two million Hutus and their leaders fled from Rwanda to Zaire and other neighbouring countries.

The 1994 massacre of Tutsis by Hutus had long historical roots in both Rwanda and Burundi. In both countries, the Hutus are a large majority of 85–90%, and the Tutsis a minority of 10–15%. While Hutus and Tutsis speak the same language, share the same names and the same predominantly Catholic religion, and intermarry, every native of Rwanda or Burundi knows whether he/she is a Hutu or a Tutsi. For centuries, a feudal Tutsi aristocracy of cattlekeepers ruled over the agricultural Hutus before the two territories became a German colony in 1899. Germany chose to rule indirectly through Tutsi monarchs, a system maintained by Belgium after World War I and World War II, when Ruanda-Urundi became a League of Nations mandate, then a UN trust territory. In 1926, the Belgians introduced ethnic identity cards differentiating Hutus from Tutsis. A Hutu revolt against the authority of the Tutsi chiefs in 1959 sparked a massacre of at least 20 000 Tutsis, leading to the exile of many Tutsis. Following the independence of both territories in 1962, with the Hutus monopolizing power in Rwanda, more killings of Tutsis took place in 1962 and 1963, leading to massive outflows of refugees to Uganda.

In 1972, the government of Burundi, then controlled by the Tutsis, tried to eliminate the educated class of the Hutus. All those with some education, government jobs or money were to be killed. Out of a population of 3.5 million inhabitants, an estimated 100 000–200 000 Hutus were killed: they offered little resistance. In August 1988, Tutsis were killed by armed bands in two northeastern communes. Military repression followed, causing more killings of Hutus and the flight of approximately 50 000 Hutu peasants to Rwanda.

In Rwanda, the Chief of Staff of the Rwandan Army, General Habyarimana, a Hutu, seized power in 1973. He set up a one-party state. A policy of ethnic quotas was adopted: Tutsis were allotted only 10% of the places in schools, universities and in civil service posts. The RPF led a failed invasion from Uganda in 1990. The Arusha Peace Agreement of 4 August 1993 was to settle the Rwandan conflict peacefully, by power sharing between the Hutu leaders and the RPF in a transitional government, under the supervision of an international peacekeeping mission – the UN Assistance Mission for Rwanda, UNAMIR. Resistance by President Habyarimana and extremist Hutu parties succeeded in delaying the implementation of the Agreement.[2] The plane crash of 6 April 1994 triggered the well-planned genocide.

THE CREATION OF THE TRIBUNAL

The creation of both Tribunals, the Tribunal for Former Yugoslavia and the Rwanda Tribunal, was approved by the UN Security Council as an enforcement measure under Chapter VII of the UN Charter. In both cases, the Council determined that widespread and flagrant violations of international humanitarian law constituted a threat to international peace and security, thus justifying the recourse to Chapter VII. In both cases, the creation of a tribunal was to contribute to halting abuses and restoring and maintaining peace. In Rwanda, it was also to contribute to the process of national reconciliation. In both cases, the creation of a Tribunal was a *post facto* substitute for an effective, timely, military intervention by the UN Security Council. In both cases, the major powers showed their incapacity or unwillingness to prevent a man-made disaster of which warning signals had been given by the UN, their own diplomatic services, and/or by international and human rights organizations – or to stop it while it was taking place.

After his mission to Rwanda in April 1993, the UN Special Rapporteur on extra-judicial, summary or arbitrary executions, Mr

Bacre Waly Ndiaye, submitted a report to the Human Rights Commission in which he concluded that there existed widespread and systematic abuses, including incitement to ethnic hatred and violence against the Tutsis. Before the genocide, between December 1993 and March 1994, UNAMIR noted on several occasions inflammatory broadcasts by Radio Mille Collines and suspicious movements by armed groups. UNAMIR received evidence that arms were being brought into the country, protested to the provisional government and conveyed this information to the diplomatic community.[3] According to press reports,[4] a cable to UN headquarters dated 11 January 1994 from the Canadian commander of UN peacekeepers in Rwanda, Major General Romeo Dallaire provided an account of the plot from an informant described as a leading member of a Hutu political party in charge of training Hutu militia. The informant had been ordered to register all Tutsis in Kigali. He suspected that it was for their extermination. In 20 minutes, his personnel could kill up to 1000 Tutsis. General Dallaire made repeated requests to the UN headquarters for reinforcements and authorization to use force to seize Hutu weapons caches. UN officials responded that political support of the major powers in the Security Council would be required, which seemed unlikely at the time. The Security Council was not informed of the Hutu plot by the UN peace-keeping department in New York, who only asked Dallaire to inform the Rwandan President and the US, French and Belgian embassies.

On 20 April 1994, the Secretary-General issued a Special Report referring to the 'torrent of widespread killings' with both political and ethnic dimensions, indicating that the deaths 'could possibly number tens of thousands'. The Secretary-General offered three alternatives: one, to reinforce UNAMIR by several thousand additional troops and to give UNAMIR enforcement powers under Chapter VII; the second to reduce the mission staffing from 2500 troops and military and police observers to about 270; and the last to withdraw UNAMIR. The Security Council adopted the second alternative, rendering the UN mission useless.[5] The lack of effective action in Rwanda was accompanied by the wilful avoidance of the word 'genocide' to describe the massacres. On 17 May 1994, the Security Council 'recalled' that the 'killing of members of an ethnic group with the intention of destroying such a group, in whole or in part, constitutes a crime punishable under international law' (Res. 918). The USA referred to 'acts of genocide' rather than genocide. Recognition that actual genocide was occurring might have obligated the USA and other powers to take more vigorous action and to punish the perpetrators under the Genocide Convention. The Secretary-General broke the taboo by stating, on 31 May, that 'There can be little doubt that it constitutes genocide, since there have been large-scale killings of communities and families belonging to a particular ethnic group'.[6] On 28 June 1994, Mr R. Degni-Ségui, Special Rapporteur of the Commission on Human Rights, stated that 'the massacres are all the more horrible and terrifying in that they give the impression of being planned, systematic and atrocious'. He identified as immediately apparent causes of the human rights violations in Rwanda the rejection of alternate political power, incitement to hatred and violence, and impunity.[7]

As for the Yugoslavia Tribunal, the establishment of the Rwanda Tribunal was preceded by a Commission of Experts. On 1 July 1994, the unanimous Security Council requested the Secretary-General to establish an impartial Commission of Experts to examine and analyse information, investigate and provide the Secretary-General with its conclusions on the evidence of grave violations of international humanitarian law, including the evidence of possible acts of genocide in Rwanda (Res. 935).

The Commission reported in October, on the basis of ample evidence, that individuals on both sides of the armed conflict in Rwanda during the period 6 April to 15 July 1994 had perpetrated serious breaches of international humanitarian law and crimes against humanity. The Commission concluded there was 'overwhelming evidence' to prove that acts of genocide against the Tutsi group were perpetrated by Hutu elements in a concerted, planned, systematic and methodical way. These mass exterminations constituted genocide within the meaning of Article II of the 1948 Genocide Convention. The Commission had not uncovered any evidence to indicate that Tutsi elements perpetrated acts with intent to destroy the Hutu ethnic group as such within the meaning of the Convention. The Commission recommended that the Security Council amend the Statute of the Yugoslavia Tribunal to ensure that its jurisdiction covered crimes committed in Rwanda during the conflict which began on 6 April 1994.[8]

On 9 August, the UN Subcommission on Prevention of Discrimination and Protection of Minorities approved a resolution demanding an immediate end to the massacres and sufferings imposed on the people of Rwanda with the complicity of certain states. It deplored the fact that the tardy and insufficiently effective intervention by the international community, including the UN and the Organization of African Unity, did not, when it was still possible, prevent the genocide.[9]

While Yugoslavia had opposed the establishment of the International Tribunal for Former Yugoslavia, the Tutsi-dominated government of Rwanda proposed the creation of an international tribunal by letter to the President of the Security Council dated 28 September 1994. On 6 October, the President of Rwanda, Pasteur Bizimungu, urged the UN to establish an international tribunal in his country quickly to bring those responsible for genocide to justice. The Rwandan government wanted to avoid any suspicion of its wanting to organize speedy, vengeful justice. Instead of a 'victors' justice', an international presence would ensure an exemplary justice which would be seen to be completely impartial and fair. The government believed that it was impossible to build a state of law and arrive at true national reconciliation without eradicating the culture of impunity which has characterized Rwandan society.[10] However, Rwanda voted against Resolution 955 which set up the Tribunal on 8 November 1994. Its main objection was that the Tribunal's Statute rules out capital punishment, which is nevertheless provided for in the Rwandan penal code. As a consequence, leaders who devised, planned and organized the genocide may escape capital punishment, while lower-ranking perpetrators 'would be subjected to the harshness of [the death] sentence'. Other objections related to the temporal jurisdiction of the Tribunal, which was considered too restrictive, and to its composition and structure – the number of Trial Chamber judges should be increased, and the Tribunal should have its own Appeals Chamber and Prosecutor. The seat of the Tribunal should be in Rwanda.[11]

THE STATUTE OF THE TRIBUNAL

The Statute of the Rwanda Tribunal is based to a large extent on the Statute of the Yugoslavia Tribunal, and includes institutional links with the latter, but it also includes a few differences due in part to the national, internal nature of the Rwanda genocide, while the Yugoslav conflict had both national and international aspect.[12]

Both Tribunals are *ad hoc*, time-limited subsidiary bodies of the Security Council, with a limited *ratione loci, ratione personae* and *ratione temporis* competence: the Rwanda Tribunal may prosecute persons responsible for serious violations of international law committed in the territory of Rwanda and Rwandan citizens responsible for such violations committed in the territory of neighbouring states between 1 January 1994 and 31 December 1994. Only natural persons may be prosecuted, not states or other institutions. *Ratione materiae*, the competence of both Tribunals is based in part on the provisions of the Genocide Convention. The list of crimes against humanity is identical for both Tribunals. However, their definition in the Rwanda Statute does not require a nexus with armed conflict as in the Statute of the Yugoslavia Tribunal, but it requires that such crimes be committed 'as part of a widespread or systematic attack against any civilian population'. Any reference to the 'Violations of the laws or customs of war' is omitted in the Rwanda Statute, in view of the internal nature of the Rwanda conflict. The reference to 'Grave breaches of the Geneva Conventions of 1949' in the Statute of the Yugoslavia Tribunal, not applicable to an internal conflict, is replaced by an article on 'Violations of article 3 common to the Geneva Conventions and of Additional Protocol II' specifically applicable to armed conflict not of an international character.

Both Tribunals have primacy over the national courts of all states, and consist of two Trial Chambers, an Appeals Chamber, a Prosecutor and a Registry. Both Tribunals are composed of 11 judges of different nationalities. However, the Appeals Chamber of the Yugoslavia Tribunal also serves as Appeals Chamber for the Rwanda Tribunal. The Prosecutor of the Yugoslavia Tribunal also serves as Prosecutor for the Rwanda Tribunal, assisted by an additional Deputy Prosecutor and staff. Other provisions are similar in both Statutes. On 22 February 1995, the Security Council decided that the seat of the Tribunal would be in Arusha, Tanzania (Res. 977). The judges of the Tribunal's Trial Chambers were elected by the General Assembly in May 1995 from a list approved by the Security Council. The Tribunal's first plenary session opened on 26 June in the Hague. On 27 June, Laity Kama (Senegal) was elected unanimously by the eleven judges as President of the Tribunal. The judges adopted their Rules of Procedure on the model of those of the Yugoslavia Tribunal.

INITIAL OBSTACLES

Created in November 1994, the Tribunal faced major problems before its installation was completed and before it became operational. While some of the problems were similar to those faced by the Yugoslavia Tribunal, some were specific to the material difficulties of setting up an ambitious, efficient international tribunal in a small African country. Paradoxically, it appeared, in 1997, that the Rwanda Tribunal had become more effective than the Yugoslavia Tribunal in obtaining custody of the main perpetrators of the genocide. In July 1995, besides the 11 judges, the Tribunal was only staffed by ten persons, including the Assistant Prosecutor, Honoré Rakotomanana, and the UN had not yet established the Tribunal's budget. The 1996 budget was approximately $40 million, and $30 million for 1997. Work had started on installing the Tribunal's seat in Arusha.

The first indictments were made in December 1995 against eight former Rwandan officials who were suspected of leading the genocide and had fled the country: their identity had not been revealed. On 19 February 1996, the Tribunal indicted two former Hutu leaders, in jail in Zambia. One was Georges Rutaganda, a businessman and a former vice president of the *interahamwe*, the Hutu militia which witnesses say carried out most of the massacres. He was accused of taking part in massacres in Kigali and Nyanza around 11 April 1994 and was thought of having played a significant role in the planning of the genocide. He was also a high-ranking official in the former ruling party, the National Revolutionary Movement for Democracy and Development, and a major investor in the Mille Collines Radio. Jean Paul Akayesu was the former mayor of Tapa, in the Gitarama préfecture, where at least 2000 Tutsis were killed. He is accused of encouraging the murder of a Tutsi teacher on 19 April 1994 in Taba, which set off widespread killings of Tutsis. Both are charged with genocide, crimes against humanity and violations of Common Article 3 of the Geneva Conventions. Both were transferred to Arusha in May 1996 and both pleaded not guilty in the initial hearing on 30 May. By June 1996, 18 Rwandans suspected of genocidal activities in 1994 were in custody: three in the Tribunal's jail in Arusha, ten in Cameroon, three in Belgium, one in Switzerland and one in Malawi. In September, a former pastor of the Seventh Day Adventist Church, who had been indicted by the Tribunal for taking part in massacres in the South-West of Rwanda, was arrested in the USA. Akayesu's trial was to start in October 1996, but was adjourned several times at the request of his lawyers. By October 1996, 25 individuals had been indicted. However, the first courtroom was only completed in November, without air conditioning. In October 1997, 21 defendants were detained in the Arusha jail.[13]

Governments' Uneven Co-operation

As for the Tribunal for Former Yugoslavia, the main reason for the slow start of the Rwanda Tribunal was the lack of support and co-operation of a number of governments. The Tribunal did not receive any substantial help from Kenya until July 1997, except for the arrest in Kenya and transfer to Arusha of Obed Ruzindana, in September 1996, accused of having participated in the massacre in the Mugonero Hospital in April 1994 and other alleged murders. 10 000 Rwandans took refuge in Kenya, including some of the leading planners and perpetrators of the genocide. President Daniel T. arap Moi stated initially that he would reject any summonses from the Tribunal and would arrest any of its members who entered the country. Mobutu's Zaire offered no help to the Tribunal. The Rwandan news agency asserted in May 1996 that Zaire gave safe haven to the 'entire former government which planned and supervised genocide in Rwanda along with the former army and Interahamwe militia'. At least four indicted Rwandans had fled to Zaire.

French justice has not co-operated with the Tribunal: at least two Rwandans accused of genocidal activities, a Catholic priest and a gynecologist, have found refuge in France. Judicial inquiries have been called off in one case, and have not been initiated in the other. Neither the French government nor the French military have offered any information or support to the Tribunal. The French attitude is no doubt linked to President Mitterand's support for Habyarimana as from the 1980s. France has provided military help to the Hutu-led government and armed forces, as from at least 1990 until April or May 1994, in material, armament and other logistical support, including the loan of instructors. Besides its humanitarian objective, the French Operation 'Turquoise' allowed Hutu leaders to escape into Zaire.

Other countries have given assistance to the Tribunal, subject to delays linked to legal extradition requirements or politics. Twelve Rwandan suspects were arrested in Cameroon in March and April 1996: one was transferred to Arusha in May 1996 and three in

January 1997. Elie Ndayambaje, former mayor of Muganza, was arrested in Belgium on 28 June 1995 and transferred to Arusha on 8 November 1996. He was charged with genocide, crimes against humanity, violations of common Article 3 of the Geneva Conventions and Additional Protocol II. His trial has been postponed to 1998. Joseph Kanyabashi, former mayor of Ngoma, was also transferred from Belgium to Arusha on 8 November 1996. Zambia has co-operated by allowing the transfer of three indicted Rwandans to Arusha in May 1996. Another suspect was transferred from the Ivory Coast to Arusha in November 1996.[14]

The USA has given substantial legal and financial support to the Tribunal, as it did for the Yugoslavia Tribunal. A US official announced in June 1996 that the USA had given $5.6 million to the Tribunal in cash contributions, as well as in personnel, goods, database development and information sharing. The USA has provided secure communications equipment, microfilm printer readers, photocopy machines, computers, cameras etc. The USA has worked closely with International Physicians for Human Rights, a Boston-based NGO, who have carried out exhumations of mass graves in Rwanda in preparation for prosecutions. A Rwanda Tribunal Documentation Center has been established in Washington, DC, which compiles unclassified documents on war crimes suspects and makes them available to the Tribunal. An additional commitment of $650 000 to support the Tribunal was announced in October 1996.

The USA, Denmark, the Netherlands and Norway have contributed expert personnel to the Office of the Prosecutor. The European Union has given ECU3 million to the Tribunal, has assisted in the protection of witnesses, and has provided legal assistance and help in setting up databases.[15] Financial problems have hampered the Tribunal's work. About 100 persons work for the Tribunal, out of a target of 350. A total of 145 investigators were to be employed, but their number has been reduced to 80: only 30 are actually working in the field, often in dangerous conditions. As there is no significant 'paper trail', prosecution is essentially based on witnesses' testimonies. Witnesses are wary of giving testimonies in the fear of retaliation.

Mismanagement

The slow and uncertain progress in the Tribunal's work and complaints submitted by Member States and staff members led the UN

General Assembly, by resolution of 7 June 1996, to request the Office of Internal Oversight to inspect the Tribunal in order to identify problems and recommend measures to enhance the efficient utilization of resources. The Office's report was submitted to the Assembly on 6 February 1997.[16] The Office found that the Tribunal was suffering from serious operational deficiencies in its management, deficiencies which developed from its inception. The tribunal's effectiveness had been negatively affected by the UN short-term funding arrangements, by the geographical separation of the Prosecutor's Office, located in Kigali, from the other organs of the Tribunal, based in Arusha, and by the lack of adequate infrastructure in both locations. In the Tribunal's Registry, not a single administrative area functioned effectively. The Registrar had (abusively) asserted that his function as Chief Administrative Officer gave him authority for all matters having administrative or financial implications. The Office of the Prosecutor had administrative, leadership and operational problems. Relationships between the Registry and the Office of the Prosecutor were often characterized by tension rather than co-operation. These difficulties were exacerbated by the recruitment of inexperienced or unqualified staff. Senior personnel in the UN headquarters' Department of Administration and Management and in the Office of Legal Affairs had failed to bear responsibility for the effectiveness of the Tribunal on the misperception of respect for the independence of the Tribunal. In fact, it seemed that the Yugoslavia Tribunal staff had been more 'nurtured' by the UN Office of Legal Affairs than the Rwanda Tribunal. Less negatively, there was no evidence of corrupt practices or misuse of funds.

Even more important than mismanagement, the Office found a serious error of strategy. The first Prosecutor had encouraged the Deputy Prosecutor to focus on national figures, a strategy which was not properly applied by the latter. This was the single most significant failing. One of the recommendations of the Office was that the Rwanda Tribunal and the Yugoslavia Tribunal should foster their mutual relationship. The latter's more established Registry should serve as a model and a relevant contact for the Arusha Registry.

On 26 February 1997, the Secretary-General accepted the resignation of Honoré Rakotomana, the Deputy Prosecutor and of Andronico Adede, Registrar. Bernard Muna (Cameroon) was appointed as Deputy Prosecutor, as well as a new Registrar, Agwu Okali (Nigeria), formerly with the UN Legal Office. The chiefs of personnel, finance and administration in the Registry were also replaced. A Deputy Registrar was appointed.[17]

1997 ACHIEVEMENTS

Following this necessary housecleaning, and as a result of political changes in neighbouring countries and pressures, the Tribunal was having more success in securing custody through extradition of high-level Rwandan former officials or personalities accused of having planned, encouraged or carried out the genocide, or of having committed other serious breaches of international humanitarian law. On 9 January 1997, Paul Biya, President of Cameroon, finally authorized the transfer to Arusha of four Rwandans accused of genocide and crimes against humanity, requested by the Tribunal six months before. Among them were: Théoneste Bagosora, former Director of Cabinet in the Rwandan Ministry of Defence, considered as one of the officials mainly responsible for the genocide; Professor Ferdinand Nahimana, an ideologist and founder of Radio Mille Collines, who is facing charges of conspiracy to commit genocide, direct and public incitement to commit genocide, complicity in genocide and crimes against humanity; and Anatole Nsengiyumva, former Lieutenant-Colonel in the Rwandan Armed Forces, alleged to have directed killings operations from the Gisenyi préfecture. They had been arrested in Cameroon in March 1996.

Following a visit to Kenya by Rwanda's Vice President, Paul Kagame, the Kenyan authorities arrested seven Rwandans on 18 July 1997, at the request of the Tribunal, to be transferred to Arusha. Among those arrested were: Jean Kambanda, former Prime Minister of the Interim Government that was promptly set up after the death of President Habyarimana; Pauline Nyiramasuhuko, former Minister of Family and Women Welfare, a member of the former President's government and of the Interim Government; Colonel, then General, Gratien Kabiligi, who served in the General Staff of the Rwandan Army until July 1994 and whose elite troops allegedly took part in the massacres; Hassan Ngeze, the journalist who published the lethal 'Ten Commandments of the Hutus';[18] – Aloys Ntabakuze, a former Commander of the Para-commando battalion of the Rwandan Armed Forces; and Sylvain Nsabimana, a former Prefect of Butare. Samuel Manishimwe, a former lieutenant of the Rwandan Armed Forces was arrested in Mombasa and transferred to Arusha on 12 August 1997. On 23 July, Georges Ruggiu, a Belgian journalist who worked with Radio Mille Collines, was transferred from Kenya to Arusha.

On-going hearings (in 1997) concerned 18 defendants. They all pleaded not guilty. Seven others had been indicted but not yet arrested.[19]

Parallel National Justice

While the International Tribunal was to judge the main organizers and perpetrators of the genocide and other crimes, the new Rwandan government was faced with the challenge of rendering fair justice to others who participated, at various levels, in the massacres. The genocide involved leaders' planning and organization and mass participation by ordinary people. The genocide had led to the breakdown of law and order and the near total destruction of the country's system of justice. Most members of the judiciary had been either killed or had fled to exile. Courts were looted, damaged or destroyed. The economy had collapsed. Between 1994 and 1996, with international assistance, Rwanda trained over 750 new judicial personnel – 320 magistrates, 90 assistant prosecutors, 250 investigators, 50 court registrars and 50 court clerks. Courtrooms and prosecutors' offices were repaired.

An 'Organic Law on the Organization and Prosecution of Genocide and Crimes against Humanity' was adopted in 1996 which classified suspects into four categories. Category 1 was reserved for the genocide leaders and their lieutenants – authorities at the national, prefectoral or communal level, or in a political party, the clergy or in a militia, sexual torturers, and 'notorious murderers who by virtue of the zeal or excessive malice with which they committed atrocities, distinguished themselves' in specific areas. In category 2 were persons whose criminal acts or whose acts of criminal participation place them among perpetrators or accomplices of intentional homicide or of serious assaults against the person causing death. In category 3 were persons whose criminal acts or acts of criminal participation render them guilty of other serious assaults against the person not resulting in death, and in category 4 were persons who committed offences against property.

The death penalty was reserved for category 1 offenders. Sentences for other offenders would vary according to a 'confession and guilty plea' programme. Category 2 offenders may be sentenced to seven to 11 years' imprisonment if they confess before charges are brought, 12 to 15 years if they confess after, and life imprisonment if convicted without confessing. Category 3 offenders, if they confess, may be sentenced to only one-third of the penalties mandated in the Rwandan criminal law. Out-of court compensation could be decided upon for offences against property. Specialized chambers, comprised of three magistrates with assessors, have exclusive jurisdiction over the genocide cases. There is no jury. Military offenders are tried by a specialized chamber of military courts.[20]

Following the genocide, more than 90 000 persons have been detained in overcrowded jails, waiting to be judged. The government has published a list of 1900 persons charged with genocide. In the first trial which started in Kibungo on 27 December 1996, two Hutus were condemned to death by firing squad for genocide. Sentences were subject to appeal. They were not assisted by a lawyer. By April 1997, 13 defendants had been condemned to death, but no executions had taken place. Two defendants were acquitted.[21]

CONCLUSION

While geography, history, culture, and political and economic conditions set apart Yugoslavia and Rwanda and their conflicts, a few similarities may be noted.

The Rwanda genocide had the characteristics of a particularly tragic episode in a long civil war, a political power struggle based on ethnic differences. The ethnic cleansing committed in the former Yugoslavia took place during demands for national sovereignty and competing territorial claims with a long history of past wars and exactions and a continuing hostility between the Orthodox Serbs, the Catholic Croats and the Bosnian Muslims. Neither Yugoslavia nor Rwanda have known democracy. In both countries and areas, the cycle of violence had been reinforced by a culture of impunity.

International intervention into these countries was possible because they are small countries, and because the public revelation of genocide and other atrocities forced the UN Security Council to focus on those crimes and to take, in both cases, measures which proved inadequate: humanitarian assistance in an on-going conflict in the case of Yugoslavia, without the benefit of military protection and without a political settlement in view – a peace-keeping mission in Rwanda reduced to a small group in the midst of a genocide.

In both cases, the creation of an international tribunal by the Security Council appears to have been a substitute, or an alibi for the lack of a timely, forceful intervention, or the lack of a credible threat of intervention. In both cases, governmental support to the Tribunals was uneven: some governments showed by their attitude, their inaction, their lack of co-operation and support, that they would be only too pleased if one or the other Tribunal proved a complete failure.

The Rwanda Tribunal was a slow starter due in part to the greater difficulties of physical installation in a small African country, and distance from major legal and research resources, in contrast with the installation of the Yugoslavia Tribunal in the Hague, seat of the International Court of Justice, with easy communications and access to universities and other learned centres. The Rwanda Tribunal suffered from serious management and staffing problems. It proved initially difficult to attract to Arusha and Kigali high-level legal specialists and experienced judicial practitioners, in view of the relative isolation of these stations from European or North American legal resources, and because of inadequate financial compensation offered to candidates.

The Rwanda Tribunal has benefited from the legal and administrative experience gained by the Yugoslavia Tribunal, an effective judicial machinery, with its own Rules of Procedures, which has overcome substantive legal obstacles and has rendered two sentences. However, the Rwanda Tribunal suffered from the decision that only one Prosecutor would serve both Tribunals: it is probable that the first Prosecutor gave more attention to the Tribunal in The Hague than to that in Arusha. It also suffered from the lack of support and monitoring on the part of the Administrative and Legal Services in the UN headquarters in New York. Both Tribunals continue to suffer from inadequate financing.

While the Yugoslavia Tribunal has completed two trials, none of the on-going cases of the Rwanda Tribunal has yet been completed, in part because of the initial internal problems of the Tribunal, in part because of the initial difficulties in obtaining custody of indicted individuals, and in part because of the delaying tactics of defendants' lawyers. However, by the end of 1997, the Rwanda Tribunal has obtained custody of several of the major leaders and perpetrators of the genocide, thanks to the co-operation of several

African and European countries. In contrast, the Yugoslavia Tribunal has not been able to obtain the arrest and custody of the main, indicted authors of the genocide and other crimes, as a result of the non-co-operation of the Yugoslavia government, the limited co-operation of the Croat government, and the refusal of the US and other Western governments to instruct NATO forces to arrest them.

There is no problem of national justice in competition with the International Tribunal for Former Yugoslavia, in so far as none of the parties to the conflict has engaged in serious judicial prosecution and trials of alleged war criminals in their country. On the other hand, there is a built-in injustice in the fact that the main perpetrators of the Rwanda genocide may only be sentenced to imprisonment by the international tribunal, while national courts may condemn those who have followed orders at lower levels of responsibility to a death sentence.

Another problem specific to the Rwanda Tribunal is that it may be accused of only trying Hutus, while the Tutsis appear to have taken revenge on Hutu returnees and Hutu refugees who had fled to Zaire. The delaying tactics of the Kabila government, which have prevented any timely and independent investigation by the UN of allegedly hidden massacres of Hutu refugees in Zaire, also prevent the identification, prosecution and judgment of perpetrators by national or international justice. This situation, which is well beyond the control of the Rwanda Tribunal, may damage its image, although the Tribunal has been properly constituted as an international tribunal and is conducting its prosecutions and trials in a fair and independent manner in accordance with its Statute and Rules of Procedures.

The principal objective of the Yugoslavia and Rwanda Tribunals is to identify, prosecute and judge those persons mainly responsible for genocide and other serious violations of international humanitarian law in the former Yugoslavia and in Rwanda. By imposing a fair and independent judicial process over individual civilian and military leaders, it was also hoped, as a consequential and perhaps unrealistic objective, that the archaic urge of revenge and physical retribution over a whole ethnic or religious group would be assuaged, a group which, in turn, should not suffer from long-term collective guilt. The 'endless cycle of ethnic violence and retribution' would finally be broken. The trials would prevent future violence and contribute to the restoration of peace.

It is premature to pass judgment on the contribution of the Tribunals to these objectives: both Tribunals are far from having completed their principal judicial tasks. An objective assessment of the possible effect of their work and judgments on the populations concerned will take years. In the meantime, on a legal and judicial plane, the creation of the Tribunals constitutes a concrete and welcome advance in the long-abandoned field of international criminal law, in spite of the political and legal problems they have experienced. Their experience, their success or their failure are being watched carefully by the governments currently negotiating the Statute of a permanent International Criminal Court, by the NGOs and by the media. The Tribunals' problems and achievements, the effectiveness of their funding, of their administration, of their legal and judicial arrangements may substantially affect these negotiations.

10 The Slow Birth of an International Criminal Court

On 17 December 1996, the UN General Assembly decided that 'a diplomatic conference of plenipotentiaries shall be held in 1998, with a view to finalizing and adopting a convention on the establishment of an international criminal court' (Res. 51/207). The Preparatory Committee created by the Assembly had noted in its report the co-operative spirit in which debates took place and 'the commitment of the international community' to this establishment. This new spirit of the 'international community', long opposed to or uninterested by the creation of an international criminal court, was related generally to the belated realization that a growing number of war crimes, crimes against humanity and genocides were being committed in a number of countries with impunity. In the lack of effective, independent and fair national justice in many countries, the need for an impartial international court had become more evident and urgent. This resolution was hailed by the promoters and supporters of an International Criminal Court as a significant victory and an historical advance for international justice.

As significant progress over the victors' justice imposed on the vanquished by the Nuremberg and Tokyo tribunals, the creation of the tribunals for former Yugoslavia and Rwanda had shown that it was possible to set up a really international criminal tribunal, to appoint judges, prosecutors, registrars and other judicial personnel, to agree on fair and equitable rules of procedure, to prosecute and judge individuals accused of serious violations of international humanitarian law. At the same time, the creation of these tribunals by the Security Council was criticized. Was it a legitimate function for the Council to set up a judiciary body? Should such a decision be taken by representatives of a small group of countries, a decision subject to the veto power of the permanent members? Linking the creation of these tribunals to Chapter VII of the Charter led to the assumption that these tribunals would be dissolved by the Council when peace and security was restored. Why choose

186

the former Yugoslavia and Rwanda, with geographical and time limitations? What about crimes committed by the Khmer Rouge, war crimes and crimes against humanity committed by Iraq, or by the USA, or by many other countries?

Some of these legitimate questions have been answered by the creation of a permanent International Criminal Court (ICC), the competence of which should eventually extend to all countries. Its creation has been preceded by multilateral intergovernmental negotiations and has resulted in a formal international treaty, to be approved and ratified by countries.

Credit must be given to scholarly and professional organizations such as the Association internationale de droit pénal (AIDP) and human rights NGOs for initiating and promoting the concept and creation of an ICC. AIDP has been a historical leader on this question since 1926.[1] In 1927, during the Paris Congress of the 'Fédération internationale des ligues des droits de l'homme' (FIDH), the Austrian League of Human Rights proposed to promote the creation of a 'Permanent International Court of Moral Justice', the action of which would ensure an effective and international protection of human rights within the framework of the League of Nations. This proposal was adopted by the Congress and has been included as one of the main demands of the Federation since then.[2] Since 1976, the Istituto Superiore Internazionale di Scienzi Criminali (ISISC) has followed AIDP's path and has, in particular, produced two documents elaborated at meetings held in Siracusa in December 1994 and 1995: the 1995 'Siracusa Draft' and the 1996 'Updated Siracusa Draft', integrating the International Law Commission (ILC) 1994 Draft Statute for an International Criminal Court with amendments proposed by a group of experts and scholars. During the intergovernmental negotiations, a coalition of hundreds of NGOs has constantly encouraged and assisted delegations with legal and other advice with the ultimate objective of creating an independent Court.

Article VI of the 1948 Genocide Convention prescribed that:

Persons charged with genocide or any of the other acts enumerated in Article III shall be tried by a competent tribunal of the State in the territory of which the act was committed, or by such international penal tribunal as may have jurisdiction with respect to those Contracting Parties which shall have accepted its jurisdiction.

In part B of the same resolution adopted on 9 December 1948 (Res. 260 (III)), the General Assembly considered that there would be an increasing need of an international judicial organ for the trial of certain crimes under international law and invited the International Law Commission (ILC) to study the desirability and possibility of establishing such an organ for the trial of persons charged with genocide or other crimes. The ILC was requested to pay attention to the possibility of establishing a Criminal Chamber of the International Court of Justice.

In 1950, the General Assembly set up a Special Committee to prepare a Draft Statute for an ICC, which produced a text in 1951, revised in 1953. This text was tabled by the Assembly in 1953 and 1954 on the pretext that the crime of aggression had not been defined, and indefinitely deferred in 1957. In reality, a number of countries were opposed to the project, including the USSR and other Socialist countries ideologically hostile to 'bourgeois' international justice. In 1989, the issue was raised again by Trinidad and Tobago in a Special Session of the General Assembly, suggesting the creation of a specialized ICC for drug-related offences. In 1990, the Assembly invited the ILC to consider the possibility of establishing an ICC or other international criminal trial mechanism (Res. 45/41). As requested by the Assembly in 1992 and 1993, the ILC prepared a Draft Statute for an ICC in 1993, revised in 1994.[3]

THE 1994 DRAFT STATUTE

The Court envisaged by the 60-article Draft Statute will be created by international treaty, not by the Security Council. It would not be part of the UN, but would have a relationship agreement with the Organization. The Court would only exercise jurisdiction over the 'most serious crimes of concern to the international community as a whole' and would be 'complementary to national criminal justice systems in cases where such trial procedures may not be available or may be ineffective' (Preamble). It will be a permanent court in the sense that it will be available when required, but it will not have a large infrastructure or permanent staff.[4] The Court would have jurisdiction over two types of crimes (Article 20):

- Four crimes under general international law: genocide, aggression, serious violations of the laws and customs applicable in armed conflict, and crimes against humanity.
- 'Exceptional serious crimes of international concern' established under specific treaties listed in an Annex. These include war crimes in the 1949 Geneva Conventions and 1977 Protocol I, crimes defined in the 1973 Convention on Apartheid, the 1984 Convention against Torture and other antiterrorism multilateral conventions, including the 1988 UN Convention against illicit traffic in narcotic drugs and psychotropic substances. The Court would only have jurisdiction under these conventions to try those crimes reaching a certain threshold of gravity, as determined by the Court.

Except in the case of genocide and aggression, the Court's jurisdiction would be explicitly consensual and limited: it would apply only to states that have become parties to the Statute and only with respect to those crimes over which that state has accepted the Court's jurisdiction (Article 21). The Court would have jurisdiction when a state party to the Statute lodges a complaint against an individual (or individuals), and the state with custody of the suspect and the state on whose territory the crime occurred agree to accept the jurisdiction of the Court. The Court would have inherent jurisdiction in the case of genocide. The primacy of the Security Council in matters of peace and security would be recognized: the Court is given jurisdiction over any of the crimes identified in the Statute if the Council, acting under Chapter VII of the Charter, had referred the matter to it. The Council has to determine that aggression has been committed before an individual can be charged as an aggressor. No prosecution may be commenced 'arising from a situation which is being dealt with by the Security Council as a threat to or a breach of the peace or an act of aggression under Chapter VII of the Charter, unless the Security Council otherwise decides (Article 23(3)).

The Draft Statute calls for 18 judges, of 18 different nationalities, representing 'the principal legal systems of the world', each elected by an absolute majority of States parties to the Treaty for a nine-year non-renewable term. The Court would have four organs (Article 5):

- A Presidency, composed of the President, two Vice Presidents and two Alternate Vice Presidents, each elected by an absolute majority of the Court's judges. Each serving a three-year term. They will have overall responsibility for the Court's management, as well as important pre-trial and post-trial judicial functions;

- A five-member Trial Chamber and a six-member Appeals Chamber, and a special five-judge Chamber to consider the application of the laws of pardon, parole, or commutation of the state in which the accused international criminal is being held. Decisions of the Trial Chamber could be reversed by the Appeals Chamber, requiring a quorum of six and a majority vote;
- The Procuracy, intended as an independent investigative arm of the Court, would be headed by a Prosecutor, assisted by Deputies and qualified staff. Both the Prosecutor and the Deputies would be elected by an absolute majority of the states party to the Treaty, by secret ballot.
- The Registry would consist of a Registrar, to be chosen by secret ballot for a renewable five-year term, by an absolute majority of the judges. The Registrar would be assisted by support staff.

In the controversial issue of trials *in absentia*, opposed by common law countries and supported conditionally by civil law countries, the ILC has leaned towards the latter by establishing a general rule and exceptions (Article 37). The general rule is that the accused should be present during the trial. The Trial Chamber could order that the trial proceed in the absence of the accused in the following cases: ill-health or security risks to an accused, continued disruption of the trial, escape from custody or breach of bail. The Chamber would ensure that the rights of the accused are respected.

The Statute endorses a number of well-established legal and judiciary principles: the principle of legality (*nullum crimen sine lege*), presumption of innocence, *non bis in idem* (Articles 39, 40 and 42). The rights of the accused (Article 41) reflect closely those set forth in Article 14 of the International Covenant on Civil and Political Rights. The applicable penalties are a term of life imprisonment, or of imprisonment for a specified number of years, and/or a fine (Article 47). As for the Yugoslavia and Rwanda tribunals, the ICC would not be authorized to impose the death penalty, in accordance with the welcome evolution of national criminal justice in many countries with the encouragement of international instruments at the global and regional levels.[5]

Review by the *Ad Hoc* Committee

In December 1994, the Assembly rejected the ILC's recommend-ation to convene an international conference of plenipotentiaries to study the Draft Statute, but decided to establish an *ad hoc* com-mittee open to all States Members of the UN or Members of specialized agencies or of the IAEA to review the issues arising from the Draft Statute (Res. 49/53). The Ad Hoc Committee met for two sessions of two weeks, in April and August 1995 and es-sentially discussed issues rather than drafting a text. The agree-ments were few and differences many. Members of the Committee expressed a wide measure of support for the establishment of an ICC which would ensure that the perpetrators of serious interna-tional crimes were brought to justice and deter future occurrences of such crimes. There was also agreement that the proposed court should be established as an independent judicial organ by means of a multilateral treaty. However, the Committee reported that the participating states differed so markedly on the major substantive and administrative issues that it would be more effective to com-bine further discussions with the actual drafting of a consolidated text of a Statute/Convention for the Court.[6]

In December 1995, the General Assembly established a prepara-tory committee, again open to all Member States of the UN and other UN agencies. The Committee was not only to discuss issues but also to draft texts, with a view to preparing a widely accept-able consolidated text of a convention for an ICC as a next step towards consideration by a conference of plenipotentiaries (Res. 50/46). It seemed that the delaying tactics of a few member states in creating one committee after another were finally unable to stop the new international impetus to create an ICC.

Review by the Preparatory Committee

The Committee met in March–April and August 1996, and in Feb-ruary, August and December 1997. Its last meeting was held from 16 March to 3 April 1998. The following review recalls the main points of agreement identified by the Preparatory Committee. Leaving aside a number of technical points, the main issue revolves on the degree of autonomy to be granted to the Court versus member states, national courts and the UN.

THE MAIN ISSUES

Relationship with the UN

The Committee generally agreed with the Ad Hoc Committee's conclusion that the Court should be an independent institution established by a multilateral treaty, in relationship with the UN. A close relationship with the UN was considered essential to establish its universality and standing. However, the terms of this relationship would determine the degree of independence of the Court vs. the UN. Other proposals such as making the Court a principal organ of the UN, in parallel to the International Court of Justice (Canada), or a UN specialized agency (France) were not retained.

The role of the Security Council in 'triggering' cases was another contentious issue. Four of the five permanent members, particularly the US and France, favoured a strong role for the Council. Some among them would limit the Court to cases referred to it by the Council, a suggestion which would be unacceptable to most states, many of whom are opposed to the 'undemocratic' role played by the Council. The US position is that the Council's responsibility to promote international peace and security requires that its interests be protected in cases that have security dimensions. In the words of David J. Scheffer, Chief US Envoy for War Crimes Issues:

> In the absence of prior Council approval, the permanent court should not hear a case that clearly pertains to an ongoing Council operation under Chapter VI (peacekeeping) or Chapter VII (peace enforcement) . . . It is equally important that the Security Council be empowered to refer cases and situations, large and small, to a permanent court and to require, if necessary, judicial enforcement under Chapter VII.[7]

In December 1997, the UK adopted a more liberal position: it opted for the 'Singapore compromise' that would allow the Court to investigate and prosecute any case unless the Security Council voted to stop its proceedings. This would require all five permanent members of the Council to agree to this decision.

The issue was that of the degree of autonomy given to the Court, and more precisely, to the Prosecutor, and of the relationship between the legal authority of the Court and the political authority of the Council. Was the Court to be subordinate to the political decisions of the Council in all cases, or only in cases when a situation has been submitted to the Council, or will the Court have broad inherent jurisdiction?

The Court's Jurisdiction

On the Court's jurisdiction, four core crimes were being considered: aggression, genocide, crimes against humanity and war crimes. There was general agreement on the importance of limiting the Court's jurisdiction to the most serious crimes of concern to the international community as a whole, so as to avoid trivializing its role and functions and interfering with the jurisdiction of national courts. However, some delegations held the view that such crimes as international terrorism, illicit drug trafficking and attacks against UN and associated personnel should be included in the list of offences to be prosecuted by the Court under the category of treaty-based crimes.

While there was general agreement to include genocide, crimes against humanity and war crimes in the Statute, the USA and the UK had opposed the inclusion of aggression. A US official said that the lack of any accepted definition for aggression, especially for the purpose of individual accountability, was the major reason for non-inclusion. The matter could be included 'ten years or so at a review conference'. On the other hand, Germany and a number of other states wanted the crime of aggression or crimes against peace, one of the counts in the Statutes and judgments of the Nuremberg and Tokyo Tribunals, included in the Court's Statute. Italy thought that the failure to include aggression in the jurisdiction of the Court would send a message of impunity to prospective aggressors.[8] Many states supported the extension of the inherent jurisdiction of the Court to cover all core crimes, and not only genocide as provided for in the Draft Statute. For them, there was no reason to distinguish between all core crimes, as crimes often overlap. As an opposite view, China considered that inherent jurisdiction for genocide 'goes against both the principle of State sovereignty and the principle of complementarity'.[9]

The principle of complementarity has been used to reflect the juridictional relationship between the new court and national courts. The USA and France joined China in their insistence that their own justice system should have primacy over the International Court, particularly in respect of their own military personnel assigned to humanitarian or enforcement operations. The final draft adopted by the Preparatory Committee in September 1997 used the 'unwillingness or genuine inability' of a state to carry out the investigation or prosecution as criteria for determining the cases over which the Court would have jurisdiction, where a case is being, or has been, investigated or prosecuted by a state with jurisdiction over it.[10] Still unresolved was the role of amnesty laws, such as those adopted in El Salvador or in South Africa.

The Role of the Prosecutor

The Draft Statute precludes the prosecutor from initiating an investigation unless a situation has been referred to him/her by a Security Council resolution or by a state. Several countries, mostly from Europe and South America, would give the prosecutor the power to initiate an investigation without the approval of the Security Council or any other organization, a power granted to the prosecutors of the Yugoslavia and Rwanda Tribunals within the more limited geographical scope of action of these bodies. Other states, including India and China, wanted cases to be initiated only by governments and to proceed only with the consent of those countries affected. The USA made a proposal under which only the prosecutor would lodge a complaint against individuals. The Security Council and governments would not target individuals, but ask the prosecutor to investigate 'situations' without specifying individuals allegedly responsible.

The Financing of the Court

The financing of the Court is also related to its independence. A number of countries have proposed that the Court should be financed by the UN regular budget, as a reliable funding basis. However, if the Court is mainly financed by the UN, an option rejected by the USA, the Court would be dependent on the organization, its member states, its critical financial position and its complex budgetary and financial procedures. The USA has proposed that the Court's general budget should be borne by state parties according to the formula of the Universal Postal Union. When the Security Council refers an aggression situation to the Court, the UN should pay for the costs of the case. When a state submits a complaint to the Court, it should contribute to the costs of the case. Voluntary contributions should be allowed.

Other Issues

There was broad support for an 18-judge court, and for a nine-year, non-renewable term. It was considered important that the judges be elected on the basis of equitable geographical representation, possibly with a gender balance. Bassiouni[11] expressed regrets that the important issue of victim compensation has not been addressed by the ILC nor by the Preparatory Committee. It was also ignored by the Statutes of the Yugoslavia and Rwanda Tribunals, which only granted to the Tribunals the right to order the return of property or proceeds acquired by criminal conduct to their rightful owners (Articles 24 and 23), i.e. the right of material restitution. A broader right to reparation, including measures of compensation and rehabilitation has been proposed in the Joinet and van Boven reports:[12] it was finally included in the Statute of the ICC.

The Joinet report has proposed that, at the national level, a victim should have the right to institute proceedings on his or her behalf where the authorities fail to do so, or to become an associated party. This option should be extended to NGOs able to show proof of long-standing activities for the protection of the victims concerned.[13] At the international level, a comparable right might be granted to victims and NGOs. As it is however unlikely that states will allow them to bring a complaint to the ICC, victims, victims' associations and NGOs should at least have the right to become an associated party ('*partie civile*') to a trial before the Court so that their interests may be properly represented and their claims considered.

THE ROME CONFERENCE – 15 JUNE–17 JULY 1998

On 17 July 1998, the UN Diplomatic Conference held in Rome decided to establish a permanent International Criminal Court by adopting its Statute by a vote of 120 in favour to 7 against, with 21 abstentions. The USA, together with China, Israel, Libya, Iraq, Qatar and Yemen, voted against the establishment of the Court. UN Secretary-General Kofi Annan declared that this was a 'giant step forward in the march towards universal human rights and the rule of law'. The Statute will enter into force following the ratification, acceptance, approval or accession of 60 States.

The vote, after five weeks of difficult, at times acrimonious, negotiations, was introducing radically important innovations into relations between States, eroding their sovereign prerogatives and establishing a new relationship between the national courts and international justice. The Statute was the final result of battles and compromises between the determination of many 'like-minded' countries to set up an independent court, with the strong support of NGOs, the fears of the US and France that their military personnel on peacekeeping missions might be indicted for war crimes by an overly independent court, the frustrated wishes of some countries to include nuclear weapons among banned weapons (India), or to add the crime of terrorism among core crimes (Sri Lanka). Some countries protested against the powers granted to the Prosecutor (China), or against the non-inclusion of the death penalty (Singapore). Most non-aligned and Arab countries opposed the creation of the Court. The US delegates objected to two key points in the Statute: the prosecutor's power to initiate investigations and the court's jurisdiction over crimes committed by citizens of non-signatory countries. After the vote, American officials promised active opposition to the ratification of the Statute by other countries and to the eventual operations of the court, in a cynical reversal of their earlier support for the punishment of genociders and war criminals, and in total contradiction to the decisive role of the USA in the creation of and support for the Nuremberg, Tokyo, ex-Yugoslavia and Rwanda Tribunals.

Only the main elements of the Statute are briefly summarized hereunder.[14]

- The Court will be a permanent institution with the power to exercise jurisdiction over persons for the most serious crimes of international concern, and is to be complementary to national criminal jurisdictions. National courts have primacy in investigating and prosecuting crimes, unless the State is unwilling or genuinely unable to carry out the investigation or prosecution.
- The Court will not be part of the UN: it will be brought into relationship with the UN through an agreement. Its seat will be in The Hague.
- Its jurisdiction will be limited to four crimes: genocide, crimes against humanity, war crimes and the crime of aggression: this list, in our view, properly excludes other crimes which might have diluted the Court's impact (Art. 17, 1, 2, 5).[15]

Although the Preamble of the Statute refers to an 'independent' Court, a number of qualifications limits its powers.

1. The Court may exercise its jurisdiction only for crimes committed on the territory of a State Party to the Statute, or of a State which has accepted to jurisdiction of the Court, or for crimes committed by a person who is a national of such a State.
2. The Presecutor's investigation has to be authorized by a Pre-Trial Chamber of the Court.
3. As another limitation to the Prosecutor's powers, no investigation or prosecution may be commenced or proceeded with for a period of 12 months after the Security Council, in a resolution adopted under Chapter VII of the UN Charter, has requested the Court to that effect – that request may be renewed by the Council under the same conditions. This reflected the Singapore compromise, which was previously rejected by the USA (Art. 12, 15, 16).

The general principles of criminal law are confirmed: *ne bis in idem, nullum crimen sine lege, nulla poena sine lege* and non-retroactivity *ratione personae* (Art. 20, 22, 23, 24). The accused 'shall be present during the trial': no trial *in absentia* is allowed except when the accused 'continues to disrupt the trial'. The presumption of innocence and the rights of the accused are confirmed (Art. 63, 66, 67).

The Court is composed of the following organs: the Presidency – an Appeals Division, a Trial Division and a Pre-Trial Division – the Office of the Prosecutor and the Registry.

As recommended by Bassiouni, Joinet and van Boven, the Court will establish principles relating to reparations to, or in respect of, victims, including restitution, compensation and rehabilitation. The Court may make an order directly against a convicted person specifying appropriate reparations to, or in respect of, victims (Art. 75). Applicable penalties include imprisonment not to exceed a maximum of 30 years, life imprisonment when justified by the extreme gravity of the crime and the individual circumstances of the convicted person – and, in addition, as applicable, a fine, a forfeiture of proceeds, property and assets derived directly or indirectly from the crime, without prejudice to the rights of bona fide third parties (Art. 77). Sentences are subject to appeal by the Prosecutor or the convicted person – either party may apply to the Appeals Chamber to revise a final judgment of conviction or sentence on established grounds (Art. 81, 84). States Parties have a general obligation to cooperate fully with the Court in its investigation and prosecution of crimes within the jurisdiction of the Court (Art. 86).

The expenses of the Court and the Assembly of States Parties will be provided by assessed contributions made by States Parties – based on the UN scale of assessment for its regular budget – in addition to funds provided by the UN in particular in relation to the expenses incurred due to referrals by the Security Council, and to voluntary contributions (Art. 115, 116, 117).

Article 124 includes a controversial transitional provision, introduced as a demand by the French delegation, itself under pressure by its military: a State, on becoming a party to the Statute, may declare that, for a period of seven years after the entry into force of the Statute for the State concerned, it does not accept the jurisdiction of the Court with respect to war crimes when a crime is alleged to have been committed by its nationals or on its territory: as stated by Amnesty International at the conclusion of the Conference, 'a few powerful countries . . . were all along more concerned to shield possible criminals from trials rather than producing a charter for victims'.[16]

CONCLUSION

The approval of the Statute of an International Criminal Court in July 1998 by 120 countries is a historical achievement for the world. It is due to those States which led the determined campaign, with the strong support of many NGOs, to create an independent Court, in order to fight against the all-too-frequent impunity of those leaders responsible for genocide, crimes against humanity, war crimes and crimes of aggression, to respond to the suffering of millions of victims, and, hopefully, to act as a deterrent for more violence and violations of international human rights and humanitarian law.

The Rome Conference was a success, in overcoming the many substantial and procedural objections raised by powerful and other countries on different grounds. The approved Statute, which benefited from the experience acquired by the ex-Yugoslavia and Rwanda Tribunals, ensures a fair degree of independence to the Court and its Prosecutor while retaining a role for the Security Council, a compromise between idealists and realists. It is unfortunate that two permanent members of the Security Council, the USA and China, have voted against the creation of the Court, as their cooperation and participation, particularly those of the USA, would be needed in the planning, installing and developing the Court. It is to be hoped that the US government and Senate will later adhere to the

Statute, after the Court has gained some experience and showed its capacity.

The new Court, like the Yugoslavia and the Rwanda Tribunals, will lack its own police force. In this respect, the Court will be dependent on governments' respect of their commitments, on their good faith and goodwill, to obtain custody of indicted individuals.

When the Statute of the Court enters into force, which will require a number of years, more years will, again, be needed to assess its usefulness and 'effectiveness' on two points.

1. Has the Court been allowed by governments or by the Security Council to indict, obtain custody of and judge the main perpetrators of the 'most serious crimes of concern to the international community as a whole'?
2. A more difficult and uncertain assessment will be to determine whether the Court's mere existence and/or its judgments have acted as a deterrent to more grave violations of international humanitarian law. While it would be unwise to set high expectations on the potential capacity of the future Court to act as such a deterrent, the creation of the ICC is in itself an impressive progress in international criminal law by providing, at the global level, an international judiciary mechanism to prosecute and judge individuals alleged to have committed the 'most serious crimes of international concern'.

11 International Justice and Politics

The dream of an independent justice has taken hold only in a few countries which believe in and try to respect Montesquieu's doctrine of separation of powers. Even in those countries, as in others, national justice is inherently part of a country's historical, political and cultural background, and related to its economic and social evolution. Judges, as citizens of their time, are not judging in an ivory tower. While called upon to apply the law, they are aware of and sensitive to their country's past and current problems, of the evolution of mores.

At the international level, in an anarchic world of sovereign but unequal and unruly nations tied by a loose network of unenforceable treaties and customs, the mere existence of international jurisdictions is almost a miracle. Or is it a mirage bound to fade away when confronted with the harsh realities and exigencies of national interest, national prestige, national and international politics?

IMPUNITY

In the world 'non-system' of voluntary international co-operation, massive exactions have been committed and are currently being committed with impunity.

- Turkish governments still deny the reality of the well-documented Armenian genocide.
- It took many years before Lenin's and Stalin's crimes were revealed, the extent of which surpassed in numbers of innocent deaths the Nazi atrocities. Soviet leaders have enjoyed total impunity in spite of the end of Communism in the new Russia.
- The Khmer Rouge leaders have not been judged, leaving aside the recent fake trial of Pol Pot.
- No charges have been levelled against the Indonesian leaders responsible for the 1965 massacres, who still rule the country.

- The Chinese Communist regime prevents the opening of any independent investigation into, or even acknowledgement for, the millions of innocent Chinese deaths caused by the regime.
- Serbs still defy the UN Security Council by rejecting the jurisdiction of the Yugoslavia Tribunal, and in refusing to arrest and transfer to the Hague the indicted perpetrators of massacres and torture. The Bosnian Serbs showed their total lack of respect for elementary humanitarian considerations by appointing, in September 1997, an alleged war criminal as chairman of their Human Rights Commission.[1]
- Tutsis are taking revenge over the Hutus by killing refugees in ex-Zaire in collusion with Kabila's forces. UN inquiry missions and human rights groups have been expelled from the country, while evidence of killings is being suppressed.
- Islamists in Algeria are slaughtering villagers, men, women, children and babies, as well as teachers, journalists, other educated professionals and government and military leaders. The terror practices of the Khmer Rouge have found a new life with the Islamist hard-liners. One of their leaders declared in January 1996: 'We are ready to sacrifice two-thirds of the population to enable the last third to succeed in Allah's way'.[2]

The 'international community', or more precisely the major powers, appear helpless or unwilling to intervene in order to prevent or stop massacres, or even to interfere with the adoption of unwelcome UN resolutions or declarations.

Repentance

In the apparent prevailing darkness, one may observe a few rays of light. One is the recognition of responsibility for war crimes or crimes against humanity, as an active or passive accomplice, by representatives of states or other institutions, even if such recognition and apologies come many years after the events. Concerning the Holocaust, President Chirac finally recognized in July 1995 the responsibility of the French state in the persecution of foreign, then French, Jews during World War II. Former French Presidents had espoused the Gaullist fiction that, as the Vichy regime was illegal, its acts did not engage France's responsibility. The anti-Jewish laws, and the role played by Vichy dignitaries and its police in the deportation of more than 75 000 Jews, were ignored. The French

Catholic Church followed, in September 1997, with a declaration of repentance, asking God and the Jewish people for forgiveness for the silence of most of its bishops on the regime's anti-Jewish measures. In contrast, by the end of 1997, the Vatican was still not ready to make a similar declaration: the Second Vatican Council had only condemned Catholic anti-semitism in 1965.[3] In May 1997, Prime Minister John Howard of Australia made a personal apology to tens of thousands of Aborigines who were taken from their parents under a former policy of forced assimilation. His government had released a human rights report stating that the forced assimilation amounted to genocide.[4]

Judiciary Advances

The Yugoslavia Tribunal received a long- and much-needed boost when, in October 1997, ten Croats indicted of war crimes and crimes against humanity surrendered to be judged by the Tribunal. The ten included Dario Kordic, charged with commanding troops who murdered Muslims in Central Bosnia. The surrender was the result of intensive political and economic pressures by the US on the Croatian President, Franjo Tudjman. The indictees were given assurance that their cases would be brought to trial in no more than three to five months.[5] Another encouraging sign is the co-operation of national justice with International Tribunals. Following Djajic's trial in May 1997 (see Chapter 6), in September 1997, another Bosnian Serb, Nikola Jorgic, was tried by a German court and found guilty on 11 counts of genocide and 30 counts of murder. The Hague Tribunal has asked national courts to assist in coping with its caseload. German prosecutors are investigating 48 other persons on charges of genocide and other war crimes in the Former Yugoslavia.[6]

AN ASSESSMENT

These limited advances do not compensate for the recurrence of mass atrocities in many parts of the world. As a consequence, one may be, or become, cynical, or at least skeptical, about the impact of international humanitarian and human rights law and of the emerging international criminal law on the behaviour and decisions of government leaders, other officials and military chiefs, or guerilla leaders. Is the creation of international law only an intellectual and diplomatic exercise devoid of practical effect? Is international humanitarian law just a dream entertained by wishful thinking international lawyers and idealists who think that a ratified convention will be respected by a fighting army or by guerillas? Do those who promoted, initiated and drafted these instruments, those diplomats who approved the final text, really believe that those governments which ratified these instruments will really apply them? Furthermore, most violations of international humanitarian law are now committed in civil wars, rather than in international conflicts. They are often carried out by undisciplined and uncontrolled rebel fighters, often children, who have no knowledge of or interest in the Geneva or Genocide Conventions. In the same vein, as the purpose of international criminal law is for national and international courts to obtain custody of individuals accused of genocide, war crimes, crimes against humanity, to judge and, as applicable, sentence them, one may wonder at the audacity, or the delusion of those (including the author) who have fought for the creation of an International Criminal Court, handicapped *ab initio* by its lack of any enforcement powers.

On the other hand, the realization that enormous obstacles stand in the way of international criminal justice should not deter those who believe that incremental progress may be obtained through the efforts of 'like-minded' governments, NGO activists, the media and public opinion pressures. These obstacles include government resistance on the grounds of national sovereignty, the magnitude of exactions, revived nationalistic, ethnic and religious hatreds, the evil side of human nature.

Judiciary progress is dependent on the advance of the democratic ideal, on political and cultural pluralism, on the building of democratic institutions, on the commitment of leaders and people. The reform of political regimes is an ambitious but necessary target. As most exactions are initiated, caused by, and/or covered by army-supported authoritarian regimes, all efforts to promote democracy should be encouraged, without ignoring the economic and social problems which may be at the origin of internal armed conflicts, while these very conflicts exacerbate economic and social problems. Mature democracy would ensure the respect of human rights and fundamental freedoms and provide, *inter alia*, for an independent judiciary. The more limited and technical judiciary approach has been that of this book. Its premise is that justice must be rendered: perpetrators of exactions must be identified, prosecuted and sentenced by independent and fair tribunals. Victims, or survivors, have the right to know, the right to justice and the right to compensation and reparation. Justice must be rendered either by national justice, or by international justice when national courts cannot offer guarantees of independence and impartiality, or are physically unable to function. As a consequence, perpetrators will no longer enjoy impunity, while potential perpetrators will fear retribution and refrain from committing exactions. The assumption is that justice rendered will eliminate the need for revenge and will lead to pardon and reconciliation.

Democracy takes a long time to grow roots. National courts of justice are as yet unable or unwilling to deal with all the crimes against humanity committed in the world. The two International Criminal Tribunals are temporary courts with a limited jurisdiction: hence the need to create a permanent International Criminal Court. The reward of the idealists will be that some of their efforts in promoting democratic and judiciary progress will succeed, even if all their expectations are not fulfilled. The approval, in July 1998, of the Statute of the International Criminal Court shows that a growing number of governments and peoples are now convinced that international justice should, if not prevail over politics, at least play the role of a legal model and moral conscience for the world's leaders.

Notes

'Nuremberg' will be used here in preference to 'Nuremburg', which is found in a number of resolutions, texts and books. *IHT* = *International Herald Tribune*.

CHAPTER 1

1. The first definition is quoted by Françoise Bory in *Origin and Development of International Humanitarian Law* (Geneva: ICRC, 1982) p. 7. The second one is in 'International Humanitarian Law: Definition', in *International Dimensions of Humanitarian Law* (Geneva: Henry Dunant Institute, Paris: UNESCO, Dordrecht/Boston/London: Martinus Nijhoff, 1988), p. xxi, note 1.
2. Adachi Sumio, 'The Asian Concept', *International Dimensions*, op. cit., pp. 13–17.
3. François de Fontette, *Le procès de Nuremberg* (Paris: Que sais-je, Presses universitaires de France, 1996), pp. 7–8.
4. Yves Beigbeder, *The Role and Status of International Humanitarian Volunteers and Organizations* (Dordrecht/Boston/London: Martinus Nijhoff, 1991), pp. 212–214.
5. Karl Joseph Partsch, 'The Western Concept', in *International Dimensions*, op. cit., p. 60.
6. Kenneth Ögren, 'Humanitarian law in the *Articles of War* decreed in 1621 by King Gustavus II Adolphus of Sweden', in *International Review of the Red Cross*, 313 (1996) 438–42.
7. Lyal S. Sunga, *Individual Responsibility in International Law for Serious Human Rights Violations* (Dordrecht/Boston/London: Martinus Nijhoff, 1992), pp. 18–19.
8. Quoted by Partsch (see note 5), p. 60.
9. The four 1949 Conventions refer respectively to (1) the 'Amelioration of the Condition of the Wounded and Sick in Armed Forces in the Field', (2) the 'Amelioration of the Condition of Wounded, Sick and Shipwrecked Members of Armed Forces at Sea', (3) the 'Treatment of Prisoners of War', and (4) the 'Protection of Civilian Persons in Time of War'.
10. Common Article 3 states: 'In the case of armed conflict not of an international character occurring in the territory of one of the High Contracting Parties, each Party to the conflict shall be bound to apply, as a minimum, the following provisions:

   1) Persons taking no active part in the hostilities, including members of armed forces who have laid down their arms and those placed *hors de combat* by sickness, wounds, detention, or any other cause,

shall in all circumstances be treated humanely, without any adverse distinction founded on race, colour, religion or faith, sex, birth or wealth, or any other similar criteria.

To this end, the following acts are and shall remain prohibited at any time and in any place whatsoever with respect to the above-mentioned persons:

a) violence to life and person, in particular murder of all kinds, mutilation, cruel treatment and torture;

b) taking of hostages:

c) outrages against personal dignity, in particular humiliating and degrading treatment;

d) the passing of sentences and the carrying out of executions without previous judgment pronounced by a regularly constituted court, affording all the judicial guarantees which are recognized as indispensable by civilized peoples.

2) The wounded and the sick shall be collected and cared for.

. . .

11. Jean Pictet, *The Fundamental Principles of the Red Cross, Commentary* (Geneva: Henry Dunant Institute, 1979), p. 60.
12. Articles I, 49, 50; II, 50, 51; III, 129, 130; IV, 146, 147; P.I, 85; P.II, 6. For instance, in I.50, grave breaches are defined as 'wilful killing, torture or inhuman treatment, including biological experiments, wilfully causing great suffering or serious injury to body or health, and extensive destruction and appropriation of property, not justified by military necessity and carried out unlawfully and wantonly'.
13. Yves Sandoz, Directeur de la Doctrine et du Droit, ICRC, 'Les Nations Unies et le Droit international humanitaire', Colloque international, Genève, 19–21 October 1995, p. 25.
14. Frederic de Martens, a Russian jurist, played a prominent role in the drafting of the Hague Conventions: see G. I. A. D. Draper, 'The Development of International Humanitarian Law' in *International Dimensions*, op. cit., pp. 72–3.
15. *International Dimensions*, op. cit., p. xxi.
16. Quoted by Paul Sieghart, *The Lawful Rights of Mankind* (Oxford/New York: Oxford University Press, 1986), p. 24. See also pp. 26 and 27 on the philosophers and the French and American Revolutions: references made by permission of Oxford University Press.
17. Ibid., p. 34.
18. UNGA Res. 177 (II), 21 November 1947.
19. UNGA Res. 1186 (XII), 11 December 1957.
20. UNGA Res. 36/106, 10 December 1981.
21. 'Report of the International Law Commission on the work of its forty-eighth session, 6 May – 26 July 1996', Doc. A/51/10.
22. For instance, Res. 51/137, 13 December 1996. The General Assembly adopted the Convention on the Safety of United Nations and Associated Personnel by Res. 49/59, 9 December 1994.

CHAPTER 2

1. On the Versailles Treaty and the Leipzig Trials, see Sunga, op. cit, pp. 22, 23; Annie Deperchin-Gouillard, 'Responsabilité et violation du droit des gens pendant la première guerre mondiale: volonté politique et impuissance juridique', and Jean-Jacques Becker, 'Les procès de Leipzig', in *Les procès de Nuremberg et de Tokyo*, Annette Wieviorka, Ed. (Paris: Editions Complexe, 1996) pp. 25–49 and 51–60. These and later references to this book are by permission of Editions Complexe. On the Nuremberg Trial, see Telford Taylor, *The Anatomy of the Nuremberg Trials* (Boston/New York/ Toronto/London: Little, Brown and Company, 1992); *The Nuremberg Trial and International Law*, George Ginsburgs and V. N. Kudriavtsev (Dordrecht/Boston/London: Martinus Nijhoff, 1990); Michael R. Marrus, *The Nuremberg War Crimes Trial, 1945–46, A Documentary History* (Boston/New York: Bedford Books, 1997), used by permission, 18 November 1997.
2. François Bédarida, *Le génocide et le nazisme* (Paris: Presses Pocket, 1992), pp. 19–22.
3. *International Herald Tribune*, 6 January 1997.
4. Yves Ternon, *L'Etat criminel, les génocides au XXe siècle* (Paris: Seuil, 1995), pp. 129 and 165, by permission (8 September 1997); see also his large bibliography. References are to the book in French, any translation is by Y. Beigbeder, not by Ed. du Seuil or University of Pennsylvania Press.
5. Taylor, op. cit., pp. 170–1.
6. In A. Tusa and J. Tusa, *The Nuremberg Trial* (New York: 1983), pp. 62, 64–7, as quoted by John F. Murphy in Ginsburgs, op. cit., p. 62.
7. Quoted by Ginsburgs, op. cit., p. 9.
8. Australia, Belgium, Czechoslovakia, Denmark, Ethiopia, Greece, Haiti, Honduras, India, Luxemburg, Netherlands, New-Zealand, Norway, Panama, Paraguay, Poland, Uruguay, Venezuela and Yugoslavia. The text of the Charter is in Appendix A of Taylor's book.
9. De Fontette, op. cit., Chapter VI.
10. Taylor, op. cit., p. 356.
11. Marrus, op. cit., p. 78.
12. Taylor, p. 429.
13. Marrus, p. 229.
14. Ibid., pp. 81–2.
15. Taylor, p. 75.
16. Ginsburgs, pp. 218–19.
17. Ibid., p. 243.
18. H. Donnedieu de Vabres, *Le procès de Nuremberg devant les principes modernes du droit pénal international*, Rec. acad., La Haye, 1947, p. 530.
19. Ginsburgh, p. 218: 336 U.S. 440 (1949).
20. Taylor, p. 66, and Ginsburgs, p. 141.
21. Marrus, pp. 229–30.
22. Taylor, p. 66.
23. Quoted in Ginsburgs, pp. 155–6.
24. Jean-Claude Favez in Wieviorka, op. cit., pp. 105, 110–11.

25. IHT, 15 October 1992; Fontette, op. cit., pp. 69–73.
26. Wieviorka, p. 116. Further comments on air bombing of Japan are in Chapter 3.
27. Taylor, p. 409; Charles Rousseau, *Droit international public* (Paris: Sirey, 1953), pp. 613–16.
28. Donnedieu de Vabres, op. cit., pp. 526–7.
29. Quoted in Ginsburgs, p. 195.
30. Donnedieu de Vabres, pp. 483, 486.
31. Sunga, op. cit., pp. 48–50.

CHAPTER 3

1. Quoted by John W. Dower in *War Without Mercy, Race and Power in the Pacific War* (New York: Pantheon, 1986) pp. 296, 299. Different authors quote different statistics based on different sources: in any case, these are estimates. We have generally quoted the more conservative figures.
2. Rhoads Murphey, *A History of Asia* (New York: HarperCollins, 1992), pp. 352, 354, 356.
3. *Le Monde*, 20 December 1990.
4. The text of the Potsdam Declaration is in US Department of State, Bulletin, 1945, pp. 137–8. The text of the Proclamation of 19 January 1946 and of the Charter of the Tokyo Tribunal are in Richard H. Minear, *Victors' Justice, The Tokyo War Crimes Trial* (Princeton, N.J.: Princeton University Press, 1971) Appendix I, pp. 183–92. For a comprehensive, factual description of the Tokyo Trial, see Solis Horwitz, *The Tokyo Trial*, in International Conciliation, Carnegie Endowment for International Peace, No. 465, November 1950. Mr Horwitz was a member of the prosecution staff at Tokyo.
5. Wieviorka, op. cit., pp. 160–1.
6. Minear, op. cit., p. 112. The Far Eastern Commission was established in February 1946. It was empowered 'to formulate the policies, principles and standards in conformity with which the fulfillment by Japan of its obligations under the terms of surrender may be accomplished'. The Commission was composed of representatives of Australia, Canada, China, France, India, the Netherlands, the Philippine Commonwealth, the USSR, the UK and the USA.
7. Wieviorka, p. 186.
8. B. V. A. Röling and Antonio Cassese, *The Tokyo Trial and Beyond* (Cambridge: Polity Press, 1993) p. 40: by permission of Blackwell Publishers (23 June 1997).
9. The majority of seven was composed of the judges from the USA, the UK, China, the USSR, the Philippines, Canada and New Zealand. New York, 1992, pp. 382–3.
10. Röling and Cassese, op. cit., p. 4.
11. *The Tokyo Judgment, The International Military Tribunal for the Far East (IMTFE), 29 April 1946 – 12 November 1948* (Amsterdam: APA University Press, 1977), B. V. A. Röling and C. F. Rüter, Eds, pp. 477–9. Further references are to 'IMTFE'.

12. Ibid., Vol. II, pp. 1035 and 1038, and Röling and Cassese, p. 28.
13. IMTFE., Vol. I, pp. 494–6.
14. Ibid., Vol. II, pp. 1116–17.
15. Ibid., Vol. I, pp. 514–15.
16. Röling and Cassese, pp. 80–1.
17. Minear, pp. 40–2.
18. IMTFE, Vol. I. p. 25.
19. Röling and Cassese, p. 98.
20. 'Defense Appeal to General MacArthur', in Minear, pp. 204–5.
21. Minear, pp. 96–7.
22. Wieviorka, pp. 124, 129.
23. Dower, op. cit., pp. 38–40.
24. IHT, 17 July 1995.
25. Haruko Taya Cook and Theodore F. Cook, *Japan at War, An Oral History* (New York: The New Press, 1992), pp. 382–3, used by permission.
26. Exhibit III in *Japanese Annual of International Law*, 8, pp. 251–2 (1964).
27. IHT, 17 September 1995, and Opinion of Judge Jaranilla in IMTFE, Vol. I, p. 511.
28. Saburo Ienaga, *The Pacific War, 1931–1945, A Critical Perspective on Japan's Role in World War II* (New York: Random House, 1978), p. 201.
29. IMTFE, Vol. I, p. 510, Vol. II, pp. 575 and 1025.
30. Röling and Cassese, p. 84.
31. *Japanese Annual of International Law*, 8/1964, pp. 212–52.
32. Advisory Opinion, para. 105 (operative paragraph). See Peter H. F. Bekker's report on the Advisory Opinion in *The American Journal of International Law*, Vol. 91, 1997, pp. 126–33. See also *International Documents Review*, 15 July 1996; *UN Observer*, September 1996. Article 2, paragraph 4 of the UN Charter states: 'All Members shall refrain in their international relations from the threat or use of force against the territorial integrity or political independence of any state, or in any other manner inconsistent with the Purposes of the United Nations'. Article 51 refers to the 'inherent right of individual or collective self-defence under certain conditions.
33. *IHT*, 18 July 1996.
34. See Wieviorka, 'Les plans japonais de guerre bactériologique et les expériences médicales sur les prisonniers de guerre', by Toshi-Yuki Tanaka, with bibliographical references, pp. 192–224; *Newsweek*, 3 October 1994 and 16 December 1996. In 'The Case Against the Nazi Physicians', 23 German defendants were tried by a US Military Tribunal in Nuremberg from October 1946 to August 1947: fifteen were found guilty, of whom seven were sentenced to death by hanging, eight to jail sentences. One was acquitted of the charges of having performed medical experiments but was found guilty of SS membership and sentenced to ten years in jail. Seven were found not guilty and freed. See *The Nazi Doctors and the Nuremberg Code, Human Rights in Human Experimentation*, George J. Annas and Michael A. Grodin, Eds (New York/Oxford: Oxford University Press, 1992), p. 105.
35. Cook and Cook, op. cit., pp. 158–67, used by permission.

36. *CQ Researcher*, 7 July 1995, '*Le Monde*', 3 August 1995, IHT, 15 August 1996 and *Far Eastern Economic Review*, 21 November 1996.
37. IMTFE, Vol. I, pp. XIII–XVI.

CHAPTER 4

1. F. Chalk and K. Jonassohn, *The History and Sociology of Genocide, Analyses and Case Studies* (New Haven/London: Yale University Press, 1990), pp. 28–31. Their definition of genocide is 'a form of one-sided mass killing in which a state or other authority intends to destroy a group, as that group and membership in it are defined by the perpetrator' (p. 23): by permission, 7 August 1997.
2. Information on the Armenian genocide is summarized from: V. N. Dadrian, 'Genocide as a problem of national and international law: The World War I Armenian case and its contemporary legal ramifications', *The Yale Journal of International Law*, 14(2), 1989, pp. 221–34, by permission (10 July 1997), see also Yves Ternon, op. cit., pp. 187, 191; and the European Parliament 'Report drawn up on behalf of the Political Affairs Committee on a political solution to the Armenian question' Doc. A 2–33/87 of 15 April 1987.
3. *The Times*, London, 3 October 1911.
4. J. S. Kirakossian, *The Armenian Genocide, The Young Turks before the Judgment of History* (Madison, Conn.: Sphinx Press, 1992), pp. 114–15, used by permission (1 July 1997).
5. Dadrian, op. cit., p. 262. In the newspaper *Il Messaggero*, the Italian Consul-General at Trebizond stated in part in an interview: 'It was a real extermination and slaughter of the innocents, an unheard-of thing, a black page stained with the flagrant violation of the most sacred rights of humanity, of Christianity, of nationality'. This is one of 150 documents published in 1916 on *The Treatment of Armenians in the Ottoman Empire, 1915–16, Documents presented to Viscount Grey of Fallodon (UK) Secretary of State for Foreign Affairs by Viscount Bryce* (London: His Majesty's Stationery Office) p. 291.
6. Dadrian, p. 280.
7. Kirakossian, op. cit., pp. 161, 164, 171–3, 186, used by permission – see note 4.
8. See *Armenian Allegations, Myth and Reality, A Handbook of Facts and Documents* (Washington D.C.: The Assembly of Turkish American Associations, 1987), Introduction, pp. ix–xii.
9. *Permanent Peoples' Tribunal Session on the Genocide of the Armenians* (Paris/Cambridge, MA, 1984) pp. 21–2.
10. 'The Whitaker Report', UN Doc. E/CN.4/Sub.2/1985/6, SR.1–SR.39, 2 July 1985.
11. *Official Journal of the European Communities*, No. C 190/119, Doc. A2-33/87, 18 June 1987.
12. On the Soviet massacres, see Chalk and Jonassohn, op. cit., pp. 290–322; and on the crimes of Communist regimes, S. Courtois, N. Werth, J. L. Panné, A. Paczkowski, K. Bartosek and J. L. Margolin,

Le Livre noir du communisme. Crimes, terreurs, répression (Paris: R. Lafond, 1997). According to the latter book, the total number of deaths caused by all Communist regimes is approximately 85 million.

13. Roy A. Medvedev, *On Stalin and Stalinism* (Oxford/New York/Toronto/ Melbourne: Oxford University Press, 1979), pp. 185, 186: by permission of Oxford University Press (8 July 1997).

14. See Robert Conquest, *Harvest of Sorrow: Soviet Collectivization of Agriculture and the Terror Famine'* (London, Hutchinson, 1986); 'No Grain of Pity' – an extract is in Chalk and Jonassohn, pp. 291–300.

15. Conquest in Chalk and Jonassohn, p. 300, 313, 314, 320.

16. See Khrushchev's secret speech to the Twentieth Communist Party Congress, 24–25 February 1956, *New York Times*, 5 June 1956.

17. Wallace Fowlie, *André Gide, his life and art* (New York: Macmillan, 1965), pp. 101–2; Victor Kravchenko, *I Chose Freedom, The Personal and Political Life of a Soviet Official* (New York: Charles Scribner's Sons, 1946); *Time*, 8 July 1946; *Newsweek*, 24 January, 7 February, 11 and 18 April 1949. In 1951, the 'Commission internationale contre le régime concentrationnaire' published a *Livre blanc sur les camps soviétiques* which revealed the reality of the gulags: see *Le Monde*, 16 December 1997.

18. Medvedev, op. cit., p. 164.

19. *L'Express*, 27 March 1997.

20. According to the *Livre noir*, op. cit., the number of deaths caused by the Soviet regime is approximately 15 million.

21. Information in this section is based on Chalk and Jonassohn, op. cit., pp. 378–83, Murphey, op. cit., pp. 405–8, *Amnesty International, Report 1995*, New York, 1995, pp. 160–3, and encyclopedias.

22. L. R. J. Rummel, *China's Bloody Century, Genocide and Mass Murder since 1900* (New Brunswick/London: Transaction, 1991), pp. v, 7 and 8: by permission (13 August 1997). According to the *Livre noir*, op. cit., the total number of victims in China and Tibet caused by the Communist regime ranges from 44.5 to 72 million.

23. Ben Kiernan, *The Pol Pot Regime, Race, Power and Genocide under the Khmer Rouge, 1975–79* (New Haven/London: Yale University Press, 1996), p. 8: by permission, 7 August 1997. On the Khmer Rouge, see also Ternon, pp. 204–33. The *Livre noir* estimate of deaths caused by the Khmer Rouge ranges from 1.3 to 2.3 million deaths.

24. Ternon, p. 224.

25. UN Doc. E/CN.4/1335/1979, 30 January 1979.

26. UN Doc. A/34/491, Annex, August 1979.

27. *Genocide and Democracy in Cambodia, The Khmer Rouge, the UN and the International Community,* ed. B. Kiernan (New Haven: Yale University Law School, Southeast Asia Studies, 1993), p. 196, used by permission (12 August 1997).

28. Ternon, p. 230.

29. *The Cambodian Genocide Program, First Progress Report, 15 September 1995* (New Haven: Yale University, Council on Southeast Asia Studies, 1995), used by permission (12 August 1997).

30. *Le Point*, 1 February 1997; IHT, 19 September 1996.

31. *IHT*, 28 July 1997 and *Le Monde*, 2 August and 25 October 1997.
32. UN Doc. A/51/930, 24 June 1997.
33. G. H. Stanton, 'The Cambodian Genocide and International Law' in *Genocide and Democracy in Cambodia*, op. cit., pp. 142–61.

CHAPTER 5

1. UN Doc. E/CN.4/Sub.2/1997/20, 26 June 1997, hereafter referred to as the 'Joinet report'; van Boven's Note is in Appendix to Doc. E/CN.4/1997/104, 16 January 1997.
2. M. P. Scharf, 'The Case for a Permanent International Truth Commission', paper presented on 21 July 1996 during 'Justice in Cataclysm', A Conference co-sponsored by Duke University School of Law and the Office of the Prosecutor of the International Tribunal for the Former Yugoslavia and Rwanda, Brussels.
3. P. B. Hayner, 'Fifteen Truth Commissions – 1974 to 1994: A Comparative Study', 16 *Human Rights Quarterly* (1994) 600–655: by permission (14 August 1997). Truth Commissions reviewed in the article are in Argentina, Bolivia, Chad, Chile, El Salvador, Ethiopia, Germany, the Philippines, Rwanda, South Africa (two ANC Commissions), Uganda (two Commissions), Uruguay, Zimbabwe. Other Commissions have been established in Guatemala, Haiti, Honduras, Sierra Leone and South Africa.
4. Hayner, op. cit., pp. 613–16.
5. 'Report of the Chilean National Commission on Truth and Reconciliation', 5–6 (Phillip E. Berryman, trans., 1993).
6. UN Doc. A/44/635 and E/CN.4/1990/5.
7. See 'Amnesty International Report 1995', pp. 96–7; Hayner, pp. 621–3; M. Ensalaco, 'Truth Commissions for Chile and El Salvador: A Report and Assessment', *Human Rights Quarterly* (1994), pp. 657–75, by permission (14 August 1997).
8. A regional peace plan was ratified in August 1987 by Costa Rica, El Salvador, Guatemala, Honduras and Nicaragua. On the peace process in El Salvador, see J. Tessitore and S. Woolfson Eds., *A Global Agenda, Issues before the 47th, 48th, 49th General Assembly of the United Nations*, UN Association of the USA (Lanham/New York/London: University Press of America, 1992, 1993, 1994.
9. ONUSAL was in El Salvador from July 1991 to April 1995. The instruments establishing the Commission's mandate are in UN Doc. S/25500, 1 April 1993.
10. Guarantees were provided by the Security Council – see Res. 714 of 30 September 1991 – and by the Group of Four Friends of the Secretary-General.
11. UN Doc. S/25500, 1 April 1993.
12. UN *Press Release* SG/SM/4950, 24 March 1993; see also Hayner, p. 629.
13. International Covenant on Civil and Political Rights, Human Rights Committee, UN Doc. CCPR/C/79/Add.34, 18 April 1994, paras. 6 and

7; A/49/281-S/1994/886, 28 July 1994, A/51/1, 20 August 1996, p. 108.

14. See UN Doc. A/48/928, 19 April 1994 and Annexes, and Res. 48/267.

15. *IHT*, 20 December 1996; *Le Monde*, 21 December 1996; *New York Times*, 7 April 1997.

16. See Hayner, op. cit., pp. 625–6, 632–4.

17. Information on the South African Commission is based in part on a paper presented by Alexander Boraine, Vice Chairperson, South African Truth and Reconciliation Commission on 'Alternatives and Adjuncts to Criminal Prosecutions' at the Brussels Conference of 20–21 July 1996 – see note 2 above (permission granted by Dr Boraine on 30 June 1997); and in part on documentation kindly provided by the South African Permanent Mission to the UN in Geneva, including 'TRC Workshop Manual', Communications and Marketing Department, South Africa, 22 August 1997.

18. 'TRC Statistics: HRV & Amnesty', Communications and Marketing Department, South Africa, 25 August 1997, Summary, p. 2.

19. *Time*, 21 October 1996; *IHT*, 23 August, 22 October 1996; *Newsweek*, 30 September 1996; *The Economist*, 1 February 1997; *St. Louis Post-Dispatch*, 14 April 1997. R. F. Botha, former South African Foreign Minister, apologized for failing to turn the tide of *apartheid* and for his reluctance to investigate the killing and torturing of political opponents by white security forces – *IHT*, 15 October 1997.

20. *IHT*, 18 July 1997.

21. *IHT*, 8–9 February 1997.

22. Annex to the Mexico Agreements, 27 April 1991, para. 2, UN Doc. S/25500, 1 April 1993.

23. Hayner, p. 652.

24. Boraine, op. cit., p. 10.

25. D. Bronkhorst, *Truth and Reconciliation – Obstacles and Opportunities for Human Rights* (Amsterdam: Amnesty International, 1995), pp. 150–1.

26. See M. Ignatieff 'How can past sins be absolved?', *Index on Censorship*, London, September/October 1996.

CHAPTER 6

1. *Newsweek*, 15 April 1996.

2. Joinet report, op. cit., Principle 21.

3. *Le Monde*, 1 January 1997.

4. *International Covenant on Civil and Political Rights*, Articles 14 and 15.

5. *Newsweek*, 13 December 1993; *IHT*, 1 and 4 July 1997.

6. *New York Times*, 4 July 1987; *IHT*, 18 July 1996, 31 January 1997; Wieviorka, op. cit., pp. 285–8.

7. *IHT*, 12–13 November and 15 December 1994; *Newsweek*, 19 December 1994.

8. TOIP is an autonomous organization jointly formed by the Ethiopian Human Rights and Peace Center and the InterAfrica Group. It is supported by a grant from USAID. Information on the trials is based on periodical 'Trial Update(s)' issued by TOIP.

9. See 'Trial Update, February 1996. The Penal Code dates from the reign of Emperor Haile Selassie. It includes provisions for war crimes, because the Emperor had hoped to bring Italians to trial for actions committed during the Fascist Italian occupation of Ethiopia in the 1930s.
10. 'Trial Update', 2 March and 4 April 1996.
11. 'Trial Update', 9 and 25 April, 11 and 20 June 1996, 20 March 1997.
12. *Le Monde*, 5 November 1996.
13. Amnesty International *Report 1995*, pp. 128–9.
14. *Le Monde*, 17 February 1994 and 12–13 October 1997; *The Nation*, 8 May 1995, *IHT*, 24–25 May, 5–6 July 1997. On Former Yugoslavia, see Human Rights Watch/Helsinki 'War Crimes Trials in the Former Yugoslavia', Vol. 7, No. 10, June 1995; A. Destexhe and M. Foret, *De Nuremberg à La Haye et Arusha* (Brussels: Bruylant, 1997), pp. 116–17.
15. Efraim Zuroff, 'Justice as a basis for reconciliation in the wake of the Holocaust: The Case of Lithuania', paper presented to the Brussels Conference (see Note 2, Chapter 5); US *Daily Bulletin*, Geneva, EUR203, 12 August 1997.
16. Joinet report, Principles 26–35, 20.

CHAPTER 7

1. The text of the Initial Complaint of the 'International War Crimes Tribunal, US War Crimes against Iraq' is at http://deoxy.org/wc-ilaw.htm, the Final Judgment is at http://deoxy.org/wc/warcrim3.htm. See also *UN Observer and International Report*, April 1992.
2. *Journal de Genève*, 7 February 1991; US *Daily Bulletin*, Geneva, 29 April 1993; Reuter's release of 20 January 1997 on INDICT.
3. J. Duffett, Ed., *Against the Crime of Silence, Proceedings of the Russell International War Crimes Tribunal, Stockholm–Copenhagen* (1968), and P. Limqueco and P. Weiss, Eds, *Prevent the Crime of Silence, Reports from the Sessions of the International War Crimes Tribunal Founded by Bertrand Russell, London–Stockholm–Roskilde* (London: Penguin Press, 1971).
4. On Peoples' Tribunals, see R. Falk, 'Keeping Nuremberg Alive' and L. Joinet 'Les tribunaux d'opinion' in *Marxism, Democracy and the Rights of Peoples – Homage to Lelio Basso* (Milan: F. Angeli Editore, 1979), pp. 811–20 and 821–30; E. Jouve, *Un tribunal pour les peuples* (Paris: Berger-Levrault, 1983); and documentation from International League for the Rights and Liberation of Peoples.
5. See http://www.idc.net/intlpeoplestribunal.

CHAPTER 8

1. Security Council Res. No. 808 and 827.
2. This was the opinion expressed by Secretary-General Boutros-Ghali in October 1993, although he added that the report provided a sub-

stantial basis for further investigations which might lead to prosecution (US *Daily Bulletin*, Geneva, EUR304, 20 October 1993). The Commission was composed of five persons appointed by the Secretary-General on the basis of their expertise and integrity and in a personal capacity. The first Chairman was Professor Frits Kalshoven from the Netherlands who resigned in August 1993. He was replaced by Professor Cherif Bassiouni (Egypt/USA). Other members were from Canada, Senegal, Norway and the Netherlands, following Professor Kalshoven's departure. The Final Report of the Commission is in UN Doc. S/1994/674. On the Commission's work, see M. Cherif Bassiouni, 'The Commission of Experts Established pursuant to Security Council Resolution 780: Investigating Violations of International Humanitarian Law in the Former Yugoslavia', Occasional Paper No. 2, International Human Rights Law Institute, DePaul University College of Law, 1996.

3. *IHT*, 13–14 November 1993.
4. Bassiouni, op. cit., p. 11 and 19; UN *Press Release* SC/94/8, 15 April 1994.
5. UN *Press Releases* HR/3141, 13 August 1992, HR/3145, 14 August 1992, DH/1667, 16 June 1994, HR/94/37, 4 August 1994, HR/94/40, 29 August 1994; US *Daily Bulletin* EUR502/504/507/513/514, 4 November 1994.
6. Human Rights Watch, 'Bosnia–Hercegovina, The Fall of Srebrenica and the Failure of UN Peacekeeping', Vol. 7, No. 13, October 1995; and *Le Monde*, 11 July 1996.
7. *Newsweek*, 22 April 1996.
8. The Statute of the Tribunal is in Annex to UN Doc. S/25704, 3 May 1993.
9. UN Doc. S/25704, 3 May 1993, para. 28.
10. Third Annual Report of the Tribunal, UN Doc. A/51/292, S/1996/665, 16 August 1996, paragraph 189–90.
11. US *Daily Bulletin*, Geneva, EUR505, 21 January 1994, UN *Press Release* GA/AB/3152, 30 May 1997.
12. UN *Press Releases* SC/294, 20 August 1993, GA/8500, 17 September 1993, SC/308, 17 November 1993, SC/310, 1 December 1993; ICTY *Press Release* CC/PIO/197-E, 21 May 1997.
13. UN *Press Releases* SC/94/5, 15 February 1994, HR/94/15, 9 May 1994, DH/1643, 12 May 1994.
14. See *UN Observer and International Report*, October 1993; Security Council Res. 877 (1993), 936 (1994), 1047 (1996), and UN *Press Release* SG/A/94/1, 21 January 1994.
15. The judgment of the Trial Chamber is in '*Prosecutor v. Tadic*, Case IT-1-T', the judgment of the Appeals Chamber is in '*Prosecutor v. Tadic*, Case IT-94-1-AR72'. See also G. H. Aldrich, 'Jurisdiction of the International Criminal Tribunal for the Former Yugoslavia', *American Journal of International Law*, January 1996, 64–9.
16. *Le Monde*, 17 February 1994, 16 July 1997; *IHT*, 8 May 1996; Tribunal 'Sentencing Judgment' of 14 July 1997, Case No. IT-94-1-T.
17. *Le Monde*, 2 December 1996; *UN Observer and International Report*, January 1997; 'Sentencing Judgment', 29 November 1996, Case No. IT-96-1-T.

18. *Le Monde*, 21 May 1996, 12 March, 26 June, 4, 12 July 1997; *IHT*, 12, 13 July 1997.
19. UN *Press Releases* DH/1942, 25 July 1995, DH/2024, 16 November 1995.
20. In December 1997, the Tribunal's Prosecutor, Louise Arbour, shocked French officials by stating that indicted war criminals could feel 'perfectly safe' in the French zone of Bosnia, because the French had shown 'total inertia' in seeking their arrest. She asked France to change its policy in order to permit military officers to testify before the Tribunal. French Defence Minister Alain Richard rejected these criticisms and this request, calling the Tribunal a 'spectacle trial'. In fact, the only NATO peacekeepers who have arrested indicted war criminals in 1996 and 1997 were British commandos: *Le Monde*, 15 December 1997; *IHT*, 16 and 22 December 1997.
21. For instance, *IHT*, 14–15 June 1997.
22. 'Application of the Convention on the Prevention and Punishment of the Crime of Genocide (Bosnia and Herzegovina v. Yugoslavia), Preliminary Objections, Judgment, International Court of Justice, 11 July 1996'. See also P. H. F. Bekker and P. C. Szasz, on the same subject, *American Journal of International Law*, January 1997 91 (1), 121–6.
23. UN *Press Releases* DH/1456, 13 August 1993; ICJ *Communiqué*, 93/9, 8 April 1993; ICJ/26, 16 September 1993.
24. Article IX of the Genocide Convention: 'Disputes between the Contracting Parties relating to the interpretation, application or fulfilment of the present Convention, including those relating to the responsibility of a State for genocide or any of the other acts enumerated in Article III, shall be submitted to the International Court of Justice at the request of any of the parties to the dispute'.
25. G. H. Stanton, 'The Cambodian Genocide and International Law', in *Genocide and Democracy in Cambodia*, ed. B. Kiernan (New Haven: Yale University Southeast Asia Studies, 1993), pp. 144–6.
26. T. Meron, 'Answering for War Crimes, Lessons from the Balkans', *Foreign Affairs*, January/February 1997, pp. 2–8.

CHAPTER 9

1. UN Doc. S/1994/640, 31 May 1994, S/1994/1133, 6 October 1994.
2. On Rwanda, see: A. Destexhe, *Rwanda and Genocide in the Twentieth Century* (London/East Haven, CT: Pluto Press, 1995); F. Reyntjens, 'Rwanda: Genocide and Beyond', *Journal of Refugee Studies*, 9 (3) (1996), pp. 240–51. On Burundi, *Le Monde*, 4–5 October 1992; J. P. Chrétien, 'Burundi: The Obsession with Genocide', *Current History*, May 1996, 206–10.
3. UN Doc. E/CN.4/1994/7/Add.1, 11 August 1993, and S/1994/640, 31 May 1994, para. 11.
4. *IHT*, 30 November/1 December 1996; *Newsweek*, 17 November 1997.
5. UN Doc. S/1994/470, 20 April 1994 and Res. 912, 21 April 1994.
6. UN Doc. S/1994/640, 31 May 1994, para. 36.

7. UN Doc. E/CN.4/1995/7, 28 June 1994, paras 25 and section B.
8. UN Doc. S/1994/1125, 4 October 1994.
9. UN *Press Release* HR/SC/94/13.
10. UN Doc. S/1994/1115, S/PV.3453, 1994, para. 14.
11. Ibid., para. 16.
12. The Statute of the Rwanda Tribunal is in Annex to Security Council Res. 955 (1994), 8 November 1994. See also P. Akhavan, 'The International Tribunal for Rwanda: the politics and pragmatics of punishment', *American Journal of International Law*, 90 (3) (July 1996), 501–10.
13. *IHT*, 21 February, 1 November 1996; *Le Monde*, 28 September 1996, 7 January 1997; *Ubutabera*, Intermedia, 25 October 1997.
14. UN Doc. S-1996-332; *Ubutabera*, Intermedia, 7 August 1997; *Le Monde*, 25 July 1997.
15. US *Daily Bulletin*, Geneva, EUR312, 6 June and EUR108, 29 October 1996; The European Commission *The Week in Europe, Week ending 21 March 1997*.
16. Res. 50/213 C, UN Doc. A/51/789.
17. US *Daily Bulletin*, Geneva, AEF304, 12 February 1997, AEF301, 26 February 1997.
18. 'The Hutu 10 Commandments', published in 1990 in the *Kangura* magazine, warned Hutus not to intermarry, fraternize or go into business with Tutsis. Commandment 8 states: 'The Hutu should stop having mercy on the Tutsi'.
19. *Le Monde*, 10 January, 20–21 July, 25 July 1997; UN *Daily Highlights*, 21 July, 12 and 18 August 1997.
20. Paper presented by G. Gahima, Ministry of Justice, Rwanda, on 'Rwanda: The Challenge of Justice in the Aftermath of Genocide', Brussels Conference, 20–22 July 1996 (see Note 2, Chapter 5). See also A. Zarembo, 'Judgment Day', *Harper's Magazine*, April 1997, pp. 68–80.
21. *Le Monde*, 5–6 January 1997; *Chicago Tribune*, 11 April 1997.

CHAPTER 10

1. See M. Cherif Bassiouni, 'Recent UN activities in connection with the establishment of a permanent international criminal court and the role of the Association internationale de droit pénal (AIDP) and the Istituto Superiore Internazionale di Scienzi Criminali (ISISC), *Transnational Associations*, 1/97, pp. 21–7.
2. 'La lettre hebdomadaire de la FIDH', No. 613–14, 16/23 November 1995.
3. The 1994 Draft Statute is in Doc. A/49/10. The International Law Commission was established by the General Assembly in 1947 to promote the progressive development of international law and its codification. The Commission, which meets annually, is composed of thirty-four members serving in their individual capacities.
4. See J. Crawford, 'The ILC adopts a Statute for an International Criminal Court', *The American Journal of International Law*, 89 (1995), 404–16.

5. UN General Assembly Res. 44/128 of 15 December 1989, 'Elaboration of a second optional protocol to the International Covenant on Civil and Political Rights, aiming at the abolition of the death penalty'; at the regional level, Council of Europe 'Protocol No. 6 to the Convention for the Protection of Human Rights and Fundamental Freedoms concerning the abolition of the death penalty', 28 April 1983.
6. The *Ad Hoc* Committee's report is in Doc. A/50/22. See also UN *Press Release* GA/95/06, 13 April 1995; *International Documents Review*, 15 April 1996.
7. D. J. Scheffer, 'International judicial intervention', *Foreign Policy*, Spring 1996, No. 102 p. 34 (18).
8. US *Daily Bulletin*, Geneva, 22 August 1996. On Italy and other countries favouring the inclusion of aggression in the Statute, see *International Documents Review*, 22 April 1996.
9. *Xinhua News Agency*, 'Chinese Ambassador on International Criminal Court', 31 October 1996.
10. See Revised Article 35, Doc. A/AC.249/1997/WG3/CPR.2. On the US position, see US *Daily Bulletin*, EUR505, 22 August 1997.
11. See Note 1. The only reference to financial compensation to victims is in Article 47.3(c), which provides that paid fines may be transferred, by order of the Court to, *inter alia*, a trust fund established by the UN Secretary-General for the benefit of victims of crime.
12. UN Doc. E/CN.4/1997, 16 January 1997, paras. 12–14; E/CN.4/Sub.2/1997/20, 26 June 1997, Principles 40–2.
13. UN Doc. E/CN/Sub.2/1997/20, Principle 20.
14. UN Doc. A/Conf.183/9, 17 July 1998.
15. The Court will however not exercise jurisdiction over the crime of aggression until a provision is adopted defining the crime and setting out the conditions under which the Court will exercise jurisdiction with respect to this crime. Under Articles 5, 12, and 123, this will not occur before the expiry of seven years from the entry into force of the Statute.
16. UN Press release L/Rom/22 of 17 July 1998, p. 8.

CHAPTER 11

1. *Le Monde*, 30 September 1997.
2. Declaration by Abassi Madani quoted by *Marianne*, 29 September/5 October 1997. Recent press reports allege that the Algerian government may also be involved in some of the massacres.
3. French lawyers, a police union and the Order of Doctors also apologized for their attitude during World War II with regard to anti-semitic laws and measures: *IHT*, 13 October 1997.
4. *Le Monde*, 29 May 1997.
5. US *Daily Bulletin* EUR403, 2 October 1997; *Le Monde*, 7 October 1997.
6. *IHT*, 27–28 September 1997.

Select Bibliography

Bédarida, François, *Le génicide et le nazisme* (Paris: Presses Pocket, 1992)

Bédarida, François, *Touvier, Vichy et le crime contre l'humanité, Le dossier de l'accusation* (Paris: Seuil, 1996)

Bettati, Mario and Dupuy, Pierre-Marie, *Les ONG et le Droit International* (Paris: Economica, 1986)

Bory, Françoise, *Origin and Development of International Humanitarian Law* (Geneva: ICRC, 1982)

Bronkhorst, Daan, *Truth and Reconciliation, Obstacles and Opportunities for Human Rights* (Amsterdam: Amnesty International Dutch Section, 1995)

Chalk, F. and Jonassohn, K., *The History and Sociology of Genocide, Analyses and Case Studies* (New Haven/London: Yale University Press, 1990)

Conquest, Robert, *Harvest of Sorrow: Soviet Collectivization of Agriculture and the Terror Famine* (London: Hutchinson, 1986)

Cook, Haruko and Cook, Theodore F., *Japan at War, An Oral History* (New York: The New Press, 1992)

Destexhe, Alain, *Rwanda and Genocide in the Twentieth Century* (London/ East Haven, CT: Pluto Press, 1995)

Destexthe, Alain and Foret, Michel, *De Nuremberg à La Haye et Arusha* (Brussels: Bruylant, 1997)

Donnedieu de Vabres, Henri, *Le procès de Nuremberg devant les principes modernes du droit pénal international* (the Hague: Rec. Acad., 1947)

Donnelly, Jack, *International Human Rights* (Boulder/San Francisco/Oxford: Westview Press, 1993)

Dower, John W., *War Without Mercy, Race and Power in the Pacific War* (New York: Pantheon Books, 1986)

Fontette, François de, *Le procès de Nuremberg* (Paris: Presses universitaires de France, 1996)

Ginsburg, George and Kudriavtsev, V. N. (eds), *The Nuremberg Trial and International Law* (Dordrecht/Boston/London: Martinus Nijhoff, 1990)

Ienaga, Saburo, *The Pacific War, 1931–1945, A Critical Perspective on Japan's Role in World War II* (New York: Random House, 1978)

Jouve, E., *Un tribunal pour les peuples* (Paris: Berger-Levrault, 1983)

Kiernan, Ben, *The Pol Pot Regime, Race, Power and Genocide under the Khmer Rouge, 1975–79* (New Haven/London: Yale University Press, 1996)

Kiernan, Ben (Ed.), *Genocide and Democracy in Cambodia, The Khmer Rouge, the UN and the International Community* (New Haven, Ct: Yale University Law School, Southeast Asia Studies, 1993)

Kirakossian, J. S., *The Armenian Genocide, the Young Turks before the Judgment of History* (Madison, CT: Sphinx Press, 1992)

Limqueco, P. and Weiss, P. (Eds), *Prevent the Crime of Silence, Reports from the Sessions of the International War Crimes Tribunal founded by Bertrand Russell, London–Stockholm–Roskilde* (London: Penguin Press, 1971)

Marrus, Michael R., *The Nuremberg War Crimes Trial 1945-46, A Documentary History* (Boston/New York: Bedford Books, 1997)

Medvedev, Roy A., *On Stalin and Stalinism* (Oxford/New York/Toronto/Melbourne: Oxford University Press, 1979)

Mercier, Michèle, *Crimes without Punishment, Humanitarian Action in Former Yugoslavia* (London/East Haven, Ct: Pluto Press, 1995)

Minear, Richard H., *Victors' Justice, the Tokyo War Crimes Trial* (Princeton, N.J.: Princeton University Press, 1971)

Pictet, Jean, *The Fundamental Principles of the Red Cross, Commentary* (Geneva: Henry Dunant Institute, 1979)

Röling, B. V. A. and Cassese, Antonio, *The Tokyo Trial and Beyond* (Cambridge: Polity Press, 1993)

Röling, B. V. A. and Rüter, C. F. (eds), *The Tokyo Judgment, The International Military Tribunal for the Far East (IMTFE)* (Amsterdam: APA University Press, 1977)

Rummel, L. R. J., *China's Bloody Century, Genocide and Mass Murder since 1900* (New Brunswick/London: Transaction, 1991)

Shawcross, Hartley, *Life Sentence* (London: Constable, 1995)

Sieghart, Paul, *The Lawful Rights of Mankind* (Oxford/New York: Oxford University Press, 1985)

Sunga, Lyal S., *Individual Responsibility in International Law for Serious Human Rights Violations* (Dordrecht/Boston/London: Martinus Nijhoff, 1992)

Taylor, Telford, *The Anatomy of the Nuremberg Trials* (Boston/New York/Toronto/London: Little, Brown and Company, 1992)

Ternon, Yves, *L'Etat criminel, les Génocides au Xxe siècle* (Paris: Seuil, 1995)

UNESCO, *International Dimensions of Humanitarian Law* (Paris/Geneva/Dordrecht/Boston/London: Henry Dunant Institute, UNESCO, Martinus Nijhoff, 1988).

Wieviorka, Annette (ed.), *Les procès de Nuremberg et de Tokyo* (Paris: Editions Complexe, 1996)

Williams, Paul and Cigar, Norman, *A Prima Facie Case for the Indictment of Slobovan Milosevic* (London: Alliance to Defend Bosnia-Herzegovina, 1996)

Index